The Black
Progress Question

SAGE SERIES ON
RACE AND ETHNIC RELATIONS

Series Editor:

JOHN H. STANFIELD II

College of William and Mary

This series is designed for scholars working in creative theoretical areas related to race and ethnic relations. The series will publish books and collections of original articles that critically assess and expand upon race and ethnic relations issues from American and comparative points of view.

The Black Progress Question

Explaining the African American Predicament

Stephen Burman

Sage Series on Race and Ethnic Relations

v o l u m e   9

SAGE Publications
International Educational and Professional Publisher
Thousand Oaks   London   New Delhi

For information address:

SAGE Publications, Inc.
2455 Teller Road
Thousand Oaks, California 91320

SAGE Publications Ltd.
6 Bonhill Street
London EC2A 4PU
United Kingdom

SAGE Publications India Pvt. Ltd.
M-32 Market
Greater Kailash I
New Delhi 110 048 India

Printed in the United States of America

Library of Congress Cataloging-in-Publication Data

Burman, Stephen.
    The Black progress question : explaining the African American
predicament / author, Stephen Burman.
        p. cm. — (Sage series on race and ethnic relations : vol. 9)
    ISBN 0-8039-5060-8 (cloth).   ISBN 0-8039-5061-6 (pbk.)
    1. Afro-Americans—Politics and government. 2. Afro-Americans—
Economic conditions. I. Title. II. Series: Sage series on race
and ethnic relations ; v. 9.
E185.615.B85   1995
305.896'073—dc20   94-36218

95 96 97 98 99 10 9 8 7 6 5 4 3 2 1

Typesetter: Christina Hill

To my mother, my brother,
and in memory of my father

Contents

Series Editor's Introduction

The "progress" of African Americans has been one of the most perplexing and paradoxical problems in American history. This is because the question of whether African Americans are "making progress" is very much a sociological and political barometer of equality in the United States. Their duration, growth, and peculiar political and economic integration in the U.S. nation-state has made African Americans even more a symbol of the lowest possible social status than are Native American peoples—even though the latter are actually the lowest on the racialized socioeconomic hierarchy of U.S. society. Thus when African Americans "progress," it is indeed the most conservative indicator that quality of life in America is moving up a notch or two.

I should add that the unique place of African Americans as the barometer of American quality of life has also included a profound moral consciousness regarding the contradictions between democratic ideals and historically specific and persistent patterns of African American oppression. The "American Dilemma," the name of Gunnar Myrdal's epic summary of this moral contradiction in the collective consciousness of dominant American culture, has been a theme of heated public debate since the Constitutional Convention of 1776 and, indeed, before. It has yet to be resolved even in minute ways.

The persistence of the dungeon-level experiences of African Americans as a reality by which to gauge American status has been enough to fuel the fires of anxiety among the dominant regarding African American progress. Have African Americans progressed or have they not? If they have progressed, how much and why? If they have not progressed, why not? Although at the turn of the century, African American progress meant being freed from slavery, by the mid-20th century, it meant assimilating the norms of whites in a rigidly regulated, biracial caste-ordered industrial society. By the late 20th century, African American progress meant the benefits of the civil rights movements and policies of the 1950s and 1960s. Some European Americans during the civil rights era and its immediate aftermath considered African American progress a positive element in a country viewing itself as a democratic nation-state. Others, however, perceived African American progress as a threat, because it implied the erosion of Euro-American racialized ethnic privilege.

The national political culture of the post-1970s is producing even more complexities in the African American progress debate, as boundaries among traditional racialized political ideologies begin to fade and as new ones begin to emerge. The development of new kinds of African-descent status categories, such as African descent immigrants, and new modes of underclasses and middle classes, is creating new kinds of social inequality debates that even further complicate the meaning of African American progress. The major complication, of course, is the continuation of the centrality of race thinking in American dominant culture. This thinking persistently stands in the way of African Americans, past or present, experiencing an improved quality of life and political empowerment during the long run. In other words, regardless of times of optimistic race relations rhetoric or the significant upward mobility of a relatively few African American superstars, the fact remains that most African Americans remain on the lowest stair of the American stratification matrix.

As a British scholar, Stephen Burman offers an excellent outsider's perspective on the paradoxes of African American progress. It is a work which I hope will stimulate needed discussion on the persistent stubbornness of the cult of racialized thinking and group feeling that continues to make the idea of African American progress politically convenient rhetoric based on only scant empirical evidence.

John H. Stanfield II
Series Editor

Preface

Some projects have longer gestation periods than others. The origins of this book go back a long way. I first became interested in race in the United States when, as a student, I had the opportunity to live and work in the American South. This was at the height of the Civil Rights Movement and, like many non-Americans of my generation, I found the turmoil surrounding me at once both the most exciting and most depressing aspect of American society. It seemed to encapsulate the love-hate relationship we felt for the United States. Later, as a graduate student, I began to put this interest into a more intellectual context and to appreciate just how significant the resolution of the race problem was to every set of ideas about the nature of American society that I encountered. Investigating the prospects for its resolution therefore became the most appropriate way to pursue an understanding of American society.

My doctoral dissertation was devoted to this task, and this book bears traces of it. It remains appropriate to acknowledge some of the debts incurred then. In Atlanta, hundreds of political, community, and business leaders were willing to give some of their time to be interviewed about the nature of their city. These interviews were conducted on the basis of confidentiality and so names cannot be named, but, perhaps because of this, many of those interviewed were startlingly frank; collectively they provided a rich fund of information on which to base an understanding of how the politics of Atlanta actually worked. Material support can be more explicitly acknowledged, which is fitting because the project could not have been completed without it. In this respect I am particularly indebted to the late J. Paul Austin and to the late Robert J. Broadwater, formerly adjunct Professor at the Georgia Institute of Technology, a man from whom I learned much in areas well beyond the scope of this book.

In the United Kingdom I was also fortunate to receive grants from the Economic and Social Research Council, Oxford University Chest, Nuffield College, Oxford, the Nuffield Foundation, and the American Politics Group of the Political Studies Association. Equally vital support, but of an intellectual nature, was provided by my dissertation supervisors, Professor Chelly Halsey and the late Philip Williams; on a more personal level I am indebted to Gaby Riesz.

Later, I was struck by another characteristic of America's race problem. This was the variability in the attention paid to it in political culture and in public discourse generally. For an issue so central and so serious, it seemed odd that it should go in and out of fashion so readily. Such fashion was inevitably dictated by white America, and the mid-1980s seemed to be a period when interest was in decline. Although the product of many factors, not least the changing interplay of white guilt and increasing economic hardship, further reflection made it apparent that this volatility had to be interpreted politically. During the Reagan years, neoconservative thought was in the ascendant. Many reasons for this had little to do with race, but one reason was the impression neoconservatism created that if the race problem had not been solved then at least progress toward a solution was firmly in process. Contrary ideas were expressed, of course, but the dominance of the neoconservative agenda was evident. Its tone was combative rather than complacent, focusing on the need to roll back what were perceived as the excessive, threatening, and unnecessary concessions made to Blacks, notably in the form of affirmative action. Nonetheless its impact was to reduce the salience of race in the political agenda because of the underlying presupposition that this was a problem that was taking care of itself.

And yet it was not so. In recent years it has become increasingly accepted that American race relations, far from becoming unproblematic, have taken on new dimensions that are frightening. The first of these is the growing division within the Black community itself since the 1960s and the concomitant growth of an underclass whose plight is an affront to the very idea of progress. The second is the increasingly evident interethnic tensions consequent upon the changed character of immigration into America since 1965. This has brought together a whole new range of minorities, all of them people of color, struggling to make their way at the bottom of the pyramid of American society. Third is the effect of the collapse of world communism and the globalization of the capitalist economy. This, combined with fears of American decline, has made imperative a restructuring of the American economy to make it more competitive. The impact of restructuring on large segments of the Black community is potentially disastrous, accentuating the interethnic rivalries that poverty already brings. It is fitting that the pressures generated by these movements should have blown up, literally, in Los Angeles, where the coalescence of the divisions, the rivalries, and the restructuring has been more inflammatory than in any other city.

At all events the introduction of a new realism into the appreciation of the plight of Blacks has focused attention once again on the centrality of race and ethnicity in American life. A vital difference is that this time there is a lack of confidence in the interpretations this renewed focus brings. It is less difficult to establish the fact of Black disadvantage than to offer a structure of analysis that points to a solution to the problems presented. From the right it is no longer possible to make confident assertions that the capitalist market is solving the problem. For liberals previous faith that education in the values and ideals of American society would gradually attenuate the problem, given tolerance, patience, and moderation on all sides, now seems naive at best, hypocritical and a rationalization of racism at worst. The weaknesses further to the left are hardly less striking. Marxist analysis is undergoing a fundamental re-evaluation in the light of the collapse of the political systems its philosophy spawned, and whatever distance is placed between the practical Marxism of formerly socialist countries and its Western intellectual version, its credibility must be brought into question. The alternative radical analysis, which brings a cultural and nationalist approach to the plight of African Americans, also seems at an impasse. It inspired much hope, and the positive approach to multiculturalism it has given rise to is one of the few optimistic signs of recent years. But the harsh realities of national politics, as evidenced by the fate of Jesse Jackson's campaigns, have cruelly exposed the limits of the Rainbow Coalition and threaten to make this yet another false dawn.

We are at a stage where the urgency to analyze race in the United States is not matched by the intellectual frameworks we have available to understand it. A reassessment of approaches to the position of Blacks is therefore timely. The concept of progress is the most appropriate single idea around which to construct this because it embodies a dialectic of explanation and action, combining theoretical and practical understanding; Black Americans' still embattled status makes this the only tenable approach to the subject. The issue it raises is not whether the position of African Americans has changed in the last generation, because this much is obvious; rather it is the less tractable issue of whether change can be summed up as improvement, advancement, or any of the other synonyms of progress. It is through analyzing the interplay between these ordinal and cardinal dimensions that thought can be organized, insight generated, and action undertaken.

The predicament African Americans continue to find themselves in is reflected in the debates about progress, and so the meaning of the idea must be discussed as an essential preliminary, accomplished in Chapter 1. This does not explore every possible meaning of the term *progress* or its etymology; but it adopts a contextual perspective in which the meanings of the idea as they have been applied to Black Americans are explored. This restriction does not reduce its complexity; more importantly the context demonstrates that an idea of progress is integral to each approach that has been taken to explaining Blacks' position and therefore also to every strategy for resolving their predicament. Just as there will never be universal assent for a single explanation or a single strategy for solving the problem, neither will there be unanimity on the meaning of progress. The concept will remain contested, but it is precisely because of this quality that it provides the ideal window onto the problem of explaining the African American predicament whose nature it shares.

Similarly in organizing the discussion in Chapters 2 through 5 into traditions of thought that have attempted to explain and resolve the African American predicament—liberal, neoconservative, Marxist, and cultural—my purpose is not to conduct a survey and least of all to pretend to an exhaustive account of so large and diverse a set of writings. Rather it is to explore the range of possibilities generated by each approach. The works cited are therefore illustrative of the underlying possibilities and a basis for a critique rather than an intellectual history of each approach. This is undertaken in a spirit of optimism, in the belief that establishing the relative strengths and weaknesses of approaches to the question of Black progress will permit building on the strengths. The development of newer models will not only analyze the position more accurately but in doing so will point the way to the most effective paths to progress.

However, the assessment undertaken in this book reveals the depth of the vested interests that underpin the various models of the Black problem. The failure, in other words, is not just an intellectual one. It would be naive to suppose that these models are purely intellectual constructs; they reflect forces in society that provide a prop to ideas that might otherwise not withstand scrutiny. It is this that reveals the essentially political nature of the African American predicament, and Chapter 6 is devoted to further exploration of the political dimension of the various explanations offered. These forces restricting Black progress are powerful and not easily overturned, as the case study of Atlanta in Chapter 7 demonstrates, and the prognosis is therefore not bright. This is not to relapse to a solipsistic frame of mind, because all the models that have been applied to Black progress are not equal; some have more to contribute to a reconstruction of the analysis of the problem than others and in the concluding Chapter 8, I suggest which elements are most worthwhile for further intellectual and thus ultimately for practical progress. The difficulty is that those of greatest intellectual value, because they more accurately capture the reality of Blacks' position, are also those which grasp the depth of the forces ranged against Blacks and which therefore prompt the most pessimistic conclusion. Pessimism of the intellect, optimism of the will, is the appropriate motto for this dilemma.

In this reengagement with the problem, I have again received considerable support. I would particularly like to mention the encouragement and practical assistance at a critical time of Professor John Stone without which this book might have languished uncompleted. Professor Rupert Wilkinson, a longtime and ever-supportive colleague at Sussex, spent much more of his time than duty required providing me with a clear-sighted, sympathetic, but rigorous analysis of an earlier version of this book, which showed me the way forward.

I began this preface with a reference to gestation periods. No doubt this was in mind because as the manuscript has grown, so has my family. While I have been bringing it forth, my wife, Candida, has been engaged in the more significant and, I believe, even more painful task of delivering a new life into this world. Even so she has found the time and energy, from where I do not know, to continue to provide the support and intellectual and spiritual companionship without which this book would be impossible, and, even more importantly, the love without which it would, for me at least, be meaningless. Our daughter, Eve, has borne more of the brunt of this production than any 4-year-old should be asked to bear, showing tolerance and maturity beyond her years in coping with a distracted father. The sentiment is obvious but no less genuinely felt: May both Eve and her new brother, George, grow up in a world in which the pain of delivery is succeeded by the joys of freedom, not just for them but for all their African American counterparts.

1

Introduction:
The Inevitability of Antinomy

The Black experience in the United States has enriched the fabric of American history and society in countless ways, many of them only recently recognized.[1] But the overarching theme of that experience is one of misery, exploitation, inequality, and discrimination. Even where the story has been one of courage in resistance, of the triumph of humanity over venality, of dignity over bigotry, and of justice over coercion, the predicate is the tragedy of lost potential and crippling racism. Within the drama and transformations of Black history there is therefore a sense of continuity for all those who attempt to reflect on and come to terms with it. And the most wrenching question this poses is, how long must this go on? How long will Blacks continue to suffer a level of misery so far in excess of that which the vicissitudes of life impose on other Americans? When will peace be achieved on an agony that has plagued American society almost since its inception?

For this is the African American[2] predicament, the continuity of pain within change, the constancy of suffering within diversity. As neither insiders nor outsiders, Blacks retain a fundamental ambivalence in their relation to the rest of American society. To know whether a resolution of this predicament is in prospect, or whether the more things change the more they will stay the same, we have to know whether Blacks are making progress toward incorporation into American society. The question of progress today, as it has always done, crystallizes the essential issues facing Blacks, and answering it provides the greatest challenge to those who wish to understand the Black experience in America.

The question is deceptively simple: The complexities associated with the idea of progress in this context mirror the multifaceted everyday experience of Blacks in American life, and unraveling the complexities of the idea can illuminate the predicament of the people. But, just as there is no universally accepted answer to the Black predicament, so there is no agreed-upon meaning of progress. Literally, progress refers to onward movement of a beneficial nature; but this does not get us very far because we have no universally accepted notion of what would count as beneficial, or even of what ultimate destination movement should be toward.

The problem is not just the result of difficulties of measurement, although they exist;[3] nor is it due to a lack of rigor or clarity on the part of those who study this problem, although this too is not unknown. Rather, progress is a good example of an essentially contested concept, one whose ambiguities and dilemmas are inherent. There are too many conflicting interests at stake, both for the fate of Blacks and for the nature of American society, for the concept ever to be susceptible to simple and agreed-upon criteria. Progress is not a neutral term that can be used to describe the means to a given end. The criteria employed to judge progress are inseparable from the goal that would meet them, and contained within each goal is a vision of American society that carries all the commitment of a worldview. A chain of significance links the criteria against which progress may be judged and conclusions as to how much progress Blacks have made to an evaluation of the whole Black experience. This, in turn, is an indispensable component of any view of the whole of American society, and it is not fanciful to argue their importance beyond even this for the prospects of harmony in societies the world over in an era of globalization.

Exploring some of the complexities surrounding the idea of Black progress is therefore an indispensable preliminary. Its contestability implies a variety of models that may be classified in many ways; but, at the minimum, there is evident both a liberal and a radical corpus that have developed sufficiently to be seen as traditions of analysis. It is now time to take stock of these traditions: The position of Blacks in American society and the analysis of it are manifestly unsatisfactory, and an evaluation of the explanations offered is overdue in order to clear the ground for further development.[4] The recognition of the inevitability of antinomy is not to be confused with a relativist, or indeed a solipsist approach. Realism, or even pessimism, is no justification for determinism or fatalism. Worthwhile distinctions can be made, some approaches are more powerful than others, and superior models to explain Black progress can be developed.

However, it must be recognized that, as the principle of contestability demonstrates, no simple answer is available and neither is its mirror image, the resolution of the African American predicament, at hand.

THE CONCEPT OF PROGRESS

The idea of progress is contestable in ways which go well beyond its direct relevance to African Americans. As Christopher Lasch (1991) has demonstrated, the concept of progress lies at the heart of the contemporary competition between liberal and conservative conceptions of American society. Insofar as the idea of progress has been predicated on the achievement of a utopia, as a secular version of the Christian belief in Providence (p. 40), then the notion has become increasingly hard to sustain in the light of 20th-century history. If its essence is the less ambitious one of a process of gradual improvement in the quality of life, progress remains central to the liberal idea of a good society. But even this conception rests on the idea of constant change as the natural state of things, and this brings the idea into conflict with values of stability based on family, ethnicity, and other enduring, not to say timeless, qualities that have received increased articulation and respect in the neoconservative backlash of recent years. Marxism, too, takes change as being of the essence and sees capitalism as its greatest driving force in history, one that, however reactionary it may eventually become, unleashes enormous productive energy. Increasingly, the negative aspect of this dynamism—especially in the cultural sphere, where it creates a rootless, anomic world—has come to be recognized by those on the left (Berman, 1983). Taken to its ultimate conclusion, the idea of change inherent in the concept of progress becomes self-destructive, because it removes the possibility not just of stability but of certainty of any type, even at the most intimate level in the construction of the self (Lacan, 1968). What begins as a desire for improvement comes to gnaw away at the criteria upon which judgment can be made, to deny the categories of better and worse, of good and evil, of higher and lower. The intellectual roller coaster initiated by the desire for progress brings into question the very categories of rationality and ultimately of reason, a problem either celebrated or bemoaned but grappled with as the central question of the age by theorists of postmodernity (Baudrillard, 1988; Jameson, 1991; Lyotard, 1984).

With such a troubling background, exploration of the idea of progress in the context of Black America may be best conceived as a journey through the problems it generates, from its troubled conception to its no less embattled destination.[5] The journey begins with the criteria on which progress might be judged; this leads to problems with the types of evidence to be employed in its measurement; this in turn exposes essential differences in the methodological assumptions upon which different strands of analysis are based; these give rise to substantive differences on the range of determinants appropriate to an understanding of the Black experience (that is, how far into realms beyond that experience it is necessary to seek to find a full explanation of it); and differences of substance complete the journey by revealing the underlying problem: that there is no agreement even on the ultimate goal of progress or the destination of the journey. The tour, then, is not a comfortable one, but it remains the essential prologue to the examination of the question of Black progress.

The Problem of Measures

The first problem to strike us is the absence of an agreed-upon basis for the measurement of progress. Progress is a multifaceted concept that covers many fields of endeavor. The difficulty lies in determining which fields are critical to an overall assessment. How can we relate the findings of studies in politics, law, employment, income, housing, prejudice, segregation, and many others? None can, by definition, provide a complete answer. This would matter little if the relationship between all these fields was consistent in the sense that they all generated similar answers, with differences only of degree serving to round out the harmonious picture they provide. But this is not the case, and we are left in search of a basis for evaluation when different fields generate contradictory indicators.

How do we, for example, weigh a decreasing income gap between Blacks and whites with a widening unemployment ratio[6] or assess the significance of increased occupancy of political office by Blacks against an increase in the index of residential segregation? Further, on what basis do we understand the causal connections between fields that produce contradictory answers? Relationships can be measured statistically to determine the degree of correlation between these fields, but to the extent— and it is a significant one—that we are not comparing like with like, synthesizing results to produce one overall conclusion becomes a formal exercise that provides only spurious cover for the essential contestability of the concept.

A natural response to such difficulties is to take refuge in the facts. Surely, most of us instinctively feel, the evidence itself must resolve many of these ambiguities. But facts can mean, or be made to mean, many things. To take one simple example from the field of politics, the fact that there has been an increase in the number of Blacks holding political office in recent years provides, for many, irrefutable evidence of progress; to others, more cynical, it suggests a form of tokenism designed to minimize rather than to promote overall Black progress. However such a dispute might be resolved, it cannot be settled simply by reference to the facts, because it is not facts but their interpretation which is in dispute. Placing faith in the facts to resolve the problems with the idea of progress is therefore naive. Interpretation is an inevitable component of analysis, and the significance any interpretation carries for the fate of Blacks and for American society at large precludes unanimity. On the other hand, facts are not meaningless; we must avoid the temptations of relativism. Even if facts cannot determine their own interpretation, interpretation and conclusions are impossible without them. The point is to avoid the twin dangers of drawing conclusions in isolation from the evidence that bears upon them, or of assuming that the evidence permits only a single conclusion; to avoid, in other words, the traps of both empiricism and idealism. Rules of logic and consistency remain applicable, but so, equally, do the values and judgments that lie irreducibly at the core of interpretation.

Underlying the problems both of the relative importance of different fields and of appropriate evidence is not just the familiar distinction between quantitative and qualitative data but the more fundamental debate between the respective roles of material and ideal factors in the explanation of Blacks' place in American society. Those who stress the former focus on income, employment, and other aspects of the economic dimension to Blacks' experience more susceptible to quantitative assessment, a predisposition that transcends the political spectrum. The same applies to those who adopt an idealist approach and who favor the study of culture, identity, sense of self, and the role of race as a constituent of such categories, in respect to both Blacks and whites. The focus here is on more qualitative data that can illuminate the processes by which such factors facilitate or hinder the Black struggle. The question is whether there can be any meeting ground, or whether these dichotomous approaches are doomed to a dialogue of the deaf in which mutual incomprehension leads to ever-greater obfuscation of the central idea of progress. Although no simple synthesis is available, and indeed should not be sought, there is one area that has critical implications for all approaches to Black progress and in which constructive communication can be developed. No approach can be complete without a political dimension, although none may be purely political in itself. In this conception politics is not just another field of activity; rather it is the site in which the struggle between the competing tensions of the Black experience and the race/class dichotomy they imply can be played out. The role of the state, therefore, becomes critical in any evaluation of Black progress because of its property of reflecting, encapsulating, crystallizing, and manifesting the diverse pressures, material and ideal, economic and cultural, whose balance governs the rate of Black progress. This focusing role is played out at all levels at which Black progress carries significance, from the local to the national and the international.

The Construction of Models

How then should we proceed in the face of this irreducible plurality of meanings? Rather than attempting the forlorn task of establishing a single basis against which progress can be judged, we must first scrutinize the internal construction of the various models of Black progress. This requires examination of the validity of their assumptions, the consistency of the hypotheses they derive, the evidence they employ, the conclusions they reach. Above all, it requires recognition of the indispensable role theoretical constructs play in the conclusions derived by each model. Arguments that claim to proceed in an unmediated fashion from the facts create only a smoke screen behind which their theoretical suppositions lurk unexamined. Examining models on their own terms, in this sense, recognizes the essential pluralism of the field but does not accept the relativist idea that all models are equally valid. Instead it provides the precondition for an assessment of the range and power of explanation of each approach. The reason there continues to be so little clarity and unanimity about the central idea of progress lies in the political and prescriptive weight attached to any conclusions about its current rate. The real political consequences of this debate for the lives of Black people in the United States create the pressure for obfuscation that works its way back into and shapes the analyses. If ever there were to be unanimity, it could only be because the fate of Blacks was settled, which would make the debate redundant. As long as the position of African Americans remains unsatisfactory, there will be political disputes as to how it should be improved, and for just as long there will be disagreement, reflecting entrenched political stances, as to what would constitute a solution to the race problem.

THE SIGNIFICANCE OF BLACK PROGRESS

But the real extent of the pressures on this question only becomes apparent if we consider its implications beyond the realm of Black experience itself. For it is in the significance of Black progress for American society as a whole, and even for social relations on a global scale, that the greatest pressures arise. Although the wider canvas is, strictly, external to Blacks' experience, the two are inextricably tied because the wider realm exerts a significant shaping force upon Black progress, just as the fate of African Americans carries immense significance for the wider realms.

A Touchstone for Debate on U.S. Society

To take American society first, there is a basic confusion about the idea of progress here. On the one hand, we have a society founded in a burst of revolutionary optimism which implied the possibility of improving the human condition, and therefore of progress, even if not of the perfectibility of humankind; on the other, we have a political system designed on pluralist lines whose object is to prevent the concentration of power on the grounds that human nature is such that any such concentration will inevitably lead to corruption, abuse, and exploitation. The combination of indefatigable optimism tempered by a pragmatism that borders on cynicism is characteristic of American society, and the position of Blacks reflects this ambivalence. As such, the Black experience becomes the touchstone for much of the debate in U.S. public life, one around which ideas of democracy, freedom, justice, and equality take concrete shape. The Black experience therefore critically influences the ideas that govern American social structure, playing an essential part in constructions of the American polity and economy and ideas about how they work and how they can be made to work better. It is not too much to claim that no major issue in American public discourse can be fully discussed without taking into account the implications for Black progress. However, the connection is more problematic than Black progress simply acting as a focus around which wider debates coalesce. The difficulty lies with the ways in which general perspectives on American society dictate views on the race issue (Horton, 1966).

The Black experience poses the greatest challenge to any benign view of American history and society. There is formidable difficulty in reconciling that experience with claims that America has represented, and continues to represent, a successful social experiment and a source of human fulfillment. All too often reconciliation is forced, exercised at the expense of a realistic picture of Blacks' condition. More insidiously, where the facts of disadvantage are undeniable, the concept of progress acts as the tool of reconciliation. For the idea of progress has the inestimable virtue of introducing a temporal dimension that creates a space in which the evident contradiction between the idea of good society and one that has treated a substantial minority of citizens so shamefully can be resolved. Even if the condition of Blacks now does not support the idea of the good society, as long as they can be seen to be progressing toward incorporation, the problem ceases to be the intractable deficiency of the social structure and becomes simply a matter of time. In this way the difficulty is turned around so that the Black problem, far from being an indictment of American society, will, when it is solved, provide the ultimate confirmation of America's capacity to live up to its ideals.

The pressure to make the analysis of Black position conform to a benign liberal perspective on American society, therefore, gives rise to a tendency to exaggerate the extent of progress. A similar, if opposite, pressure arises with critical or radical perspectives on American society. There is no less at stake here; those who see the primary characteristics of the American experiment as being founded on racism and/or class exploitation need the Black experience to conform to this thesis, if it is to carry weight. Insofar as the temporal element is introduced here too, it is the absence of significant progress that is required to validate the enduringly exploitative and discriminatory nature of American capitalism and racism. The resulting pressure to distort is just as great as with the benign view. Black progress must, therefore, be seen in this wider context: Whether Blacks are making progress or not will either confirm or deny a general perspective on American society, and no such perspective can be complete or convincing unless it incorporates a view on Black progress consistent with its general premises. Once this is understood it is not surprising that the evidence has been bent into very different shapes to provide the appropriate link in the chain of intellectual support for competing perspectives on American society.

The Impact of Globalized Capitalism

The external significance of Black progress does not stop at the U.S. border. Increasingly, the Black experience is affected by developments in the rest of the world, specifically the process of the globalization of capitalism that is the hallmark of the current era in world affairs. The postwar era of American hegemony saw a massive increase in the exchange of goods and services between countries as the United States used its dominant role to promote freer trade. But even the massive movements involved in this process have been superseded by the new phase of enhanced integration of the world economy that has accelerated with the collapse of communism. This has involved a quantum jump in the mobility of capital within the world economy, combined with a similar acceleration in the mobility of labor as new political-economic formations take shape to capitalize on the opportunities presented by the post-Cold War world. The consequences of these trends are important, not only for America's role in the modern world, but more particularly for Blacks in America.

The connection involved here requires some elaboration (Burman, 1991): For much of the postwar era, the U.S. economy was in a sense insulated by its economic preeminence from the problems of the rest of the world. This is not to suggest America's overseas relations were unimportant, or that economic preeminence did not benefit the U.S. domestic economy and Americans' standard of living. On the contrary, the international economic system that America promoted after World War II, based as it was on classic liberal principles of maximum feasible free movement of goods and capital, exerted a powerful shaping influence on economic development in other countries, as well as making a major contribution to domestic prosperity. The point is, however, that the American-inspired postwar international economic system was not a zero-sum one; American gains were not necessarily made at the expense of other countries. The fact that the United States benefited from the new international economic order did not preclude other countries from doing so as well. Of course, not all countries benefited, particularly those in the Third World; and among those that did there were great variations. But it is because the benefits of the postwar international economic order were sufficiently widely disseminated that U.S. domination took a hegemonic form rather than the more coercive one employed, for example, by the Soviet Union in its sphere of influence, where economic prosperity was much less evident. Further, it is because this form of world economic development was beneficial to a sufficiently broad spectrum that the pressure existed to extend it to a new phase of international integration, once the potential became available.

What the period of American hegemony did mean is that the domestic society was sufficiently cushioned to provide a wide degree of freedom in addressing its major problems, such as that posed by the position of Blacks. The Great Society programs of the 1960s, for example, were targeted to a significant degree at improving the lot of Blacks, but they were in turn facilitated by a level of prosperity that owed much to the success of America's international role in the postwar years. Similarly, the transformation of race consciousness among African Americans stimulated by the Civil Rights Movement owed much to an appreciation of the parallels with anticolonial struggles by people of color throughout the world (Blauner, 1972, part 1), a situation in which the U.S. state did not always support the forces of liberation, thereby providing African Americans with lessons concerning their own path to freedom. In sum, the impact of America's international role on Blacks in this earlier era was arguably benign on balance, but it was in the main indirect and relatively minor. The question is whether, as we move into a new era of heightened internationalization of capitalism, this will continue to be the case.

American hegemony, and the prosperity associated with it, gave rise to the imperative for globalization of the capitalist economy. It will continue to be in the interest of the United States to participate in this new international economic order. Indeed the United States will have little choice; the issue is whether or not it will remain as leader. What has become questionable is whether this interest extends to Blacks and other poorer sections of American society. It is more likely that as the new international economic order develops, we will—indeed are—witnessing a bifurcation of interests in American society. The gap is between those who benefit directly from its operation, namely capitalists and much of the predominantly white middle class, and those strata, the underclass, most Blacks, and the poor generally, for whom American participation in internationalization is, in the short run at least, likely to be a disaster. No doubt such a schematic view will prove too clear-cut, but even if partially true, how can this have come about?

The U.S. Role Abroad

The situation has its origins in the American decision after World War II not to retreat to an isolationist position but to use its power to gain access to overseas markets, in the process supplanting the British and other European powers as the major investor of capital overseas. This thrust was supported by a system of managed exchange rates, aid, and reduced barriers to trade, backed up by political-military alliances, facilitating a massive increase in the integration of the world economy and ushering in a period of prosperity that extended to many of the advanced capitalist powers. It was a system of cooperation that could only have developed in a stable fashion after the cataclysmic upheaval of the war through the agency of an hegemonic power that could act as guarantor of a framework for the development of a freer, more integrated international economy. The United States provided this critical element; in doing so it increased its own prosperity as well as that of other countries and brought about a period of relative stability characterized by steady economic growth in the developed capitalist world.[7] It was the very success of the U.S.-sponsored system that undermined, as it was bound to do, American preeminence. General economic growth permitted other countries to catch up on the vast superiority enjoyed by the U.S. economy after the war. The immediate postwar U.S. position could not have lasted, and it was not in America's interests that it should, because the United States also benefited from the expanded overseas markets growth provided. Much has been made of the consequent decline in American economic power. The argument, which is often made in a determinist fashion, suggests that the United States is merely the last in a long line of imperialist powers condemned to overstretch itself and doomed to terminal decline as other powers supplant it on the world stage. Jeremiads abound on this subject and are generally unwarranted (Kennedy, 1988; Nye, 1990).

This is not to deny that American-sponsored internationalization will present important new challenges for America's role in the world. The most obvious of these is the collateral one of the decline in communism, a change that has deprived the United States of one of the key sources of its hegemonic power, its role as protector of all the other capitalist powers in the struggle against the communist threat. Although the decline of communism relieves the United States of some of the military burdens associated with its protective role, it also exposes the country to greater competition from other capitalist powers whose dependence on it for military protection from the external threat is now diminished. What has changed, therefore, is that the fall of communism has eliminated the disciplining effect the Cold War had on friendly as well as hostile powers. This is happening at a time when these friendly powers have reached a level of economic strength which makes them able to take advantage of the opening up of the former communist world and perhaps to take over from the United States the leading role in developing the world economy. In sum, the consequence of the new world order is that the United States is much more vulnerable to economic competition in a world where there is great potential for development and economic expansion. It is thus challenged at its most vulnerable point, the relative weakness of its economy and the reduced competitiveness to which this has given rise.

The New Challenge

Although the challenge has arisen because of the success of the United States in promoting world growth and defeating communism, it is no less real for that. If it is to retain its leading role in world affairs in the 1990s, America must respond by improving its economic competitiveness in a way that cooperates with, rather than resists, the now irreversible tide of internationalization (Burman, 1994). This will involve capitalizing on its hidden strengths as an economic power, strengths that are too little recognized in the pessimistic analyses of American decline. American economic weakness is often exaggerated because the differences between the structure of its economy and those of its major competitors are not recognized. The U.S. economy is continental in character and much more differentiated than smaller economies. It has a high tech, high productivity sector in parts of which it is a world leader; but its economy also encompasses a substantial low-wage, relatively low value-added sector in services, agriculture, and manufacturing. This differentiation is easily submerged in comparative economic statistics that are constructed at a macro level and are therefore average indicators. U.S. performance is often underestimated because its differentiated structure pulls its average down, giving rise to invidious comparisons with other countries, whose economies are more concentrated in the advanced sectors.

The point is that differentiation is not necessarily a weakness; it is only made to seem so by the process of averaging. For some countries, it may be possible to concentrate almost entirely on high value-added sectors and construct national economies around this. Even where this is possible, a pool of cheap labor will still be needed for basic manufacturing, services, and agriculture. The problem is how to secure this. Increasingly this is done by exportation of capital and jobs, because cheap labor is not available domestically and its importation raises too many social problems. But this is not a satisfactory solution because the conditions of accumulation are difficult to secure abroad. These constraints will prove to be the Achilles' heel of the advanced and apparently supercompetitive economies that claim to be overtaking the United States. For America such a strategy is neither desirable nor appropriate. Its greater size and differentiation give it the alternative option of developing both advanced and cheap sectors predominantly within its own borders. Both sectors can be developed to maximum efficiency and competitiveness, but the advanced sector will compete with other advanced capitalist countries, whereas the cheap sector will compete with newly industrializing countries. If the appropriate basis of comparison is chosen, the United States can be competitive across a broad range and has the unique strength of combining both elements in one, integrated political, economic, and military structure, with all the advantages of security and stability this entails. Such a strategy will not be without difficulties, but the development of the North American Free Trade Area, combined with recent revitalizing Asian and Hispanic immigration—where, it should be noted, the United States has a much better record of absorption than its competitors in Europe and Japan—suggest the possibilities available to the United States in respect to securing the appropriate supply of cheap labor. Providing the requisite highly educated labor force and investment capital for the advanced sector remains a problem, but it is not an insuperable one, as is demonstrated by America's impressive record in certain key advanced industries.[8]

The Implications for Blacks

It is the implications of this strategy for maximizing American economic competitiveness, and hence its potential for world leadership until the end of the century, that are disturbing for Blacks. If the key to increased competitiveness lies in developing a large pool of cheap labor and in creating a properly funded stratum of high tech jobs, the problem will lie with those groups that do not fit easily into either category. And the majority of Blacks lie precisely in the middle stratum that is threatened with superfluity.[9] Some Blacks will make it into the highly educated advanced sector, indeed some already have. They form part of the much-heralded new Black middle class, although much of the rest of this group is dependent on publicly funded professional jobs that are not likely to fare so well in the economic restructuring increased competitiveness will promote. The real problem lies with those left behind, who will have to compete with the new cheap labor of Asian and Hispanic origin that American capital is rushing to tie up with.

There has already been a substantial drift of capital from the central cities, where Blacks have typically come to reside, to either overseas locations or to newly industrializing parts of the Mexican American border areas, leaving Blacks locked into declining central cities, unwanted and unneeded spectators to this dynamic coupling of U.S. capital and Hispanic and Asian labor, lacking the education or training to enter the advanced sector but equally unable to compete with the wages for which Hispanic and Asian labor will work. This, it should be clear, is not a cultural problem of whether Blacks are willing to work for the market rate. Conservative critics such as Charles Murray (1984, 1988) have made much of the absence of a proper work ethic as being at the root of Blacks' failure to make more progress. The scope of the implications of global economic restructuring can be gauged from the fact that the costs involved in existing in their immediate urban environment make competition in this sector literally unsustainable for Blacks, regardless of the cultural attributes that may be spuriously assigned to them, and even assuming the owners of capital would be prepared to create jobs in such an environment. Their circumstances make much of the Black community unable to meet the challenge posed by the dramatic economic restructuring resulting from changes in the world political economy, changes which America has little choice but to accept even if it has to do so at the expense of Blacks and other unskilled, impoverished workers in its own country.

To recap the sequence that has brought Blacks to this impasse: The United States, in its period of unquestioned postwar hegemony, promoted economic growth in the advanced capitalist world through a system of free trade and mobile capital. This fostered the process of internationalization, which has taken a quantum leap with the disintegration of much of the communist world. The new global economy presents the United States with severe challenges to its economic competitiveness; to meet these it must restructure its economy in such a way as to capitalize on its unique economic strengths. The means by which it must do this will leave many unskilled workers, notably a large proportion of the Black community, superfluous to the needs of the labor market and unable to compete in it. Without an economic underpinning, the prospects for further pathological disintegration of the inner city communities where so many Blacks live are grim.

Can Government Help?

The enhanced mobility of capital on a world scale which is characteristic of globalization has shifted the balance of power between capital and labor in the United States. Just as the Black community was establishing a stake in traditional, unionized working-class jobs in manufacturing and the public services, these have declined, leaving a trail of unemployment and demoralized workers in the wake of capital flight. Lacking the economic muscle to remedy the decline in their fortunes, it has been natural for Blacks to look to politics as a means of redressing the balance. The restructuring associated with internationalization thus raises problems of a fundamentally political nature. In such circumstances it is the role of the state to ensure that conditions for the efficient accumulation of capital on which competitiveness depends are sustained, while simultaneously containing the potential for disruption and conflict these upheavals inevitably entail (Dunleavy & O'Leary, 1987, pp. 266-270; Jessop, 1990). This task is made more difficult by the fact that the mobility of capital threatens to outrun the power of any given state, even the American one, to control it. Although it is a fallacy to assume that capital can operate in a nonpolitical, that is to say, an unregulated market environment, either domestically or globally, this does not mean the balance of power between capital and the state cannot shift to the former's advantage. To the extent that globalization has brought this about, the tensions out of which the U.S. state has to produce a stable social compromise are weighted in favor of capital.

This does not augur well for the Blacks' prospects of incorporation. More likely than extensive and expensive state programs designed to improve the lot of Blacks and other groups of the poor displaced by globalization[10] is a minimalist containment strategy that relies for the diffusion of tension on the incorporation of a minority of middle-class Blacks into the mainstream and keeps the rest isolated in ghetto environments characterized by drugs, crime, and welfare dependency, with a reserve of repressive measures available whenever and wherever Blacks threaten to break out of their apathy into active or violent resistance. This strategy, although prompted by global economic developments, will operate through state activity at all levels of society, international, national, and local. Black political domination of the inner cities in which they form a majority is unlikely to create sufficient political force to counteract those pressures arising from the wider restructuring. The limited power Blacks enjoy in national politics will also prove inadequate in face of the competing pressures on the state generated by the new mobility of capital. In sum, the development of a new international division of labor, to which the United States will have to adapt if it is to compete, has as one of its effects the redundancy of that sector of the domestic American workforce of which Blacks make up a disproportionate part. The change will enhance the opportunities for the Black middle class in the advanced sector of the economy, but for much of the rest of the Black community, it offers only a prospect of becoming an underclass on the margins of society, superfluous to the requirements of the economic mainstream, mired in poverty, isolation, and neglect, and locked into the inner cities, where they lack the political resources to engineer an escape from their economic desolation.

A Change in Ethnic Relations

The economic restructuring prompted by internationalization will also promote a new set of ethnic relations. These will arise indirectly out of new relations with newly industrializing countries to which American capital will export jobs. More significant for Blacks will be the new domestic ethnic mix arising from the increased mobility of labor associated with the new economic order. One aspect is the increase in immigration from Asia, particularly to the West Coast of the United States, but this will be outweighed by the massive influx of labor from Hispanic areas. The consequence of this remix of peoples of color within American society may be to set Blacks in competition at the bottom end of the labor market with workers of Hispanic and Asian origin. There is obvious potential for strife here, as was graphically illustrated by the Los Angeles riots. In the recent past, problems of this sort have arisen primarily between Blacks and neoethnic white groups; the future prospect is for a new phase of competition between nonwhites in which Blacks risk being leapfrogged again in the race for upward social mobility. If this proves to be the case, it will demonstrate how the classic ladder model has not worked; as their turn for upward movement comes, new groups enter the competition and overtake Blacks, leaving them trapped at the bottom, just off the ladder. The fact that this competition is the result of a restructuring designed primarily by white-owned capital to protect its interests will do nothing to diminish the virulence of the competition and the animosity it will produce.

Such a prospect is not predestined. It is also possible that economic restructuring will create alliances between adversely affected groups by enhancing the role of color as the basis for struggle. Whether this prospect materializes will depend on the construction of their own identities by the groups involved. It may be that Blacks will see their position as unique, in the sense that their history in America gives them a singular perspective on exploitation and suffering,[11] with a consequent reluctance to enter political alliances with groups of a different heritage. Perhaps similar considerations will apply to Asians and Hispanics, who may not want to blend their cultural traditions with the very different ones of Blacks. More particularly, the seeds for competition may lie in the difference between groups who see their present status as merely a temporary stopping point on the march toward the American dream and those who have lost the optimism about such faith. The balance between ethnic separatism and integration, or between competition and alliance, is a perennial problem for a multicultural society such as the United States. A successful solution in terms of social stability will avoid the excesses of separatism and of cultural submersion. There is no guarantee that the balance will be struck in a way that promotes the common struggle against exploitation or that furthers Blacks' prospects for progress.

The relevance of these issues is not only to demonstrate the ways in which Black progress is influenced by wider movements but also to show how it is of significance for the wider stage. One of the major problems facing the world as globalization progresses will be the tensions emerging from the new juxtapositions of ethnic groups. For globalization will involve increased movements of labor in response to economic forces; the process is not simply one of capital moving to where the cheap labor resides but of increased mobility of both, creating new and more productive economic patterns. These patterns will, however, break down traditional barriers between societies, open up new contacts between people of differing cultures, and threaten the stability of political patterns based on older, more discrete systems of international relations. In this context the American experiment in multiculturalism takes on added significance. This is true not just because America's history has been a model for the construction of an effective society out of diverse ethnic heritages; it is also because the United States is renewing its own ethnic constitution in response to globalization and thereby setting itself yet again the challenge of absorption, of creating social justice and harmony out of potential competition and conflict. American claims for the success of its multicultural experiment will be put to the test again by the new waves of Hispanic and Asian immigration, but the problem spanning both the historical experiment and the contemporary one is Black incorporation. Just as historical claims for American success at creating a multi-ethnic society have always been challenged by the position of Blacks, so too will contemporary ones.

Whatever the fate of the new immigrants, multiculturalism will not succeed unless at this juncture Blacks also are incorporated into American society. Just as America will be in the vanguard of the great experiment in multiculturalism prompted by globalization, so its value as an example for the new era will be determined in large part by how it treats its Black minority. In short the social problems presented by globalization are unlikely to be resolved satisfactorily if the United States, with all its historical experience in this area, cannot solve them in its own society, and the United States will not solve them unless it produces a satisfactory answer to the question of Black progress. There is, therefore, much more at stake than just the fate of Blacks themselves; their fate will be a signal for the whole of the modern world as it attempts to grapple with the massive dislocations and opportunities presented by the hypermobility of the postmodern world.

CRITERIA FOR BLACK PROGRESS

The weight this wider significance puts upon the question of Black progress only serves to increase the pressure to make analysis of it fit preordained patterns and exacerbates the difficulties of obtaining a clear and consistent set of definitions and criteria on which to base discussion. The fact that the implications of contemporary movements in international political economy carry such potentially negative consequences for Black progress in America demonstrates that it is impossible to understand fully the question of Black progress by looking only at the Black experience itself. The concept of progress has at the very least to be broadened to incorporate these exogenous pressures, even though this makes evident how difficult it is to draw the boundaries to this question. This brings us back to the basic issue, which is what it is we are trying to measure when we talk of progress in this context.

Integration: A Color-Blind Society

The first possibility is that of complete integration; this implies an ideal of a society that is color-blind, a society in which position, wealth, and status are allocated solely on the basis of individual merit, and in which all inalienable characteristics such as race, and indeed ethnicity, gender, sexual preference, and other historical bases of discrimination play no part. This concept of society is one of an aggregate of autonomous individuals in which the achievement of each member of society is determined solely by his or her talents and the effort made to fulfil them. The image is a classic liberal one of a meritocracy, its underpinning a universalistic concept of the sanctity and supremacy of the individual. In such a vision, progress is measured by the extent to which race becomes an irrelevant category in society.

The most famous exposition of this vision was made by Martin Luther King, Jr., in his "I have a dream" speech in Washington, DC, in 1963. Few would question the rhetorical genius or emotional appeal of that speech, or indeed that at the time it encapsulated and defined in the most moving way the hopes and dreams of those who aspired to a solution to America's race problems. Although it provided a defining vision of progress for its day, from the perspective of more than a generation later, its aspirations now seem not only dated but also impractical and, to many, undesirable. It is impractical because it ignores the primary role played in social life by groups; in effect it ignores the way America has worked as a society in which individuals have made progress not solely through their own efforts but through exercising their talents within a network of group-based mutual support. Where rewards are distributed on a competitive basis, individuals are a weak force when faced with the cohesion of the group. The superior effectiveness of groups in securing upward social mobility for their members is one reason groups have retained their vitality for so long in American society.

Such groups are not necessarily constituted on the basis of race or ethnicity; they may equally be class-based associations arising from common economic interests, although the two criteria have rarely been discrete historically. In either case the goal of complete integration based on individualism denies Blacks legitimacy for the primary basis, association by race and/or class, upon which they, like so many other groups before them in America, can organize to pursue advancement. In the name of the ideal of liberty, the goal of integration, therefore, denies Blacks the means to achieve progress. Further, integration devalues the importance of group culture, denies the importance of common heritage, and deprives individuals of the positive sense of identity that derives from an awareness of this commonality and the sense of belonging it engenders. If it were to be realized, integration would therefore create not an ideal commonwealth composed of rational, autonomous individuals but an atomized, anomic society in which individuals were rudderless, deprived of the basic need for association, or at least the affective form of association based on common ethnicity for which no amount of voluntary association based on a contractual sense of obligation can substitute. If the impracticality of integration as a goal is rooted in its ineffectiveness as a basis for social mobility, its undesirability ultimately lies in the cultural and emotional denial that it would wreak on Blacks. The liberal ideal of integration is a chimera that cannot be realized for the same reason it should not be realized. Group association survives as a basis of social organization, in America as elsewhere, because it is functional in the competition for scarce goods and status and because it meets basic human emotional needs. Integration would involve its denial to Blacks both as a means to and the end of progress. It would remove one of the principal weapons other groups have employed in their paths to social mobility and in doing so it would deny the value of their culture, which is critical to a sense of positive identity for Blacks, irrespective of its usefulness in facilitating mobility.

Separatism: Equality of Groups

These flaws inevitably conjure up separatism as the alternative vision, which recognizes the group-based character that the goal of progress must embody. The thread of equality remains common to both ideals. But this raises the doubt that this goal also is impractical because, as the Supreme Court among others has famously argued, separate is inherently unequal. Any doctrine to the contrary does less to liberate Blacks than to provide a rationale for their continued subjugation. Even this begs the more fundamental question of what is meant by equality in this context. Advocates of integration have to specify whether it is equality of opportunity or of result that forms part of the ideal, but confronting this dilemma from a separatist perspective reveals even more clearly what a tangled web these concepts can weave. Whichever type of equality is specified, it would, in the separatist view, of necessity refer to groups rather than individuals. In concrete terms this would mean that the goal for Blacks would be to replicate exactly the socioeconomic profile of whites because this would be the minimum necessary to satisfy even the criterion of equality of opportunity. But this has the consequence of reconciling progress with the continued existence of Black poverty because the criterion would be met so long as Black poverty was proportionate to white. In theory, that would mean the goal of progress could be achieved by reducing the group profile of whites to that of Blacks by increasing the proportion of poor whites until it matched that in the Black community. Evidently this is not the intention behind separatism, which must therefore imply the improvement of Blacks rather than the decline of whites and which, by the same token, also carries some connotation of equality of result.

If this is so, does it follow that income is the criterion for equality? Would it, for example, meet the criterion of progress if Blacks were to develop a proportion of middle-class income earners equivalent to whites, but do so on the basis of publicly funded employment at various levels of government whereas whites achieved these income levels predominantly in the private sector? This is not an entirely fanciful notion because much of the recent growth in the Black middle class has been in precisely the professional level of government employment. We might argue that public employment is, and indeed should be, subject to political control in a way that private wealth, whose origin in private property is sacrosanct in a capitalist society, is not. This would suggest that in a predominantly white democratic society, Black middle-class professional employment persists at the pleasure of the white majority. If so then income equality would mask a continuing imbalance of power between the races. Imbalances of power are presumably incompatible with true equality, but it is much more difficult to establish criteria for measuring the elimination of such a relational and multidimensional concept. It becomes apparent then that behind even the severe but apparently straightforward criterion of equality of result there lurk further twists to the problem.

What if we attempt to sidestep this underlying problem of power by rejecting income equivalence as the criterion for equality and insisting that the latter requires literal replication by Blacks of whites' job distribution? This would mean that Blacks as a group must not only earn the same as whites but do so by doing the same number of jobs as whites in each socioeconomic category. If Blacks constitute some 13% of the American population, does this mean that 13% of all doctors or any other high-status occupation must be Black? Further, must they replicate the distribution of whites between the higher status parts of the medical profession, such as heart surgery, and the less salubrious sectors, such as the casualty wards of public hospitals? Clearly such comparisons become absurd long before they reach their logical conclusion. The serious issue underlying them is to ask at what point do we draw the line and argue that the criterion of equality has been achieved. At the very least, it is important to recognize that traveling down this path would rapidly become incompatible with individual choice because, in the name of equality, it would require such a rigid form of quotas as to preclude it. All of this applies even to a simple Black-white race model; we can reach a position of absurdity much more quickly if we define progress in ethnic terms and require equality of this type between all the ethnic groups of which American society is composed. The scope for antagonism between groups is evident in any society that attempted to follow this path; separatism would lead to uncontainable conflict long before it would lead to equality. Any complex society that attempted to organize the distribution of roles along these lines would be doomed to disintegrate in a conflagration born of recrimination and resentment before it could achieve the intended goal of equality or indeed of Black progress.

CONCLUSION

When viewed as ideal types, both of the possible goals of progress, complete integration and separatism with equality, although they have differing strengths and weaknesses, end up being both impractical and undesirable. We cannot therefore pretend to choose between them on objective or analytical grounds. There is no higher authority to which it is possible to appeal to resolve the debate as to which might be preferable or, to put it another way, which should be the "real" goal of Black progress. All these possibilities are inherent in the idea of progress itself, and which of them is stressed will vary with whoever is talking. Consensus is impossible and in consequence the idea that progress can be achieved in any universally agreed-upon sense becomes equally untenable. The usual refuge in the face of this is to suggest that ideal types are just that; they are not meant to be actualized in the real world. Rather they provide a standard against which real world developments may be measured and understood. This may be so, but the fact that the actual condition of Blacks is likely to contain elements of both ideals should reinforce the message of the inherent irreducibility of this problem and its nonsusceptibility to simple or consensual solutions.

Discussion of its goals completes the picture of the contestability of the concept of progress this chapter has explored: We have seen how it is irredeemably value-laden in its assumptions, its measurement, its internal and external determinants, and in its goals. What this demonstrates is the impossibility and indeed pointlessness of attempting to reduce the question of Black progress to any simple definition. It is essential to resist the illusion that the problems posed by the discussion of Black progress can be solved or that the choices inherent in them can be resolved by appeal to any single set of criteria. The malleability of the concept has permitted different traditions of answering the question and explaining the position of Blacks to arise and endure. If this chapter has achieved its purpose, it will have shown that the debates between such traditions cannot be resolved wholly in favor of any one of them. The dichotomy thus expressed arises inevitably out of and reflects the fundamental ambivalence of the African American predicament. A constructive approach must proceed from the basis of the inevitability of antinomy, seeking to capture rather than deny this ambivalence through the exploration of the principal explanations of Black progress, with the message of contestability in mind. Avoiding the Scylla of dogmatism and the Charybdis of eclecticism, we can by this process build a more rounded perspective, which, although it too cannot command universal assent, can perhaps be employed to advance the cause and study of Black progress.

NOTES

1. The most notable change here has perhaps been in the field of popular culture and in literature, where contemporary African American writers such as Toni Morrison and Alice Walker have become prominent in ways that transcend any confines of race. That they are only the most prominent recent examples of a rich cultural tradition is an idea forcefully and effectively advocated by a band of Black cultural critics, of whom the most prominent is Henry Louis Gates, Jr. Gates (1992, p. 31) is himself associated with the attempt to create a canon of African American literature, which will create a tradition, as well as defining and preserving it. Nor does the interest in recovery stop at America's boundaries; for an interesting and highly successful exercise which combines gender and the African Diaspora, see the anthology *Daughters of Africa,* edited by Margaret Busby (1992).

2. I will use the terms *Black* and *African American* interchangeably, although it may be argued that they have different connotations. Shelby Steele (1990) suggests that the adoption of the designation *Black* in the 1960s was healthy, in that it confronted not only whites but also the anxiety of inferiority Blacks had internalized until then. The coinage of *African American,* on the other hand, he sees as a euphemistic compensatory mechanism, "a self-conscious reaching for pride through nomenclature (which) suggests nothing so much as a despair over the possibility of gaining the less conspicuous pride that follows real advancement" (p. 47). Henry Louis Gates, Jr. (1992, chap. 8) goes further in an elegant discussion of the meaning of Blackness: "The ultimate sign of our sheer powerlessness is all of the attention we have given . . . to declaring the birth of the African-American and pronouncing the Black Self dead. Don't we have anything better to do?" (p. 138).

Others would see its adoption as a symbol of increased sophistication. In the 1960s the confrontational connotations of Black may have enhanced pride and political effectiveness, but by defining the situation as dichotomous, it left Blacks as a relatively small and powerless minority confronting a homogenous white majority. What was liberating, therefore, became limiting. *African American* represents an escape from this trap because it is a term which not only "effectively evokes the specific cultural dimensions of . . . identity" (Williams, 1991, p. 257), it also helps redefine American society as a series of minorities rather than one divided along race lines in a form of conflict which Blacks must lose. It therefore opens the path for the inclusion of African Americans in this pluralist mosaic on equal terms. Ultimately it is for the subjects to weigh the merits of such arguments and determine their own preferred designation. It is because both terms remain in current usage that the advantage of employing both as a contribution to elegant variation in the text remains legitimate.

3. Difficulties of measurement arise at even the most elementary level because it is well-known that the U.S. Census seriously undercounts the number of Blacks in American society (Farley & Allen, 1987). If even such basic facts cannot be reliably calculated, it does not give grounds for faith in any statistically based answer to the question of progress.

4. This is not to suggest there have been no previous assessments. See, for example, Forsythe (1977), Vander Zanden (1973), Lyman (1972), Frazier (1972), and Hughes (1963).

5. See Derrick Bell, 1987, *And We Are Not Saved: The Elusive Quest for Racial Justice,* for an exploration of the alternative paths to progress through the medium of a dialogue that combines fantasy and acute practicality to generate insight in a most creative way.

6. It is a puzzling fact that although a case can be made for some degree of progress in most areas of Black life such as education, income, or formal political representation, this does not seem to be the case for employment. Here the position of Blacks relative to whites seems unequivocally to have worsened. On this see Reynolds Farley and Walter Allen, 1987, *The Color Line and the Quality of Life in America,* Chapter 9.

7. There is much debate as to whether America's role can be construed in quite so benign a fashion as this, less because of its specific characteristics than because of the weakness of any theory of hegemonic stability. On this see Snidal (1985), Webb and Krasner (1989), and Grunberg (1990).

8. The priority which the Clinton administration has given to foreign and domestic economic policy suggests an acute awareness of what is needed to restore competitiveness. Much of its focus has been on asserting national self-interest in trade and restoring the advanced sectors of the economy after decades of distortion and neglect brought about by a preoccupation with political and strategic balance in the Cold War era. However, securing "flexibility"—the much-used euphemism—at the cheaper end of the labor market is an equally important if less publicized component of the strategy and the one likely to have the greater impact on Black progress. For indications of the thinking behind the Clinton administration approach, see Reich (1993), Thurow (1985), and Tyson (1992).

9. These international trends provide one possible explanation for at least the recent evidence concerning the puzzle in note 6. Employment trends are particularly vulnerable to international factors in the post-Cold War world, and this is an arena where Blacks have even less ability to affect the agenda than they do in other areas governed more by domestic considerations.

10. It is worth noting in passing that the implications of restructuring also undermine the credibility of a color-blind strategy for Black progress, as advocated, for example, by William Julius Wilson (1987), in which improvement for Blacks arises from programs targeted at all poor Americans rather than being based on race, on the grounds that to do the latter creates

an impression of special treatment and so produces a backlash that makes it self-defeating. Leaving aside the evident lack of appetite among the majority, middle-class tax-paying sections of the population for such redistributive programs in an era of economic constraint, such programs, by reducing the pool of available cheap labor, would be inimical to a strategy for increased competitiveness that depends in great part on maintaining just such a pool. The harsh truth is that competitiveness requires continuing poverty as a discipline on wage levels, and no government can be committed to both simultaneously.

11. See Gates, 1992, on the debilitating effects of Blacks claiming uniqueness in their suffering.

2

These Things Take Time:
The Liberal Tradition and Black Progress

The defining characteristic of the liberal approach to Black progress is optimism. There are differences of degree and in the bases on which optimism is founded, but the invariable element is that the problem of Blacks' place in American society is gradually being solved. This common premise is the uniting thread that justifies the idea that there is a tradition of liberal analysis and makes the differences variations on a theme rather than simply a random collection of responses to the question of Black progress. Tradition also suggests evolution, and the balance between the changes this implies and the continuity of the basic element of optimism will, together with an assessment of the adequacy of the tradition in explaining the rate of Black progress, provide the focus for this chapter.

ORIGINS OF THE LIBERAL TRADITION

Park: The Race Relations Cycle

Liberal optimism received perhaps its clearest articulation in the work of Robert E. Park. Writing in the 1930s, Park brought to the field the key concept of the race relations cycle (Park, 1950, pp. xii, 149-151, 189-195). This he formulated as a general law applicable to all situations of racial contact, as well as providing a framework for understanding the development of race relations in the United States. He argued that the cycle proceeds in four stages: contact, conflict, accommodation, and assimilation. The first stage occurs when two races meet and are obliged to interact. Conflict then arises as the races compete for scarce resources. This eventually gives way to accommodation in which a stable, but invariably unequal, social order is established. Finally, accommodation is superseded as the races assimilate through a process of cultural and ultimately physical merging, to the point where the society becomes homogeneous in its racial dimension. At this point, Park believed, class would succeed race as the main axis of social conflict.

Park treated the race relations cycle as virtually ineluctable. He insisted that race relations invariably pass through these four stages, and one need only calculate where a given race is in the cycle to know what its past was and what its future will be. It is a guide both to history and to the contemporary world, explaining the past as well as current events in terms of their evolutionary propriety. The concept of the cycle thus contained an implicit lesson for the future of race relations in the United States; it implied that their path of development would be one of integration and assimilation. The object of sociological research would therefore be to chart developments along this given path, documenting the progress toward integration that was Blacks' allotted role. The assimilationist bias that Park's cycle thereby infused into the study of race in the United States was its principal legacy to the liberal tradition.

In contemplating the United States specifically, Park (1950) was interested "most of all in studying the details of the process by which the Negro was making his slow but steady advance" (p. viii). But the more he tried to fit the facts of the Black experience with his idea of progress, the more stress he was forced to place on those aspects of the situation that slowed down the working of the cycle. His comments became a virtual catalog of the obstacles hindering the progress of Blacks. However, he did not accept such negative evidence as a refutation of his argument. He attributed any problems to the conservatism of individuals and institutions. These could resist progress but never, he was convinced, halt it altogether. All barriers to progress could be explained away by reducing them to the status of temporary obstacles. This, as has been repeatedly pointed out, (Etzioni, 1959, pp. 255-262; Lyman, 1972, pp. 227-270; Metzger, 1971, pp. 627-647), is the fundamental weakness of the theory of the cycle—it is, as employed by Park, unscientific because it cannot be disproved. Any amount of contradictory evidence can be dismissed by the argument that it points to delay in the working out of the cycle rather than a refutation of it. All criticism can be deflected by extending the time span over which the theory will operate. It can thus be preserved in all circumstances. The theory of the cycle is therefore a form of historicism, one that fails to meet the criterion of falsifiability (Popper, 1959), and one that becomes ultimately an endlessly woven tapestry of loopholes and caveats.

As a corollary of this historicism, Park's theory is also determinist. It implies the helplessness of human actors in the face of massive impersonal historical forces. By denying the capacity of people to alter fundamentally the course of events, it denies their responsibility for their actions in bringing them about. Park sees the march of history as benign and its inevitability as comforting. However, race relations is an area in which man's inhumanity to man has flourished, and theories invoking history have shown themselves more susceptible to justifying such behavior than to combating it. Park's theory should for this reason, if for no other, be treated skeptically.

Myrdal: The American Creed

One of those to criticize Park for determinism was Gunnar Myrdal, another founding father of the liberal tradition, who argued that Park's work encouraged a do-nothing approach to the problem. Myrdal also criticized works inspired by a Marxist approach for being teleological, that is for assuming to know the direction in which history is inevitably heading and what its final point will be, on the grounds that this must give rise to fatalism. In view of this it is curious that Myrdal's own approach reveals the same weakness (Medalia, 1962).

To see why this is the case and yet why his thesis dominated the study of race relations in the United States for 20 years after its publication and established a liberal orthodoxy (Higham, 1975, p. 217; Jackson, 1990, p. xi), we need a brief exposition of Myrdal's monumental survey of the condition of Blacks in America, *An American Dilemma* (Myrdal, 1944).[1] Although enormously wide-ranging his argument is in essence a simple one: Myrdal saw the position of Blacks in America as a moral problem:

> The American Negro problem is a problem in the heart of the American. . . .
> it is there that the decisive struggle goes on . . . at bottom our problem is the
> moral dilemma of the Americans . . . the American dilemma is the conflict
> between his moral valuations on various levels of consciousness and gener-
> ality. (It) is the ever raging conflict between, on the one hand, the valu-
> ations preserved on the general plane which we shall call the American
> creed, where the American thinks, talks and acts under the influence of

high national precepts and, on the other hand, the valuations on specific planes of individual and group living where personal and local interests, economic, social and sexual jealousies, considerations of community prestige and conformity, group prejudice against particular persons or types of people and all sorts of miscellaneous wants, habits and impulses dominate his outlook. (Myrdal, 1944, p. 1)

Myrdal takes the creed to be the most distinctive feature of American society and argues that the United States has the most explicitly articulated system of ideals in reference to human action of any nation. The creed may not always be realized in practice, but all Americans are conscious of the ideals that ought to rule their actions. This awareness is the product of a thorough indoctrination process whereby the elements of the creed are espoused on every possible occasion and public discourse on any major issue is only possible in terms of it. The importance of the American creed is that it is a social force. The failure of Americans to live up to its precepts, in race relations as elsewhere, is not taken by Myrdal as a sign of hypocrisy or cynicism because historically the creed has triumphed, albeit not yet completely. It has provided the main impetus for change, causing a reduction in inequality and preventing rigid class or caste stratification (Warner, 1936). For Myrdal, any condition short of consistency between the creed and social organization creates a strain in American society which can be temporarily alleviated but which must ultimately be resolved by establishment of those social relations fully consistent with belief. For this reason he is able to echo the keynote of optimism in his conclusion, "Not since Reconstruction has there been more reason to anticipate fundamental changes in American race relations, changes which involve a development towards the American ideals" (Myrdal, 1944, p. lxi).[2]

Underlying what he takes to be this distinctive perspective, Myrdal stresses the importance of the methodology that produces it. The crucial aspect is the emphasis he places on beliefs and the efficacy of human intervention. Having rejected perspectives that leave no scope for human agency, he adopts a standpoint in which the problem is analyzed in terms of the valuations and beliefs of the social actors concerned, on the premise that when people define situations as real, they become so because action is predicated on those beliefs. However, Myrdal overreacts against the neglect of belief systems in the study of race relations and gives them undue emphasis. He falls into the idealist trap of considering the impact of values sui generis, without taking into account their interaction with class or group interests. His anxiety to avoid the straw man of economic determinism leads him to neglect proper consideration of the divergent material interests and power relationships that are integral to the study of race relations.

This flaw in his approach permits his optimistic conclusions as to the prospects of progress for Blacks. Evidently, if the creed contains ideals of equality and justice, and if it is a major force in society, then the outcome is a foregone conclusion. If, however, there are classes in society whose material interests or privileges depend on racial exploitation, or indeed if the whole social structure is predicated on the division of labor implied by racial discrimination, then one might be considerably less sanguine about the prospects for the triumph of the creed. Myrdal fails to take seriously this latter possibility because by giving primacy to the efficacy of beliefs in general and to the creed in particular, he has himself constructed, despite his strictures against determinism, an image of a vague and powerful force that will determine social organization and resolve the race problem. Far from turning Park's analysis around, his notion of the creed is used to fill the gap left by the rejection of the cycle, and the creed becomes the vehicle of an evolutionary teleology parallel to that of Park. Myrdal's conservatism may be of a somewhat softer kind, but it still vitiates his claim to a new sociology of race based on free will and the inherent human capacity to remake the world. On this analysis the end result of Blacks' experience is again assumed to be integration and full equality. Little more need be done than observe the implementation of the creed. The path may be tortuous, the opposition strong, but "we" always know where we are going and that we will get there in the end. All signs of positive change are interpreted as evidence confirming the correctness of the analysis; all contrary evidence is dismissed as a temporary setback or a detour from the true path. The weight given to the two types of evidence is thereby systematically distorted by the concepts informing the analysis, as indeed is the direction in which evidence is sought. The result is an overriding optimism, the complacency of which seems matched only by its lack of convincing substantiation.

To place as much faith in the creed as Myrdal does hardly stops short of the "facile optimism of romantic abstraction" (Cox, 1959). The mass of empirical detail in *An American Dilemma,* valuable as it is in other respects, tells us little about the question of progress. On this issue we are offered only the power of the creed, just as with Park we are offered the power of the cycle. If we lack faith in the essential goodness of white Americans, then we are offered little else that would support an optimistic prognosis. The problem with this lies not so much with the concept of the creed itself. The elements of American culture it encapsulates are undoubtedly very striking, particularly to an outsider, as Myrdal was. The extent to which social and policy issues, including those of race, are discussed in terms of their precepts is indeed worthy of note. The error is to draw from this the conclusion, as Myrdal did, that the ideals of the creed, because they shape discussion, somehow force their own implementation. It is not necessary to go so far as to argue that ideals are always a rationalization of self-interest to be able to suggest that Myrdal's view is crude and naive in the overarching role he ascribes to the creed and the consequent neglect of social structure. It may be that Myrdal and Park will prove to be correct; but if they are, and if the liberal tradition is to offer a sociologically convincing argument for why Blacks will progress, it will need more effective concepts than the American creed or the race relations cycle.

A Natural Antipathy

Before considering some alternative concepts that have served as a basis for liberal optimism, however, we must take note of another aspect of the tradition which was evident in its earlier exponents and has remained influential subsequently. This is the assumption that racial conflict is rooted in some instinctive impulse of repugnance that produces a natural antipathy between the races. Although Park (1950, p. 280), for example, does not subscribe to theories of biological inferiority, he does see racial conflict as being based on universal psychological traits.[3] The problem with this approach is that it abstracts from the structural factors that produce these traits in particular groups. The aspects of personality to which prejudice is ascribed by Park—sexual urges, jealousies, we-they feelings—are roots of action common to all people. As universals, they cannot logically be invoked to explain the specific properties of the system of racial discrimination that has developed in the United States. Because these factors are, by definition, present in all situations of racial conflict, they cannot in themselves explain what has shaped race relations in America into their unique configuration (Gordon, 1978).

Similarly, Myrdal places great stress on individual race prejudice among whites. This is again taken to be a psychological syndrome based on roots as described by Park. That this is more than a rationalization of economic self-interest is exemplified for Myrdal by the power of prejudice in governing the behavior of lower-class whites. Even though the economic interests of the lower class should dictate solidarity with Blacks, most of whom belong to the same class, they are at least as prejudiced as any other element of white society. However desirable solidarity between exploited groups may be, it is wishful thinking, because the psychological drives manifesting themselves in prejudice will invariably supersede economic self-interest. The focus on individual prejudice assumes, but does not demonstrate, that there are no structural barriers to integration. It leads to the conception of the problem as an individual matter and thus diverts attention from the systemic factors that shape individual psychology. It therefore obviates the need for the study of power in relation to race; it substitutes a social-psychological perspective for one derived from political sociology:

> It is a distortion to posit the perceptual subjective notion of prejudice as the central and independent variable in analysing social and political reality. . . . Myrdal's ethical-moral approach begs the question, what are the social, economic and political origins of the relationship of racial inequality and what are the social, political and economic factors sustaining such relationships. (Katznelson, 1973, p. 6)

One of the more problematic implications of this line of thought is that it contradicts the idea embodied in the American creed and the race relations cycle. These suggest that racial antipathy is temporary, whereas the psychological perspective suggests racism is a permanent feature of society. There seems little room for compromise because, on the one hand, we have universal and unchanging traits of human nature, and on the other, the iron laws of history. Truly an irresistible force and an immovable object.

Notwithstanding the contradiction, both elements have left their mark on the liberal tradition. This can best be explained by the one thing they have in common; both divert the focus of investigation away from the social structure of American society. The psychological perspective implies that prejudice should be studied at the individual level because its roots are located in the human psyche and not in the social structure. The notions of creed and cycle imply that the social structure is irrelevant to the development of race relations because the structure cannot contain any insuperable barriers to assimilation. If it did, history could not achieve the goal preordained for it by the creed and the cycle.

As a result of the influence of this common factor, sociological investigations of race in the United States tended to concentrate on monitoring the gradual and inevitable decline in the racial prejudice that was perceived as the crux of the problem. This was coupled with suggestions for piecemeal amelioration and recourse to moral exhortation as befitting a belief that better information and education and an appeal to whites' higher nature would hasten the pace of Black incorporation.

One consequence of this was to deny Blacks anything more than a passive role in the resolution of the race problem (Lasch, 1991, pp. 439-445). Integration was so firmly established as the goal of history that the idea of Blacks developing their own values and culture independently of the creed was not countenanced; they were viewed as white Americans with different colored skins, whose only path to progress was to become so like whites as to be indistinguishable. The patronizing element of this early manifestation of the liberal perspective leaves it open to Ralph Ellison's (1967) objection:

> Can a people (its faith in an idealized creed notwithstanding) live and develop over 300 years simply by reacting? Are American Negroes the creature of the white man or have they at least helped to create themselves out of what they have found around them. Men have made a way of life in caves and upon cliffs, why cannot Negroes have made a way of life on the horns of the white man's dilemma? (pp. 315-316)

To sum up, although sociological research did gradually come to distance itself from the historicism of the earliest exponents of the liberal tradition, it carried over the crucial idea that relations between the races were gradually improving and Blacks were moving toward integration.[4] Optimism as to the pace of the process was tempered by the reality of continued discrimination, but the underlying idea of progress was scarcely questioned. And the sanguine perspective persisted because there were not seen to be any fundamental barriers in the American social structure to prevent the incorporation of Blacks.[5]

EVOLUTION OF LIBERAL THEORY

Parsons: Pluralism Replaces Integration

But if the American creed and the race relations cycle became dated as the conceptual underpinning for liberal optimism, newer ideas came to the fore to perform the same function, ideas which had the advantage of addressing the structural level rather than reducing the problem to one of individual prejudice. The first and necessary conceptual advance was the introduction of a distinction between inclusion and assimilation as the path of progress (Gordon, 1964). This was made most notably by Talcott Parsons (1965, 1975); he argued that full inclusion into society is compatible with the maintenance of a distinctive ethnic identity for Blacks, contrary to the assimilationist perspective that implies their total absorption into the dominant culture. Inclusion suggests pluralism as the goal and rejects the vision of integration favored by Park and Myrdal. Indeed Parsons's pluralistic vision allowed him to welcome the rise in Black consciousness, even a degree of polarization around the axis of color, as a sign of progress because, he argued, without it Blacks would not have sufficient identity, cohesion, or internal organization to take their place as equals in the mosaic of ethnic groups he saw as the hallmark of American society (Parsons, 1968; 1975, pp. 71-79).

The idea of inclusion is an important departure because it shifts the liberal focus away from full integration of the individual into a homogeneous culture, and toward the group and its participation in a diverse, pluralistic culture. The merit of this is that, because it presents a more realistic picture of the nature of American society, it lays the groundwork for a more cogent analysis both of the means and the goal of Black progress. It thereby restores the possibility of optimism, which the insistence on integration had undermined. Indeed in Parsons's formulation, this departure permits the claim that it will fall to Blacks to set the seal on the Marxian error in respect to American society. Far from their condition being a challenge to the idea of America as a just society, their predicament will become its vindication as Blacks demonstrate that equality does not require revolution, that integration without loss of identity, integration into pluralism, is the path of the future. The healthiest result, as well as the necessary precondition, of this process is the building up of Black solidarity and the sense that being Black has a positive value. There are dangers of an unworkable and counterproductive separatism in this, but the pluralist solution involves neither separation nor assimilation but rather a repetition of the success story of full participation achieved by Jewish and Catholic immigrants in less than two generations.

This conception of pluralism rests, in turn, on the idea of modernization as a liberating force in American society. Modernization involves a process of differentiation which gives rise to a more complex social structure. Thus Parsons, for example, sees a general development of American society towards emancipating the individual from the older types of paternalistic involvement and toward making the individuals in the various contexts of social relations increasingly independent of each other. . . . In the present position the special position of the Negro as occupying a total status by virtue of his race has become increasingly anomalous. (Parsons & Clarke, 1966, p. xxi)

In a pluralistic system, ethnic membership does not determine the whole of an individual's status because this is also affected by occupation, education, religion, political affiliation, and so on. The trend toward pluralism as used in this sense leads then to an increasing looseness of fit between the components of status. This means that Blacks' position in society is no longer determined solely by race but is also influenced by these diverse elements. The point is that on these criteria Blacks suffer no inherent disadvantage compared to other groups, and one may assume that the practical disadvantage they suffer will decline as these other factors become increasingly independent of ethnic status. The process of differentiation bringing this about is fostered by the structural changes of industrialization and urbanization, and by adopting such fundamental processes in support of optimism, the liberal perspective is made more substantial.

If there is improvement in this respect, at a deeper level the perspective remains unchanged. The premise of pluralism remains a value consensus that provides the basis of agreement on the distribution of roles in the stratification system. Whatever the criteria adopted to determine this, be they occupation, kinship, ethnicity, or anything else, it is still necessary, if this model is to work in a way that permits entry of Blacks, for there to be a shared set of values governing the rules of the game. At most, ethnicity can be seen as a deviation from an agreed-upon pattern, giving rise to a system in which members of a particular group are not accepted in roles for which they would otherwise be qualified. It is a moot point whether it is other than a truism to characterize the stratification pattern of any society as being based on an agreed-upon value system. But it is undeniable that such an analysis contributes little to our understanding of those situations where there is substantial resentment of, and resistance to, the allocation of rewards. And Blacks' situation in America is just such a situation. Ethnicity cannot cause a deviation from an agreed-upon value pattern because there is no mutually accepted pattern for it to deviate from, no shared value system as to the allocation of roles among

Blacks and whites on which such a stratification system could be based. It is true that white America is a case in which it is more than usually appropriate to apply the notion of value consensus. This is because of the unusual degree of self-consciousness of the nation at its founding, the explicitness of its ideals as formulated then and expounded ever since, its largely voluntary composition as a result of immigration, and the mobility of its population. In view of this a significant measure of value consensus would not be surprising. The point, however, is that it is precisely these conditions that have not applied to Blacks. They formed the one group that in no sense chose to come to America; they are the major group to which the traditional ideals have not been addressed; and they are the largest group not to have benefited from their implementation.

The reason that Blacks have historically done relatively little to successfully challenge the consensus is not so much because they subscribe to it as because they are powerless to do anything about it. It is because the experience of Blacks in America has been so different that their situation is problematic. Only by effectively ignoring these differences and extending assumptions applicable to white America can the pluralist model generate optimistic predictions as to the prospects of progress. The extrapolation to Blacks of factors that have affected white America is typical of the liberal perspective; it thereby evades the central issue, which is the extent to which racial barriers make Blacks' experience so different as to preclude any analysis of their position in terms applicable to the rest of society.

Historical Analogy: Another Immigrant Wave

Another form of extrapolation is the use of historical analogy as a means of predicting the fate of Blacks (Hills, 1970; Kristol, 1972). On this analogy Blacks are the last in a long line of immigrant groups to be absorbed into the mainstream, even if they were one of the earliest to arrive. The first great test of the norm of freedom for all groups came in the aftermath of the great wave of immigration that ended after World War I. These immigrants came mostly from southern and eastern Europe and violated more sharply than previous waves the WASP norm that had predominated up to that point. The absorption of this wave led to a generally raised level of ethnic awareness and a crisis for the American community of much the same variety as posed by the position of Blacks today. The accepted fact that the crisis was weathered is taken as good cause for believing that the contemporary one will be as well. Blacks' turn has come last because until recently they were isolated from the process of inclusion by living in the rural South. But now that is no longer the case, and they will become part of the process by which the United States has always been protected from serious class conflict, namely the upward mobility of large parts of the working class that have been recent immigrants. Now that Blacks are at last on the same ladder of social mobility as everyone else, they can begin their ascent of it. Of course, the suggestion that if others could make it starting from the bottom, then Blacks should be able to do so simply does not follow. The difference between the historical position of immigrant groups and of Blacks is immense. To pose the problem in this way manages to avoid these differences and begs the question of why after 350 years Blacks remain the most unequal and alien group in America when much more recent immigrant groups have been incorporated with relative ease. To base optimism only on analogy or extrapolation is as weak as placing faith in the providence of the creed or the cycle. It seems a curious way to analyze a social problem: by looking at everything except the actual situation at hand.

Parsons: The Concept of Citizenship

A final illustration of this form of reasoning is evident in the use made, again notably by Parsons, of the concept of citizenship (Marshall, 1950). In Marshall's formulation full citizenship has three components: the first is the civic or legal aspect by which the individual or group is guaranteed equal rights of person, property, religion, and association before the law. This stage is especially important for Blacks because they are the one group, apart from Native Americans, that did not secure these rights automatically. It is on this component that demands for equality can most effectively be made in terms of the American creed, and patently there has been significant progress in this area, as witnessed, for example, by the Civil Rights Acts of the 1960s.

The second component is full political rights. This involves Blacks not only gaining the franchise but participating in the lobbying process, obtaining access to the media, and doing whatever else is needed to allow them to affect the policy-making process in their best interests. Increases in Black voter registration and the election of Blacks to political office are taken to provide ample evidence of the advances being made in this area. These elections are seen to be of double significance, for besides helping to give Blacks the second component of citizenship, they also provide the resources by which the third and final component, and thus the solution to the Black problem, will be achieved.

The third component is social and concerns the attainment of the resources and capacities that are the prerequisites for gaining equality of opportunity. The first category of resources is economic, whereas the second relates to Blacks' capacity to function in their environment with the same effectiveness as other groups and involves the provision of equal health, education, and housing. Writing at the height of the Great Society programs, Parsons claimed that attention was being turned to the area of social rights. He argued that the programs needed to achieve these rights for Blacks were accepted by society at large, that the federal government, as the agency most committed to the implementation of the creed, had begun to enact them, and that when they had achieved their objective, the citizenship cycle would be complete and Blacks would be fully included in American society. It is clear that Parsons saw Blacks as having reached the penultimate stage in the cycle and regarded the prospects for completion as bright. Today, the faith that Parsons, echoing Myrdal, placed in the federal government as the agency that would overcome the remaining obstacles to universalism seems naive. It is now clear that cutting poverty programs and shifting responsibilities to local government, where particularistic forces are stronger, has drastically reduced the federal government's role in combating racism. If such extreme changes can take place in the role of the federal government in so short a period, it is clearly shortsighted, to put it no higher, to seize upon one period and suggest that the government must always act as an agent of inclusion. This is an excellent illustration of how the tendentiousness of the liberal approach causes it to press every possible factor into the service of the preordained goal, in this case elevating short-term influences to a level of historical significance that is both inappropriate and misleading.

But the tendentiousness is even more apparent in the employment of the citizenship concept itself. It is Parsons's equivalent of Park's cycle and Myrdal's creed, a teleological device used to predetermine the issue and thus relegate investigation to the secondary level of monitoring inevitable progress. One of its uses is to focus attention on areas where progress for Blacks is undeniable, that of legal and political rights, although this is not to suggest that legal advances are themselves unproblematic.[6] Parsons lays great stress on these first two elements and suggests that because they have been achieved, it only remains for the third and final element to be brought into the pattern. The impression thus created is that this will follow naturally from the other two because they are all part of the same process, the citizenship cycle.

It is, of course, not justified to imply such a connection. There is no logical reason why civic and political gains will produce social and economic ones. It is only made to appear that such a relationship exists by the characterization in terms of the citizenship concept. This characterization is, however, an artifact: It may be a useful way of conceptualizing the problem but it is invalid to suggest that a conceptual relationship must be reflected in the real world. Parsons's assumption that power at the ballot box and in public office will obtain economic equity for Blacks is no more than an assumption and one which, when tested against recent experience of Blacks, displays none of the inevitability associated with it through its representation in the citizenship cycle.

WHY DOES LIBERALISM FAIL?

Having explored some of the ways in which the liberal analysis is deficient, we must now ask why this is the case. The answer lies in the fact that the real object of this approach is to fit Blacks into the general conception of the United States as a pluralistic, consensus-based society that is the embodiment of liberal ideals. The primary purpose is to defend this view of America, and it is because the Black experience does not fit easily into it that it becomes necessary to have recourse to a selective use of history and elaborate conceptual distortion. Conceptually, the liberal view is deficient because it contains no adequate theory of racism. The reason is that racism is not seen as a relevant property of contemporary American social structure; it is neatly confined to history and such importance as it is conceded today is mainly viewed as a legacy of the old South. The liberal refusal to come to terms with the unpalatable fact of American racism precludes it from generating a proper understanding of the limits on Black progress and fosters the sanguine optimism that bedevils so much of the work in this tradition.

It is the same with the conception of power (Giddens, 1968; Katznelson, 1971; Parsons, 1966). This is seen as a generalized capacity for social action. If society is to achieve its agreed-upon goals, some members and institutions must have power in order to organize effective action in pursuit of those goals. As society becomes more complex it needs more authority structures, more power, to achieve its ends. The analogy can be drawn with money, the supply of which must expand as the economy becomes more complex in order to facilitate an increased number of transactions and meet the needs of the market. Power then, like money, is a means, not an end. More significantly it is not a zero-sum concept; it carries no connotations of conflict because its distribution rests on a value consensus regarding goals, and if society agrees on the goals, it must agree on the means. Power is thus, by definition, legitimate in the eyes of those subject to it and conflict is inappropriate. The idea of power as a means of exploitation or of oppression is excluded. Consequently, the exploitative and oppressive elements of the Black experience are effectively downgraded. Instead of an appreciation of the fact that Black gains have had to be struggled for and painfully extracted from the white majority, we are given the notion that these gains have been obtained as a result of whites' faith in democratic ideals or have followed inevitably from modernization. The insistence on the consensual nature of American society thereby eliminates the problem of power as a barrier to Black progress and gives rise to a bias in the analysis that vitiates its own optimism.

The complacency thus produced was rudely shattered by the events of the 1960s. The freedom rides, the ghetto riots, the rise of the Black power movement, and all the other manifestations of the Black upsurge threw into question the liberal assumption of gradual, orderly progress. Those writing in this tradition were placed on the defensive as the incorporation process did not seem to be proceeding smoothly. The response to this crisis reveals more facets of the liberal approach.

Blaming the Victim

One is the familiar syndrome of blaming the victim (Ryan, 1971), a tendency well exemplified in a classic analysis of this period, Glazer and Moynihan's (1963) *Beyond the Melting Pot*. This adopted a rather iconoclastic tone by attacking the conventional wisdom on the role of ethnicity in American life. Glazer and Moynihan argued that the vitality and importance of ethnic groups were not in decline, as the received wisdom would have it, but remained as relevant as when the immigrants first arrived, and would continue to be so, a thesis they illustrated by examining the pattern of ethnic politics in New York City. Their claim took group-based pluralism rather than individualism and assimilation as its cornerstone, and on this basis the authors were able to reach an optimistic conclusion in the first edition of their book:

> [One] concluded that the political course of the Northern Negro would be quite different from that of the Southern Negro. He would become part of the game of accommodation politics—he already was—in which the posts and benefits were distributed to groups on the basis of struggle, of course, but also on the basis of votes, money and political talent, and one concluded that in this game Negroes would not do too badly. (1970, p. x)[7]

By the time Glazer and Moynihan wrote a new introduction to the second edition of their book in 1970, events had caused them to revise this conclusion. The rate of gains made by Blacks had not kept pace with their rising expectations, and their sense of well-being actually seemed to decline. As a result Glazer and Moynihan were forced to recognize that it was not satisfactory to consider Blacks as simply another in a line of ethnic groups that had been successfully absorbed. Rather it became necessary to define them as a racial group and as such unique, a group to which the conventional analysis did not easily apply and for which new concepts would therefore have to be employed. The initial response to the events of the late 1960s thus required those writing from a liberal perspective to confront the problem of race more directly and brought about a retreat from the easy optimism displayed earlier.

The late 1960s also produced a direct challenge to the adequacy of the pluralist model, both as a description of American society and as an agent of Black progress. In response, Glazer and Moynihan (1970), rather than abandoning the incorporationist perspective, instead shifted the basis of their advocacy from description to prescription. They argued that pluralism was still the desirable system, even if it could not be claimed that it was the existing one, for Blacks at least. This argument was justified on the grounds of realism. If the Black problem was to be solved, then the only possible way was through incorporation into the existing system. Any other alternative would be unacceptable to white America and thus impracticable. The real threat to the possibility of successful accommodation was taken to be the rise of Black militancy and separatist tendencies. In a deft reversal, this allowed the proposition that the real reason for the failure of pluralism was Black rather than white racism. Black militancy had gone beyond acceptable limits and was preventing Blacks from taking their place in the system, partly by reducing their desire to do so and partly by antagonizing whites and so reducing their willingness to extend the benefits of the system to Blacks. The upshot of the argument was that if Blacks did not resist the temptations of militancy, they would be frozen out of society and would certainly end up suffering more than anyone else as a consequence (Glazer & Moynihan, 1970, p. xl).

This argument shifts the responsibility for failure away from the pluralist system and on to Blacks themselves. Lectured on the virtues of moderation and told that by challenging the rules of the game they were causing their own lack of progress, Black leaders were castigated and their demands caricatured. Militant Black spokesmen were described as "irresponsible demagogues whose chief claim to leadership is their ability to get on television by making outrageous remarks" (Glazer, 1969, p. 38). Vituperation was preferred to an analysis of how frustration may have led Blacks into militancy, and the portrayal of Blacks' demands as mindless and nihilistic contributed to the vicious circle of Black exclusion by reinforcing whites' fears and exacerbating their intransigence. To accept that Blacks were employing militant rhetoric because they were not gaining access to the system would have meant acknowledging that the problem lay with a system that was not working for Blacks. It was easier at this stage to avoid the issue by blaming Black militancy, protecting in the name of realism the essence of the liberal perspective, commitment to the status quo, even though to do so helped exaggerate the very phenomenon the analysis deplored.

Blaming History

In this tactic of shifting responsibility, Black militancy was not always the culprit. In another notable case, it was history that was to blame. In 1965 Moynihan produced a report on the Black family in which he argued that Blacks were at the bottom of the scale not because of some inherent inferiority or because of current racism, but because the breakup of the Black family under slavery had produced a preponderance of female-headed families in the Black community, and this had restricted the ability of Black children to compete with those from more conventional family backgrounds (Moynihan, 1965; Rainwater & Yancey, 1967). The historical validity of this argument has since been widely challenged (Gutman, 1976), but the point is that it was used in such a way as to imply that Black inadequacy was the problem, and it is this theme that recurs even though the explanation for that inadequacy may change.[8] The argument is pragmatic rather than moralistic: Black social patterns are seen as simply not allowing them to keep up in the socioeco-

nomic race (Banfield, 1974). The breakdown of traditional cultural re-
straints, as evidenced in such pathological traits as rates of drug use,
enjoyed renewed currency in the 1980s to explain why so much of the
Black community was trapped at the bottom of the social structure
(Glazer, 1988). The proposition remains that mobility is open to all who
have the ability to take advantage of the opportunities that exist. If
Blacks fail to do so the fault must therefore lie with their history or with
another of their attributes. This view of the problem as rooted in Black
pathology harmonizes with the benign liberal view of American society
even as it reduces optimism as to the likely pace of progress for Blacks.
It therefore gives liberals an explanation of the slow rate of progress
without requiring them to reevaluate the capacity of the present social
system to incorporate Blacks. Or, to put it more harshly, it provides a
functional substitute for racism by resolving the peculiarly liberal problem of reconciling humanitarian impulses with self-interest (Valentine,
1968).

The question that again arises in relation to this line of response to the
Black upsurge of the 1960s is why liberals remain attached to the unal-
tered pluralist model. The answer lies in the increasingly prominent prescriptive aspect of their analysis. Its proponents are rarely content to
describe trends or present hypotheses on future developments. They are
concerned also to prescribe the best means of Black advance and expose
the limitations of alternatives. This suggests the heart of the matter, that
the liberal model is more normative than positive, more ideological than
scientific. Consequently, it is not easily susceptible to refutation. When
one defense of the values it embodies is undermined, new lines will be
sought rather than reject the basic preferences inherent in the model. The
primary commitment is to moderation, orderly progression, and action
within the social system as presently constituted. The model is a crystal-
lization of a view of the whole of American society, and it is the more
general perspective that dictates the approach to the Black experience.

Blaming Class Differences

Another response to the events of the 1960s that has become increasingly significant shares with the blaming the victim syndrome the advantage, from the liberal point of view, of arguing that white racism is not
the barrier to Black progress. The emphasis here is on the distinction
between the effects of class, as opposed to race per se, in determining
Blacks' position in society. The argument is that many of the behavior

patterns that impede Black progress are in fact lower-class patterns. Edward Banfield (1974, p. 86), for example, has argued that if social class is held constant in making Black-white income comparisons, then the difference between the races is significantly diminished, albeit not eliminated. Similarly, it is a well-attested fact that the poorer elements of society, both Black and white, have higher birth rates than the middle class. The result is that the ratio of dependents to income earners is higher in the Black community than in the white, which in itself explains part of the income differential between the races. So the source of inequality is demographic differences that work to Blacks' disadvantage, and these are, in turn, the consequence of differential class backgrounds rather than of racial discrimination.

The strongest evidence for the liberal invocation of class in support of the liberal perspective is, however, the bifurcation of the Black population in recent years as a result of the growth of both the Black middle class and of a Black underclass. The trend was noted by a variety of commentators (Freeman, 1974) and elaborated by Moynihan (1972). The most rigorous and comprehensive statement of the argument was made by W. J. Wilson (1978) in his *The Declining Significance of Race,* where he argues that to talk of the Black experience as if it were monolithic is misleading because an elaborate class structure has developed within the Black community. The bottom third of the community is in a deteriorating position and consists of female-headed families, the unemployed, welfare recipients, and so on; the middle third is a relatively stable working class concentrated in the semiskilled blue-collar occupations; and the top third, benefiting from the dismantling of formal segregation and discrimination since the 1950s, as well as increased access to the higher education vital for middle-class jobs, now occupies white-collar, professional, and skilled blue-collar jobs. The conclusion to be drawn from this development is that "class has become more important than race in determining Black life-chances in the modern industrial period" (Wilson, 1978, p. 150). If a significant number of Blacks are now able to make it into the middle class despite their race, it must follow that race cannot be an insuperable barrier to social mobility, the absence of which for the majority of Blacks must therefore be explained in class terms.

A sanguine interpretation of recent events does not follow inevitably from Wilson's thesis (Washington, 1979). Indeed Wilson (1987, p. viii) took pains to dissociate himself from just such an interpretation of his work, and there is no lack of irony in the fact that the skill and forcefulness of his exposition has led his arguments to be taken up by those who put an interpretation upon them with which he would profoundly disagree. Given Wilson's argument, it is possible to focus at least as much on the increasingly severe problems of the Black underclass as on the gains of the Black middle class, as he himself has done. And because class problems are no less intractable within the present social structure than race problems, it is perfectly possible to construct a radical analysis of the need for structural change to solve the Black problem on the basis of the bifurcation of the Black community (Brooks, 1990). But not surprisingly, this is not the line of interpretation that has been followed in liberal commentary on the trends examined by Wilson. Rather, the emphasis has been on using bifurcation to demonstrate the existence of Black progress, interpreting the growing gulf between the Black middle class and the lower classes as showing that Black social and economic patterns are becoming more like white patterns, and to this extent may be seen as evidence of Black incorporation.

This is a less rosy picture of incorporation than some earlier ones because it accepts that there will continue to be poor Blacks just as there will continue to be poor whites. But this is not the element that is stressed. Instead the rapid progress of college-educated Blacks toward equality with their white peers is emphasized as the precursor of full incorporation for Blacks. The flaw in this argument lies not in the emphasis on the gap between Black lower and middle classes, but in the conclusion that this in itself is proof of the emancipation of Blacks. To take one factor that suggests an alternative explanation, most Black middle-class employment takes place in the public sector. Disproportionately few Blacks have achieved high position as corporate executives or entrepreneurs. It is among these latter groups, and the capital they control, that power and wealth is concentrated in the American social system. Thus Black wealth has a more fragile basis;[9] that which is given by the government can be taken away by the government. Blacks have not moved into positions of wealth creation where they could, if necessary, successfully defend their wealth. Despite higher income, their position remains one of dependency, albeit of a different kind.

Moreover, the changes that have occurred in the Black pattern do not suggest it will eventually come to mirror the white one. Because Blacks are gaining entry only to limited sectors of the middle class, this advance may be seen as a form of tokenism as well as a harbinger of full equality. It may be argued that just enough Blacks are being given just enough stake in the system to forestall the development of Black radicalism. If this threat is the spur to Black advance, then far less than full equality will be necessary to forestall it. In addition, Blacks remain disproportionately represented in the working- and underclass. Their absorption into working-class jobs may be seen as occurring only because whites are vacating them to move to better ones, thus preserving existing differentials. And the position of the Black working class is made less secure both by rapid technological innovation, which is eliminating their jobs with disproportionate impact, and by globalization, which is exporting "their" jobs to locations where labor is cheaper. If this continues to happen, the Black working class will become as economically marginal as the Black underclass already is, and the gap between them and those who have escaped into the new, technologically advanced industries will become greater than ever.

The point is not to argue that class does not matter in determining the position of Blacks or to deny that Black income and occupational patterns are changing, in some respects for the better. Rather it is to suggest that these changes cannot be interpreted as evidence of some linear form of progress toward full incorporation. On the contrary, "[T]he pattern has traditionally been one where 'windows of opportunity' were promptly closed just as the gains began to produce significant reduction in Black-white economic disparities" (Farley & Allen, 1987, p. 419).

There is more to a class analysis of Blacks' position than monitoring changes in income gaps between Blacks and whites. Class is a relational concept, and the growing similarity of income within each race does not imply increasingly equal power relations between them. It is perfectly possible for some Blacks to obtain higher incomes without all Blacks gaining any more power to control their lives, a simple but fundamental distinction to which the liberal perspective seems blind. Nor does it prove that the same forces govern the distribution of income within each race. Even if Blacks and whites develop increasingly similar patterns of income distribution, factors such as tokenism may continue to mean that the similarity is misleading because what governs the pattern for each race continues to be an unequal distribution of power between the races resulting from the still quite distinct positions they occupy in the social structure.

The liberal fallacy is to interpret change as incorporation and so remove racism from its location in the social structure. It is because the substitution of class for race in this sense is one means of achieving this object that it has been seized upon in such a tendentious fashion. The growth of the Black middle class is undoubtedly a significant development, but its real significance lies not in pointing toward the advent of

Black equality but in demonstrating that the more things change the more they stay the same.

CONCLUSION

The incorporation of class into the liberal perspective on Black progress signals the transition between the defensive phase of the liberal tradition and its rebirth in a more neoconservative manifestation, which has defended the social order with greater assertiveness and élan than at any time since the early days of faith in the creed or the cycle. Before we examine the neoconservative response in more detail, we must ask, by way of summary, what are the principal strengths and weaknesses of this tradition? Park and Myrdal, as its founding fathers, imparted the essential characteristics of optimism and determinism, which minimized the role of the social structure in creating racial deprivation. Attempts were made to provide a more substantial grounding for this optimism in the structural processes of modernization and its corollary of pluralization. But the liberal analysis remained too dependent on unsatisfactory techniques of extrapolation and analogy to give its optimism intellectual conviction, as the events of the 1960s subsequently demonstrated. Resort was then taken to a prescriptive position, which shifted responsibility for the absence of greater progress onto Black militancy or other failings of Blacks themselves, before defensiveness was finally abandoned in the neoconservative renaissance of the liberal tradition.

The major strength of the liberal tradition is its ability to describe and capture the undoubted areas of progress that have occurred for Blacks. Indeed, the credibility of the tradition may be said to rest on the extent of these improvements, so closely is its analysis identified with them. In fact, however, this strength is only the mirror image of the tradition's weakness, its one-sidedness. It can only account for progress, not for its absence, or, more strictly, its limitations. Liberal accounts of the negative side of the picture tend to be feeble, as with Park's doctrine of obstacles or the attribution of the problem to the leftover effects of past discrimination. The overriding animus is to avoid making the choice between the liberal system, which has served white America, and progress for Blacks. The more progress Blacks can be seen to be making, the less the need for such a choice; hence the systematic bias that exaggerates the extent of progress and distorts liberal analysis.

Even in this context, the liberal tradition is stronger at monitoring progress than explaining it. The concepts employed—the race relations cycle, the American creed, the modernization process, the immigrant analogy—have all been found wanting. What is lacking is the capacity to go beyond the celebration of progress to the explanation of how much progress there has been, why that much and not more or less. In responding to this, the tendency is to fall back on description or on idealism —Americans' commitment to equality, justice, and so on. It is manifestly obvious that although ideals have a role to play, if they were as paramount as liberals proclaim there would never have been a race problem in the first place. To understand the degree of progress, we need to investigate the balance of power underlying racial interaction, not merely to monitor the closing of income gaps; we need to investigate the relations between the races, not just their income, occupational, or educational levels. To confine analysis to the latter abstracts from the central factor of racism by suggesting that Blacks' position is somehow produced independently of whites and their relation to the white community.

This brings us to the central flaw in the liberal perspective, its notion of progress itself. The liberal idea of Black progress is limited to incorporation into the status quo. It takes the existing social structure as a given and restricts the definition of the problem to how Blacks can be brought into it. By dismissing any argument that Blacks cannot be incorporated into this structure, it is blind to the idea that it is precisely this structure that keeps Blacks in an inferior position.

The liberal perspective therefore fails to come to terms with the idea that Black America is what it is because white America is what it is, and the position of one cannot change without changing the position of the other. Underlying this failure is a refusal to accept that race relations are power relations of a zero-sum kind. The implications of this are that Black advance can only be made at the expense of whites, that whites are unlikely to forgo the privilege they derive from Black disadvantage, and that therefore to answer the question of whether Blacks will advance we must investigate the resources each group brings to what in essence is a relationship of conflict. These resources and the balance between them are what constitute the social structure in this context, and so investigation of it is the key to understanding the issue. The liberal tradition as we have considered it so far treats the social structure as neutral or benevolent and effectively ignores it; it remains to be seen whether this fundamental deficiency is remedied in the neoconservative strand that has become its primary expression in recent years.

NOTES

1. A major recent study, which, if it does not replicate Myrdal's work, certainly updates its tradition, is Gerald D. Jaynes and Robin M. Williams, Jr.'s (1989) *A Common Destiny: Blacks and American Society*. Walter A. Jackson's (1990) *Gunnar Myrdal and America's Conscience: Social Engineering and Racial Liberalism 1938-1987*, provides a comprehensive treatment of the origins and influence of *An American Dilemma*, whereas David W. Southern's (1987) *Gunnar Myrdal and Black-White Relations: The Use and Abuse of "An American Dilemma,"* 1944–69 demonstrates clearly the influence of Myrdal's work on legal and social practitioners in the field of race relations in the quarter century after its publication.

2. Nor, we may note, was Myrdal's optimism dimmed for a considerable time. In his preface to the 20th anniversary edition of *An American Dilemma*, he claimed to have been proved right by events in the interim and to have observed the power of the creed in improving the lot of Blacks (Myrdal, 1962).

3. A related form of determinism is apparent in the more recent past arises in debates on sociobiology. See, for example, Van Den Berghe (1981).

4. One area in which the influence of this perspective was evident was in the landmark 1954 Supreme Court decision, *Brown v. Board of Education,* Topeka, Kansas, which may be said to represent a high-water mark of the idea that integration and assimilation were the object of race relations. In writing the opinion, Chief Justice Earl Warren cites the influence of *An American Dilemma* on the Court's thinking (Cruse, 1987, p. 39).

5. Myrdal himself did become less optimistic later in life. Writing in the 1970s he became concerned at the bifurcation of the Black community and the creation of an underclass and also at the failure of leadership which he saw manifested in the tendency of Black and white leaders to forsake the goal of integration in favor of an ill-defined pluralism that was dangerous in its celebration of ethnicity (Myrdal, 1974). It is significant, however, that despite this he was never able to embrace in the American context the more radical approach he adopted to the problems of the Third World (Myrdal, 1968) or to advocate fundamental structural reforms. Instead the continuing power of his definition of the problem in moral terms led him to persist in stressing the importance of exhortation and education as the keys to resolving America's race problem (Jackson, 1990, pp. 352-359).

6. A generation after the passage of the Civil Rights Acts, Kristin Bumiller (1988) has demonstrated that the role of legal redress against discrimination is limited not only by a narrow focus, its inability to embrace the structural roots of discrimination, and its bias toward dealing with the problem at an individual level, but also by the fact that those subject to discrimination are unwilling to employ this avenue. This is partly the result of the costs associated with legal proceedings; but a more significant factor is the internalization of discrimination by its victims, their belief that, although the law can provide justice in the abstract, it cannot and will not do so for them. The paralyzing effect of this is less an act of collusion with their victimhood than a testament to the power of the ideology of the law. The consequence is a paradoxical exacerbation of discrimination rather than the alleviation that is the ostensible role of civil rights legislation. Derrick Bell (1987), in *And We Are Not Saved,* similarly exposes the limitations of civil rights legislation and goes further, arguing that "reforms resulting from civil rights litigation invariably promote the interests of the white majority" (p. 63), even though as a civil rights lawyer he retains his commitment to legal redress, not in the belief that it will ensure Black progress but because of the absence of a better strategy (pp. 73-74).

7. Moynihan's subsequent career as U.S. ambassador and U.S. senator has led him to deal more with international matters, and in this arena, too, he argues that the power of ethnicity is not only underestimated and understudied but that the collapse of communism will reveal the true extent of its continuing vitality and importance in human affairs. He is, however, less sanguine about the implications of this in the international context than he and Glazer were in the American one. See Moynihan's (1993) *Pandaemonium: Ethnicity in International Politics.*

8. It is possible, as Shelby Steele (1990) has shown, to discuss the problems of Black culture sympathetically, demonstrating the weaknesses the historical legacy has left Blacks, without descending to the level of blame. Steele discusses these issues with sensitivity, insight, and eloquence, but even he goes too far in arguing that the internal problems are a greater barrier to progress than the external facts of discrimination, racism, and political and economic weakness.

9. One indicator of this is the fact that, as Farley and Allen (1987) point out, "Blacks and whites differ greatly in their wealth holdings, with the typical white household having assets about eleven times those of the typical Black household, a difference that is very much larger than the racial difference in current income" (p. 313).

3

America Right or Wrong:
The Neoconservative Response

The neoconservative response to the question of Black progress has been to reduce the criteria against which satisfactory progress might be judged; the goalposts have been shifted in order to permit a more vigorous defense of the status quo. This response has been given greater force by being in tune with the demonstrably more conservative mood evident in the country at large in the 1970s and 1980s, as compared with the classically liberal period in the 1960s. However, the appellation is misleading to the extent that it implies neoconservative writers proceed from a different—that is, conservative—philosophical tradition. Just as the general case can be made that liberalism, despite its many guises, remains the preeminent tradition of social thought in America (Hartz, 1955/1991), so neoconservative premises in the analysis of Black progress are well within the liberal tradition. The increasingly conservative slant of the analysis is not a repudiation of the liberal view of the place of Blacks but a creative reaction to the limits of the traditional liberal perspective. The analysis has become more conservative precisely in order to maintain the validity of the liberal view.[1] The neoconservative phase is therefore both a defense and an extension of the liberal tradition. It has built on those aspects of that tradition discussed in the previous chapter, but has rounded them out in ways that are sufficiently significant to warrant consideration in their own right (Steinfels, 1979).

AN INSISTENCE ON BLACK PROGRESS

Perhaps the least intellectually convincing aspect of the neoconservative analysis is the renewed insistence on the fact that Blacks have clearly
been making steady progress toward full incorporation in recent years.
The quantity of evidence employed in support of this contention has
increased considerably, but the presentation is often heavily skewed to fit
preexisting liberal concepts (Zashin, 1978). A notorious early example
was the well-known article by Wattenberg and Scammon (1973), in
which they argued that the majority of the Black community had become
middle class, a claim justified by stretching the terminology in a manner
that verged on the scurrilous (Bryce, 1973). More temperate accounts
from the period (Farley, 1977, 1984, 1985; Freeman, 1978; Levitan,
Johnston, & Taggart, 1975) have argued that the most rapid progress was
made in the late 1960s but continued through the 1970s despite a worsen-
ing general economic picture. The greatest gains were made by those
Black women who work outside the home and by young Black men with
advanced education, who have made spectacular gains in middle-class
employment as barriers of discrimination have broken down. Most
widely cited was the fact that young Black college-educated couples had
achieved parity with their white peers (Sowell, 1984, pp. 52, 80). The
failure of overall Black family income to continue making gains relative
to whites is explained by the increasing proportion of Black families that
are female-headed and of persistently low income. The gains have in fact
continued for Black husband-wife families, and the two trends have in
effect canceled each other out.

The problem with the considerable number of analyses of census data
on income and occupation which elaborate on points such as these, however, is that the evidence is more often than not one-sided. Favorable
facts are seized upon and repeated in a wide range of books and articles.
Where facts are inconvenient they are ignored, systematically down-
played, or put in a context that casts the most favorable possible light on
them. Time spans and other bases of comparison are manipulated to create an impression and sometimes an illusion of progress. This is partly a
reflection of the deeply polemical nature of the neoconservative perspective. In a complex area where no simple conclusions are possible, neoconservatives appear most animated by what they perceive as a conspiracy of silence on the gains that have been made, a refusal to recognize or
even to deny the facts as they see them (Greeley, 1974). Far from accepting that this is an area where the idea of progress itself is inherently

contested and there can be no simple answers, and that the problem is often one of perspective over which reasonable people can and will continue to differ—should one be optimistic because Blacks have made some progress, or pessimistic because they still have so far to go? Is a glass half empty or half full?—neoconservatives attack, in particular, Black leaders and federal bureaucrats. Both groups, it is claimed, have a vested interest in denying the reality of the situation. For the bureaucrats this is because continuing Black deprivation means continuing federal programs to alleviate it, programs they are employed to administer. For Black leaders, Black deprivation allows them to maintain pressure on government and employers for preferential programs for Blacks, programs whose benefits accrue more to middle-class Blacks such as themselves than to the poor Blacks they are intended to help. The criticism, often vitriolic, probably adds more heat than light to the debate. It is a further example of deflecting attention away from the social system that produces Black deprivation, a polemical technique that, despite its occasional effectiveness, amounts to little more than an exercise in scapegoating.

THE ECONOMIC ARGUMENT

Significant as such tendentiousness is, the more important question is whether the revitalization neoconservatism has brought to the liberal tradition entails any new theoretical arguments that might add weight to the perspective. One body of work that might lay claim to meeting this criterion is that of a number of economists, including some Blacks, who have in recent years built a powerful case for a laissez-faire approach to Black progress, one that has been seen as a significant challenge to the previously dominant liberal interventionist approach (Boston, 1988; Jencks, 1983; Sowell, 1975, 1981b, 1984; Williams, 1983). Their starting point is an inversion of the view, commonly held in the radical perspective but subscribed to by many liberals as well, which explains the persistence of racial discrimination in terms of its value as a source of profit for whites. Instead, they take their cue from theoretical work by Nobel prize-winning economists, Gary Becker (1957/1971) and Kenneth Arrow (1973), who have shown that discrimination is not compatible with long-run market equilibrium. Discrimination is perceived as profit forgone because employers can increase their profit by employing those workers who are discriminated against to do the same work as privileged workers, but at lower wages. In a competitive market, and assuming the substitutability of labor, the employers seeking maximum profit have an incentive to act in a way that will eliminate discrimination.

Competitive markets are, therefore, not merely nondiscriminatory in the sense that they are color-blind, but their workings actually serve to eliminate discrimination. The implication of this is that discrimination will most readily be achieved by letting markets find their own equilibrium without restriction, regulation, or hindrance. This will have the further virtue of allowing those affected by economic transactions to register their own preferences through the price mechanism and remove the influence of third parties who would intervene in such transactions in order to impose their conception of the "public interest." Free competition, free entry to markets, and flexibility of prices and wages will improve Blacks' economic position rather than outside intervention, because these conditions will make it in the employers' interests to employ Blacks. So, on this analysis, government intervention is the problem, not the solution.

Minimum wage laws are a classic example of where the intention is to improve the wages of the poor but the effect is to reduce employment opportunities for them by eliminating the flexibility in the price of their labor. The consequence is to raise wages above the level of productivity and so prevent the clearing of the employment market. Trade unions, protected by government, act similarly by restricting entry into labor markets. By doing so, in the name of protecting workers' rights, they prevent Blacks who want to work and employers who want to employ them from freely negotiating a price (wage) at which such a mutually beneficial transaction can take place.

Substantiation of the argument that politics is the problem and not the solution is provided by the example of Chinese and Japanese Americans, who have largely eschewed political involvement and yet have made considerable economic progress, demonstrating that political power is not a necessary precondition for, nor its absence a necessary barrier to, progress. As Sowell (1983) suggests, "Historically the relationship between political success and economic success has been more nearly inverse than direct" (p. 169). Much more important in explaining the economic success of the Chinese and Japanese communities in the United States and many others societies has been their culture's stress on the ethic of strong family support and hard work, traits which much of the Black community appears to lack, partially accounting for their poor adaptation to an environment that puts a premium on such attributes (Sowell, 1979).

Leaving aside the fact that this ignores the effects of the vast difference in size between groups—it is surely more difficult for American society to fully incorporate some 26 million Blacks than to adjust to the progress made by groups, like the Japanese, whose numbers run to less than 1 million—it is significant that, despite its ostensible and innovative concentration on economics as the root of the problem, neoconservatism still has to resort to cultural explanations to provide a full account of the barriers to progress. In this it reveals its continuing ties with liberal responses, particularly those that lend themselves to blaming the victim.[2]

In other respects the neoconservative approach does appear to turn traditional liberalism on its head. It continues to stress the argument that factors other than pure discrimination account for a much higher proportion of Black disadvantage than is generally accepted. As well as cultural attributes, the particular age and geographic distribution of the Black community contributes to observed Black disadvantage. Where neoconservatism seems to part company with much of the traditional approach is in its diagnosis of the remedy for this.

The Free Market Solution

True to its faith in the ability of the market to eliminate Black disadvantage, the argument is that if markets are allowed to operate more freely they will eliminate disadvantage more quickly and more democratically than any alternative mechanism. Where the liberal approach in the 1960s had placed great faith in the power of the federal government to solve the Black problem, this faith now seems to have been transferred entirely to the market, with the government, far from being the savior, having become the villain of the piece.

In fact the rupture is not so great. Liberal faith in the efficacy of government in the 1960s was specifically confined to the elimination of formal or legal discrimination as a basis for creation of equal opportunity. The neoconservative argument builds on rather than repudiates this by suggesting that once formal discrimination is removed, the role of the government is complete, and any further intervention, however well meaning or however much it is intended to further Black progress, can only serve, in what remains a market-driven economy, to distort the workings of the market and thus ipso facto to undercut Blacks' best means of advance (Sowell, 1978). Emphasis on a market solution should therefore be seen as a development of, and a complement to, the traditional liberal view of the role of government in this area. It is a development that has its roots in a long and intellectually distinguished tradition that advocates a minimalist role for the state (Friedman, 1962; Gray, 1984; Hayek, 1960; Nozick, 1974). But no matter how distinguished the intellectual antecedents the question remains of how appropriate is the application of this faith in the free market to the solution of the problem of Black progress.

The problem with this approach is that it is bewitched by the logic of its own abstractions. Rather than demonstrate that free markets are incompatible with persistent discrimination, the issue is resolved as a matter of definition; markets are simply defined in such a way that they must undermine discrimination. As a corollary, because racism is made dysfunctional to the logic of the market, it becomes inevitable that its origins must lie elsewhere. The only role open to the market is then the virtuous one of combating the influence of those spheres in which racism is generated. Once the concept is defined in this way, it is not surprising that it should become so attractive that if the real world fails to match its elegance, then the assumptions underlying this approach become prescriptive and the case inverted, so that it becomes the real world that is lacking and that should be transformed to conform to the idealized concept of a free market society, rather than the other way around (Kristol, 1978).

In this instance the prescription is to remove politics from the market. But this is an impossibility; all markets, "free" or otherwise, require a political framework. Laissez-faire does not remove political choice; it *is* a political choice, just as is every other conceivable framework for economic activity. The fallacy of this economic neoconservatism lies in its denial of Blacks' problem as an essentially political one; a denial of critical importance because it is in the political arena that Blacks' capacities are so limited. Even if we accept that Blacks' best interests lie in a free market, we would still not overcome the political weakness that prevents them from achieving this framework, as it prevents them from achieving any framework that they might believe to be in their interest. The irresponsibility of the neoconservative denial lies in its failure to recognize that free markets are a political impossibility in the United States. There are too many vested interests with a stake in government intervention, and Blacks could not change that even if they wanted to. Therefore, the most likely consequence of the advocacy of free markets is not Black emancipation but selective deregulation, with the effect of eliminating precisely those safeguards Blacks have achieved since the 1960s.

This is true because even if we accept that free markets would benefit Blacks, it does not follow that movement to half-free, less regulated markets would benefit them half as much. It is more likely to leave them with the worst of both worlds, enjoying neither the bracing effects of open competition nor the protections of government intervention. The most probable consequence of a halfway application of the free market philosophy, within a conservative American political culture replete with powerful vested interests with privileges to defend, is to provide a rationale for a do-nothing policy for an administration inclined to that approach anyway, as the history of the Reagan administration demonstrates. Neoconservative scholars cannot absolve themselves from such predictable political consequences of their analysis. Before rushing to eliminate politics from the issue of Black progress in pursuit of an infatuation with the logic of competitive markets, they would do well to incorporate into their analysis the nature of actually existing markets and the political realities that underlie them.

The Impact of Other Market Forces

The second problem with locating discrimination within the polity is the danger of confusing an analytical distinction with empirical behavior. By separating the logic of market behavior, profit maximization, from the environment in which this logic works itself out, the modifying effects of the environment on the final outcome are neglected. The assumption is too easily made that capitalists will maintain the goal of profit maximization in an environment where racial discrimination is entrenched by changing that environment, a heroic adoption of economic determinism that would sit more easily in a Marxist framework than a conservative one. A more plausible emphasis would be on the capacity of capitalists to adapt the profit imperative to the exigencies of an environment characterized by racial discrimination (Greenberg, 1976). The costs to employers of undermining a social system based on racial discrimination can be much higher than the benefits of employing Black labor in "white" jobs. In consequence, capital is more likely to take the environment as given and pursue profit within the constraints it imposes. To suppose that the mere fact of competition will always drive employers to undermine racial discrimination, no matter how deeply embedded it is in a culture, is to ignore the complexity of the influences affecting the pursuit of profit; it leads to a misinterpretation of the relation between the capitalist class and continuing racial disadvantage.

The excessive emphasis on just one of the factors governing capitalist behavior, which stems from the neoconservative preoccupation with pure market forces, not only leaves out this adaptive element, it also ignores those factors that give employers an interest in perpetuating discrimination. Given the tendency of markets to reduce discrimination, the liberal explanation of its continuance is usually couched in terms of imperfect information or statistical discrimination. The latter refers to the phenomenon whereby race is taken by employers as a possibly objective but certainly cheap index of differential productivity between Blacks and whites, which leads either to their unwillingness to employ Blacks or to employ them only at a lower wage. But even this fails to consider the benefits to the capitalist class as a whole of the divisions in the working class that racial discrimination engenders. The methodological individualism of the liberal perspective, with its focus on individual employers, does not permit such consideration, because it requires the acceptance of the concept of social classes to make it intelligible. The focus on the individual is directly related to the downgrading of the role of politics in relation to the Black problem, because it precludes the notion of a collective interest of the capitalist class that might run counter to the interests of individual capitalists. It is the resolution of the tension between these that constitutes one of the essential roles of the state in a capitalist society, a resolution which is inherently political in character but a dimension of the problem to which the neoconservative approach is therefore blind.

The essence of the collective capitalist interest is the idea that racial antipathy enhances the power of capital in the class struggle by facilitating divisions in the working class. This permits the capitalist class as a whole to increase the rate of profit by holding down Black and white wages, even if it means some members of that class have to forgo the additional profit they could obtain in the short-term from the employment of cheaper Black labor. The argument is a powerful one because, with the incorporation of an appropriate role for the state, it is both compatible with the logic of competitive markets and can account for the persistence of discrimination. The inability of the neoconservative approach to reconcile these factors—and its unwillingness to accept a political analysis that can do so—drives it to a less than satisfactory explanation in terms of minimization of the role of discrimination in explaining

Black disadvantage and the emphasis on age, geographic distribution, and so on.

The point then is not to deny the crucial neoconservative insight into the logic of markets and the color blindness of capital or to argue that other factors necessarily force capital to discriminate. It is to question both the identification of the capitalist class with pure market forces and the explanatory primacy accorded to those forces. Other factors, economic, political, and cultural, are also at work, and they affect the capitalist class in contradictory ways. The balance between them, and thus the net responsibility of capital in contributing to Black disadvantage, is not a matter to be resolved by the application of simple economic first principles. The neoconservative economic analysis, although quick to focus on the abuses of government or trade unions, is limited by its infatuation with the virtues of the market and so is unable to give a balanced interpretation of the role of employers. Despite the apparent coherence and rigor of its approach compared to some of the tendentious liberal analyses previously considered, the partiality and selective application of this rigorous economic analysis raises once again the charge of one-sidedness. It suggests that perhaps the contribution of this economic strand of neoconservatism is not as different from the rest of the liberal tradition as it would like to present itself.

The Impact of Unequal Resources

This suspicion is reinforced by the fact that even in discussing the market, this approach neglects crucial aspects of its operation that undermine its contribution to Black progress. The idea that markets tend to eliminate discrimination rests in part on the assumption of perfect competition, specifically that the preferences of each participant are given equal weight in determining outcomes. Although acceptable as an analytical abstraction, this assumption may not match reality, creating problems for neoconservative theory. If participants come to the market with unequal resources, the competition itself becomes unequal, and so therefore does the resulting distribution of resources. The pursuit of self-interest in a market situation will tend to magnify inequalities, not simply because that produces the most efficient distribution of resources but because the preferences of the privileged are systematically given more weight than those of the disadvantaged. When all are required to play by the same rules in such a situation, the rich get richer and the poor get what is left. The apparent neutrality of the market is, in the absence of equal weighting of preferences, a mechanism for reinforcing privilege. The relevance of this is that most actual markets, including those where Black labor and white-owned capital interact, are imperfect in exactly this fashion. The fact that Blacks have historically lacked resources such as skills and education to compete effectively in markets has always been at the heart of their failure to make more progress, and it is the essence of the rationale for government involvement in the marketplace. It is only by ignoring this negative aspect of the market mechanism that economic neoconservatism can miss so central a dimension of the Black experience and avoid the obvious policy implications.

The failure to observe the point that laissez-faire favors the strong is apparent in the advocacy of flexible wages and free entry into labor markets, on the grounds that if Blacks are allowed to offer to sell their labor power at a sufficiently great discount compared to whites, they will always be able to find employment (Sowell, 1978; Williams, 1983). Given the fact that poor Blacks to whom this remedy is addressed lack the human capital to gain anything but menial jobs, it remains to be demonstrated, first, how they undercut whites, the overwhelming majority of whom operate in a more skilled labor market which by definition Blacks cannot enter, and, second, how Blacks are to move out of these menial jobs into the more skilled and higher-paying labor markets. American myths notwithstanding, upward mobility is a minority phenomenon and the bulk of the working class, including its Black component, remain in working-class jobs through the generations. The labor market itself contains no mechanisms to solve these problems of mobility, and in their absence advocacy of laissez-faire and flexible wages will result only in cheaper labor for capital and a growth in inequality, with the bulk of unskilled Blacks condemned to a deteriorating position at the bottom of the labor market—hardly the path of Black progress.

The Impact of Government

Despite its radical posture, the free market dimension of neoconservatism, rather than contradicting the premises of the liberal tradition, takes them to their logical conclusion by the paradoxical process of invoking the classic principles of 19th-century laissez-faire liberalism as the key to Black progress. The centerpiece of this reversion is the belief that the competitive market can resolve Blacks' problems if allowed to operate freely, a faith, as we have seen, that is as exaggerated as its exposition is one-sided. The neoconservative justification of this reversion to first principles is that government activity has palpably failed to solve the problem of Black incorporation and continued intervention is doomed to ineffectiveness because it interferes with the real economic solution. The truth is more nearly the opposite. The rediscovery of the virtues of the market has become necessary, not because government is ineffective but because it threatens to become too effective in solving Blacks' problems. The problem is that in being even as partially effective as it has, government intervention demonstrates just how much interference with the market would be necessary to secure Black incorporation. If the interference with free market distribution associated with quotas and affirmative action has been required to win even the relatively small advances for middle-class Blacks that have occurred since the 1960s, how much more interference would be necessary to win full incorporation for Blacks? The implication of government action since the 1960s is that more of the same might eventually solve the problem of Black progress but only at the cost of fatally compromising the free market system.

The pursuit of liberal programs into the realm of reverse discrimination has exposed the contradiction between liberal commitments to both freedom, understood as a free enterprise economy, and to equality. It has forced liberals to choose which is their primary commitment, and the neoconservative response is clearly to put their conception of economic freedom first. But in rediscovering the virtue of the free market, they have argued that not only does it guarantee freedom but that it will also solve the Black problem. The beauty of this argument, and the source of its attraction, is that it removes the necessity for the difficult choice between principles. Moreover, it does so in a way that emphasizes the benign aspects of a social system, the defense of which has consistently been the principal liberal motivation. The essence of the neoconservative rediscovery of the market, then, is an attempt to rescue liberalism from its own contradictions. But this is to try to square a circle; rather than reconciling contradiction it is confirming the principal trait of the liberal tradition, the commitment to a capitalist social system even, if necessary, at the expense of Blacks' equal participation in that system.

The market, and neoconservative faith in it, joins the list of liberal concepts such as the race relations cycle, the American creed, and the citizenship cycle, which all attempt to show how the American system provides the best of both worlds, freedom and Black equality. Its distinguishing feature is a radical rhetoric that stands many earlier tenets of the liberal tradition on their head. But it shares with them a commitment to a liberal social order, and it is this, and the fact that the inversion only became necessary because previous defenses of that order were beginning to threaten it, which shows this new trend for the dialectical inversion of earlier forms of liberalism that it really is. In having been transformed in this way the liberal tradition gained a new lease of life. But the economic stand of neoconservatism cannot be said to have resolved the underlying liberal dilemma, and its one-sidedness makes it perhaps not even the strongest response of which neoconservatism is capable. Other forms, which face the relation between freedom and equality more squarely, offer the prospect of a more substantial contribution to the discussion of Black progress, and it is these we must now consider.

THE ETHNICITY ISSUE

Equality of Opportunity or Outcome

Much recent debate within the liberal tradition has revolved around the question of whether the liberal commitment regarding Blacks should be to equality of opportunity or to equality of outcome. The response has not been uniform. Some, claiming to take liberal principles to their logical conclusion, have argued that eliminating formal discrimination is insufficient. If Blacks are to take their rightful place in society, they must be given special help and opportunities to overcome their disadvantages (Livingston, 1979). Equality for Blacks is here interpreted as equality of result, and this view supports whatever programs are necessary, be they busing, affirmative action, or quotas, to achieve this goal. Although this philosophy has remained very influential, the neoconservative attack on it has proven formidable.

The starting point of the attack is to inquire what was the intent of the Congress in abolishing legal discrimination in such legislation as the Civil Rights Acts of the 1960s (Glazer, 1975, 1979). It is argued that it was explicitly to provide equal opportunity in voting, housing, education, and jobs and not to guarantee Blacks equality of result with other groups in these areas. This was done on the assumption that Blacks would eventually achieve the latter; indeed, it would be racist to assume otherwise if they really were given equality of opportunity. But more importantly, it was argued that even if they did not, for whatever reason other than unfair competition, it was no business of the liberal state to guarantee equality for Blacks, or indeed anyone else. The role of the state is to set just rules to the business of competition for advantage, not to manipulate the outcome in any direction or in favor of any person or group. It is suggested that the practice has been very different. An unholy alliance of the federal judiciary and bureaucrats have contravened the intent of Congress and attempted to impose their vision of substantive equality for Blacks on American society. This has been done by the use of occupational quotas, by busing to achieve equality in education, by threats to withhold federal grants and contracts from those who fail to comply, and by a variety of other means. An unrepresentative and irresponsible elite has battled with a resentful and unwilling white population that has resisted the imposition of a definition of equality to which they do not subscribe and which they feel to be deeply unfair.

The neoconservative critique of these trends rests on the argument that it is necessary to choose between equality of opportunity and result because they are incompatible. It is not possible to enjoy both simultaneously or to employ one as a means to the other. Human beings are of differential endowment in all areas of activity. Therefore, to the extent that they compete equally, the outcome of competition must inevitably be inequality of result.[3] Any attempt to organize the terms of competition so as to provide equal results must handicap those with greater ability and must therefore violate the principle of equal opportunity. There is no alternative but to choose which principle to guarantee.[4] This realization overturns the often-made argument that it is necessary to temporarily favor Blacks in order to overcome the effects of past inequality and to ensure equal opportunity for the future, at which point racial discrimination can be dropped. Such temporary measures, neoconservatives argue, are inevitably self-defeating, and never temporary. They create vested interests that will not be given up as the favored group progresses. They will only enshrine equality of result as a permanent objective, and the other principle will ipso facto have been discarded.

Furthermore, the idea of favoring minorities would lead to absurdities in practice. How is it possible to determine which minorities should be given preference, and to what extent? The majority is, after all, but a collection of other minorities—no single ethnic group in American society constitutes more than approximately 15% of the population. The idea would require a constantly shifting hierarchy of privilege whereby advantage would be offered to whichever group found itself at the bottom. Each year a new minority would be singled out and helped accordingly. It would then rise on the social scale, only to be replaced by the new minority of the year, which would then undergo the same process. Taken to its logical conclusion this notion becomes farcical, if only because it would institute a permanent cycle of disadvantage and compensation, turning the social structure into a roller coaster and trapping ethnic groups in a nightmare ride up and down the social scale. It would also quickly prove politically, legally, and socially impossible. The only alternative is to define disadvantaged minorities by fiat on a permanent basis. This has been done, for example, for Orientals who are an officially designated minority, eligible to benefit from affirmative action, despite their rapid rise on the socioeconomic scale to the point where their per capita income is considerably above the national average. Clearly, a no less absurd result. According to this line of attack, the fundamental misconception involved here is to equate difference with discrimination. Because of it, laudable efforts to remove discrimination become misconceived attempts to perform the undesirable and impossible task of eliminating differences (Sowell, 1976). The assumption behind such attempts is the untenable one that in the absence of discrimination, all ethnic groups, including Blacks, would be distributed in every area of society in exact proportion to their numbers in the population. This leads to the belief that, for example, employers who have a lower proportion of Blacks on their payroll should be instructed to raise their numbers to the appropriate level, because failure to achieve proportionality can only be the result of persistent discrimination. This puts the burden of proof on employers, who are obliged to demonstrate that they are not guilty of discrimination if they are to escape the strictures of the federal bureaucracy. By presuming bad faith and making outcome the only criterion, the approach ignores the diversity of human ability and social experience. Any policy that requires its advocates to do this must be misconceived.

Equality of Individuals or Groups

This is not to suggest that neoconservatives favor discrimination. Rather they are arguing it should be opposed on a case-by-case basis, as distinct from a statistical one. Where discrimination is proven in a given case, it should be punished and removed. What is unacceptable is to leap from this to arguing that failure to achieve statistical parity between groups in any area of communal life must constitute discrimination and that the government therefore has the right to intervene to ensure parity. To adopt this attitude is to contravene the first principle of a liberal society, that government should secure equal rights for all individuals, without regard for group membership or position in the social structure. Beyond that, advancement and position should be the consequence of individual merit. This strand of neoconservatism thus shares with its economic counterpart and with the traditional liberal view the strictly limited role assigned to the state and thus to politics in the solution to the Black problem.

Such an argument, powerful as it is, is not without its problems. It lays the role of ethnic groups entirely open to question (Bumiller, 1988, pp. 13-14). If individual citizenship is the basic unit of American society, what role can group membership play except to compromise the preeminence of the individual? Are ethnic groups consequently to be considered worthless or even dangerous? On the contrary; Glazer, for example, argues that they should be seen as a cornerstone of American life, one whose impact is undeniably favorable both for the individual and for society. No understanding of American history can be achieved without recognizing the overwhelming importance of ethnic loyalty, organization, and group advancement (Sowell, 1981a). As we have seen, one of the central planks of the liberal argument is precisely that Blacks should and will follow the pattern set by earlier immigrant groups, advancing on the basis of their group's cultural and social resources. It may be fairly asked whether this does not amount to an attempt to have the best of both worlds. We may turn the initial point around and suggest that the principles of individualism and ethnicity are in this context incompatible. No social system can rest on both simultaneously. It is unreasonable to stress the positive role of ethnicity in discussing white America and then revert to the principle of individualism to deny Blacks the means to make progress when they try to use that same principle for group-based advance. To do so smacks suspiciously of intellectual expediency.

The Role of Ethnicity

It must be said that, of the neoconservatives, Glazer at least faces up to the issue by attempting to develop an interpretation of America's ethnic pattern that is sufficiently flexible to accommodate both principles. For him America is unique in being a nation defined by its ideals and not, as other nations, by ethnic heritage. It is by subscribing to the ideals of liberty, equality, and citizenship that Americans define themselves and not by appeals to a common ethnicity, for the simple reason that no common ethnicity exists. At the constitutional level, America is a nation that rests on the individualist principle. Consequently, there has not been and cannot be any independent ethnic politics in the United States—which is why Black separatism is fundamentally anti-American. At the same time, however, at an everyday level, ethnic groups do exist and flourish in American society. No group has been required to give up its character and distinctiveness as the price of membership of American society. The principle that has evolved has been one of compromise:

> No formal recognition of ethnic and racial groups, but every informal recognition of their right and desire to self-development, assimilation or integration at their own chosen rate, to an independent economic base, independent social, religious and political institutions and political recognition as part of a united country. (Glazer, 1972, p. 175)

This expresses the genius of the American pattern, which has warded off the twin dangers of developing either permanent, castelike subordinate groups in the name of the ethnic principle or an excessive and unworkable homogeneity in the name of the individualist principle.[5] This is the pattern to which Blacks are now being offered entry. An attempt to gain entry on the basis of statistical parity would ruin this compromise because it would establish permanent categories and so undermine a system whose fluidity is its essence. It would, moreover, do so in a way that would be bound to harm Blacks in the long run, for if definitions by group were to be fixed and made preeminent in public policy, white groups, at present vaguely and unofficially defined, would mobilize to ensure their fair share of resources. If Blacks were to force this definition on a racial basis, they would lock themselves into a minority role. They would be in no position to compete with the white majority, which would define itself in opposition to them. They would, in other words, for the sake of short-term gains, define themselves in a position of permanent inferiority. Far better for them to concur with the existing compromise that has served other groups so well, whatever the short-term difficulties of so doing. In such a pattern they are just one group among many, larger than some and with more potential resources than others, and so with better prospects than they could ever enjoy as a permanent minority.

This is the most powerful attempt to reconcile the contradictions of the liberal position. It is not clear, however, that it adds anything but sophistication to the argument. It is an artful defense of a system that has benefited most white groups, but it still begs the question of why this system will be extended to Blacks now, when it has so obviously not been in the past. Its intellectual ingenuity cannot rid it of the air of rationalization, the rationalization of the merit of a system by those who have benefited from its operation. This is a system that Blacks are welcome to try to join but that will not be changed if they fail to do so. It is a system that will be firmly defended if Blacks seek to change it, and in a way that will be worse for those who make the challenge. There is a patronizing, even menacing undertone to this, but it usually remains well below the surface because the accompanying argument is, as we have seen, that Blacks are indeed making progress toward incorporation into this system. To that extent arguments about what will happen if they are excluded become superfluous. Blacks will only be excluded if they reject the system and bring exclusion upon themselves, and the evidence suggests that most Blacks have no desire to do this.

Because it brings the argument back to this same basis, it becomes apparent that this is essentially an updating of familiar arguments rather than a new departure. But if the thrust of the neoconservative position remains that Blacks are making progress toward incorporation and that this obviates the need for special measures to try to achieve equality of result, measures that in any case would be self-defeating and would contravene the liberal principles upon which the American social fabric rests, there remains still a third element that requires elaboration.

Ethnicity as a Defense

This revolves around the revival in recent years of the importance of ethnicity in American life and is implicit in Glazer's notion of the balance between ethnicity and individualism in American pluralism. This revival is seen as in part the consequence of attempts to give Blacks equality of result. It is a response by elements of the white population to the very success they perceive Blacks as having achieved through mobilization of the ethnic principle. This success has made ethnicity appear a successful basis for political action, and white ethnic groups have reasoned that if it has worked for Blacks then if they mobilize on the same basis it can work for them, too (Bell, 1975). The revival is concentrated among working- and lower-middle-class groups, who feel most threatened by Black progress because they are the closest to Blacks on the social scale. It is their jobs that are threatened by Blacks and their neighborhoods and schools that are "invaded" as Blacks become upwardly mobile. There is a great deal of resentment in their response. This is directed, on the one hand, at Blacks, whom they feel are gaining unfair advantages, advantages never given to their ethnic forebears when they were struggling for respectability. On the other hand, it focuses on middle-class white, often WASP, liberals whom they see as advocating Black advance from a bastion of privilege that ensures that they themselves are protected from the consequences of that advance. The jobs, neighborhoods, and schools of the WASP elite are not at risk, and it is easy for them to urge sacrifice to compensate for past injustice when it is not they but working-class whites who have to do the sacrificing. Resentment at such hypocrisy is compounded by the feeling that it is the WASPs who have benefited from past exploitation of Blacks and who are now trying to assuage their guilt at the expense of the white working class (Novak, 1973; Ryan, 1973).

Resentment is not confined to the white working class; it is also found among middle-class groups, particularly Jews, who have advanced through meritocratic individualism by such means as educational success (Glazer, 1969). Even though their capacity for success has been rooted in their strong group culture, they advanced by observing the rules of the game and resent the prospect of their achievements being undermined by Black advances based on group membership alone, rather than any principle of merit. The issue in this case focuses on the idea of quotas for desirable positions. Strictly applied, this would reduce the number of Jews in high-level jobs because they overachieve occupancy of these relative to their numbers in the population. It is too much to expect Jews to accept a change in the universalistic rules through which they have struggled for success in order to facilitate advances by Blacks just because they are Black. It is the resentment at the threat—not, it must be stressed, of Black advances as such, but of Black advance based on reverse discrimination—that has undermined traditional Jewish liberalism and brought about rising tension and hostility between the two communities in recent years.

Ethnicity as Racism in Disguise

The question that arises about the revival of ethnicity is whether it is anything more than a "reactionary impulse" (Patterson, 1977). Is it anything more than racism in a modern guise, covert, subtle even, but racism nonetheless, a defense of privilege and the status quo masquerading as a positive ideal? Patterson is unequivocal in his view: Such a revival is, on the intellectual level, a desperate attempt to deny the reality of assimilation, to reinvest fragments of the past with a reality they cannot sustain; on the economic level it is a rationalization of the interests of the petit bourgeois group that has achieved a tenuous hold on the lower steps of the good life, a means to thwart those below clambering for a place on the ladder; politically, it is a key to personal advancement for those who would place the monopoly of their own little turf above the harmony of society; and psychologically it is a pathetic attempt to enhance dignity and status at the expense of the less fortunate. More generally, Patterson (1977, pp. 147-185) argues that this ethnic revival, far from reinforcing the genius of American pluralism, contradicts the essence of a liberal society, which is its tolerance of individual diversity. The diversity allowed in the pluralist world is that of groups, not individuals, and there is an inverse relationship between the autonomy of the group and that of the individual. As the role of the group strengthens, that of the individual weakens; the strength of the group is bought at the expense of the individuality of its members. Furthermore, by replacing the individual with the group as the basic unit of society, ethnic identification promotes conflict and ultimately intolerance. As ethnic groups become interest groups they must, in the competition for resources, stress the obverse of their own positive character, the negative character of all other groups and cultures. They become intolerant of others and, in the name of promoting their own ideals, they promote their interests by generating conflict and hostility with outsiders. Universalism, as the one genuine form of individualism, is the only way to break out of the vicious circle of group conflict. Its subversion by neoethnicity in the United States is a retrograde step, not only for Blacks, whose only true hope for progress comes from the universalism that takes no cognizance of race, but also for the prospects of a genuinely liberal American civilization.

The debate over the true nature of the ethnic revival is significant because whichever viewpoint is adopted dictates, in turn, a view of Black progress in recent years. If the neoconservative view of ethnic revival as an inevitable white response to Black attempts to make progress by unjustifiable means is accepted, it becomes a perfectly natural and reasonable mechanism for self-defense, one that, moreover, is consistent with the delicate balance between individualism and ethnicity that is the genius of American society and that is praiseworthy in the values it upholds. On this view, it follows that Blacks and their fellow travelers are the villains of the piece. By trying to get too much too soon, Blacks are forcing others to defend themselves and reassert traditional values. If this slows down Black progress, Blacks have no one to blame but themselves. If, on the other hand, Patterson's critique of neoethnicity is accepted—namely that it is a racist rationalization of privilege, which will only undermine the values of a liberal society just as it keeps Blacks in a position of permanent subservience—then it is clear that the blame will attach to the neoethnics and those who justify them.

The neoconservative view is clearly informed by a favorable attitude toward ethnicity and the values it embodies, irrespective of its relation to Black progress. It is no less clear that Patterson's (1973, 1976) view is influenced primarily by a concern for Black welfare. He fails, for example, to make any distinction between the intended and unintended consequences of neoethnicity, a distinction that might be thought crucial to an evaluation of its nature but is of little consequence for Blacks, for whom the result is the same. Further, both views stem from different general ideas on the nature of society. Those who see ethnicity as an axis of modern society quite as fundamental as class or nationalism are unlikely to accept any analysis reducing its role to that of merely rationalizing self-interest (Glazer & Moynihan, 1975). On the other hand, there are those who see history as a form of progress toward the universal humanism that is the only system that can liberate human potential by emancipating it from all particularistic ties. They will view the revival of age-old loyalties in the one society predicated on the attempt to achieve this ideal as nothing short of a tragedy (Patterson, 1972, 1976).

Which Theory Is Liberal?

In assessing these arguments, it is notable that they both claim to proceed from classic liberal premises, and both have some justification for doing so. Neither derivation is easily dismissed: There is clearly more to the ethnic revival than just racism, yet there can be no question that one of its consequences has been to put obstacles in the path of African Americans' attempts to make progress. Where is one to draw the line between legitimate defense of interests and racist activity? If there is racism, it is rarely expressed directly. In resisting busing, were white ethnic parents protecting the quality of their children's education and the integrity of their communities,or were they using the busing issue because of their dislike of Blacks, as a tool to keep them in their place? What do they see as "their place"? Separate certainly, but subservient? The answer is not so clear. And yet if the undercurrent is not racist, is it not too much of a coincidence that whites rediscovered their ethnicity just when Blacks were beginning to make substantive progress, and found in it a tool that has been made all the more effective because it has been made legitimate by the Blacks themselves? By the same token, however, if racism did explain the revival of ethnicity, how would we account for the fact that there has been a worldwide upsurge of ethnic identification, often in areas where racism is of no relevance.

If a measure of even handedness is clearly in order in this assessment, it is notable that although it strengthens the liberal perspective, the neoconservative analysis of the ethnic revival takes the tradition in a direction where it flirts with setting itself firmly against recent attempts by Blacks to make progress, even with becoming associated with a racist perspective. In doing so, it has moved some distance from the liberal universalism prevalent in the era when assimilation was taken to be the goal of a liberal society and ethnic groups were seen as an obstacle to the individualism that was its key. Patterson's analysis, overstated and unrealistic though it may be, at least remains true to those principles and is a brilliant contemporary statement of the classic liberal position attuned for more combative times. But the fact that the analysis continues to revolve around these poles demonstrates how deep-rooted are these dilemmas within the liberal tradition; for all that neoconservatism has brought an extra dimension to the liberal perspective, even bringing it into conflict with its classic universalist, individualist assumptions, this has only brought the tradition full circle. Nothing could demonstrate more clearly that neoconservatism has failed to provide an answer to the question of Black progress that can transcend these dilemmas.

CONCLUSION

This then appears to be the distinctive contribution of neoconservatism, to provide not an answer to the question of Black progress but an intellectual rationale for a reconciliation of liberal principles and white self-interest in the face of Blacks' attempts to make progress; to provide, as Stephen L. Carter (1991) has put it, a justification for "a society that prefers its racial justice cheap" (p. 72).[6] In providing this, it is undoubtedly in tune with the times, but it leaves contemporary liberal analysis intellectually unconvincing because the suspicion of rationalization persists. The compromise between individualistic and group principles is too expedient; the assertions of continued Black progress are too dogmatic; the revival of ethnicity is too convenient; it all fits too neatly. Neoconservatism is impressive in its capacity to turn the defensiveness of the earlier liberal position around. In vigorously defending both the liberal ethos and the prevailing social system, it assuages the guilt that often plagued the liberal response to Black problems in recent years. But the attempt to accommodate principle and privilege is to square a circle. It is, it would seem, Blacks who must change and not the system that put them where they are, for somehow that system is not at fault. One is left wondering why there is a Black problem at all. Perhaps if the neoconservative analysis attempted a little less to do away with the problem so completely, one could believe its arguments a little more.

The liberal approach to the question of Black progress is a broad church, but one that suffered a schism under the pressures generated by the upheavals of the 1960s. The instrument of division was the realization that the legal and social reforms of that period, which followed liberal policy prescriptions, were insufficient to ensure the rapid incorporation of Blacks into the mainstream of American society. Some argued that the goal of incorporation must take precedence and government should extend its role, through measures such as affirmative action, to ensure its achievement. This attitude pushed liberalism dangerously close to a radical posture but did find support in some branches of government. It enjoyed relatively little success, however, in the sense that the gains resulting from such measures have remained limited to the Black middle class. Even this strand of liberalism has been unwilling to contemplate redistributive measures necessary to reverse the deteriorating position of the Black underclass, if only because it became increasingly evident that the problem of Black poverty could not be divorced from poverty in general and thus from the creation of a much more egalitarian society for all Americans. Awareness of how substantial were the implications of Black incorporation for American society helped to give preeminence to the alternative response; many former liberals, brought face to face with the limits of traditional liberalism, responded more creatively by developing a line of argument that came to be known as neoconservatism. This, as we have seen, attempted to circumvent the problem by denying that any choice between the status quo and Black incorporation needed to be made. A renewed faith in the power of the free market to reconcile these competing goals has been one distinctive vehicle of this optimism, and an elaborate defense of the continuing validity of the distinctive American pattern of ethnic pluralism as offering the opportunity for Black progress has been the other. Although artful, neither strand has solved the basic dilemmas of the liberal tradition when confronting the problem of Black incorporation.

This suggests that although liberal principles can accommodate widely differing policy implications, they cannot respond adequately to the question of Black progress because the scale of the problem requires solutions that go beyond what liberalism can countenance. Unwilling to acknowledge the choice between the existing social structure and Black incorporation, neoconservatism continues the liberal tradition by refusing to accept that the social structure is the source of the problem. In doing so its priorities become increasingly clear: The choice is to favor the status quo, even if that means the Black problem will not be solved. The liberal tradition reveals its true nature and its own inadequacy by treating the American social structure as neutral or benevolent in relation to the question of Black progress. But there is an alternative, radical perspective which focuses on the social structure as the essential stumbling block to Black progress. Thus is the basic issue joined. To this alternative premise and the adequacy with which the radical tradition elaborates on it we now turn.

NOTES

1. This argument applies specifically to neoconservative discussion of African Americans. On other topics a better case can be made, despite Hartz, for the argument that neoconservatism proceeds from genuinely conservative premises and thus represents a significant departure in American social thought.

2. It also shares with the liberal perspective a blindness to the importance of different historical experience of the various minority groups in explaining economic achievement. Harold Cruse (1987, pp. 299-322) has an interesting demonstration of the relevance of this factor to comparisons with other "Black" groups, such as West Indians in New York. Sowell (1981a, 1981b, 1984) makes much of this comparison to demonstrate the importance of factors other than racism, but Farley and Allen's (1987, chap. 12) careful analysis of the 1980 U.S. Census demonstrates that the differences between native-born and immigrant Blacks are greatly exaggerated, particularly in respect to differences in entrepreneurial accomplishment, a factor critical to any cultural explanation.

3. The point applies for individuals; it does not necessarily follow for groups.

4. It has been argued that this is a false dilemma. Roy L. Brooks (1990), for example, in *Rethinking the American Race Problem,* suggests that equality of result is a red herring because no one is advocating that. The point is that the agreed-upon goal of equality of opportunity cannot be achieved without special treatment under the law for disadvantaged groups. Therefore, to insist that the law remain color-blind, (or worse to insist that intent has to be demonstrated in cases of discrimination), as is the logic of the neoconservative line of argument, is to will the end but not the means and to use the law to collude in the perpetuation of discrimination.

5. Part of the animus behind Glazer's rhetoric could perhaps be explained by the fact that the balance in American society to which he is evidently so attached is reminiscent of the distinction between public and private life drawn by Hannah Arendt (1958) in *The Human Condition.* Arendt wrote against the backdrop of her experience of European societies of the

first half of the 20th century, which manifestly did not achieve such a balance, and with such tragic consequences. The immense fear lurking behind this analysis is that if America loses its quintessential balance between the spheres under pressure for Black emancipation, it might be doomed to repeat in some form the European experience.

6. Carter (1991) is referring to the restriction of the civil rights agenda to a bilateral paradigm "under which all that really matters is what specific entities do intentionally to other specific entities" (pp. 81-92). A legalistic frame of reference is thereby invoked to narrow the conception of racial justice to a form avoiding the need for any solutions that are systemic in origin or that require redistribution of wealth.

4

Everything and Nothing:
Marxism, Capitalism, and Black Progress

The premise of the Marxist analysis of Blacks in American society is that their position is the result of conflict, rather than consensus as liberals would have it, and that this conflict is located deep in the class structure of the society. There are a number of variations on this theme, indeed the very breadth of its categories lies at the root of the problems associated with the Marxist approach, but, paradoxically, all of its strands share with the liberal tradition optimism as to the resolution of the Black problem. The grounds for this optimism are, however, very different.

CLASSIC MARXISM

The principal tenet of the classic Marxist perspective on race is simply stated: Racism is a product of capitalism. Race relations are "the phenomenon of the capitalist exploitation of peoples and its complementary social attitude" (Cox, 1959, p. 21; Miles, 1980). Doctrines of racism that purport to explain the differential success of races in terms of inherent characteristics are rationalizations of a system of repression and exploitation of one race by another within a capitalist framework (Aptheker, 1946; Boggs, 1970; Breitman, 1965; Harris, 1964; Ofari, 1970; Sweezy, 1953; Williams, 1944). The fundamental imperative of capitalism is the accumulation of capital. Capitalists are compelled by the workings of competitive markets to pursue maximum profit if they are to survive. This in turn requires them to obtain labor power at the cheapest possible cost, and racism exists because it facilitates a reduction in the cost of labor. Moreover, capitalism generates a system of social relations of which class antagonism between capitalists and the proletariat is the principal feature. Racism, by creating division within the proletariat, weakens its capacity in the class struggle and thereby not only allows greater economic exploitation but also increases the control of the capitalist class over the system of social relations (Perlo, 1975).

This explanation is a functional one; racism arises because of the contribution it makes to and the beneficial effect it has on the reproduction of capitalism. The more specific functions it has fulfilled in the history of American capitalism have been, first, to reconcile a dominant liberal ideology with the practice of slavery; then to facilitate restoration of the power of the white oligarchy in the South in the Jim Crow era; and, with the urbanization and proletarianization of Blacks in the 20th century, to divide the working class on racial lines and so forestall the coalition of Black and white workers that would make exploitation more difficult (Spero & Harris, 1931).

Thus in the classic Marxist analysis, because race relations are in the last analysis a form of proletarian-bourgeois relations, it follows that they require no special theoretical categories for their explanation. In particular, the employment of race itself as an explanatory category is perceived as a basic error. It is racism as a social construct that must be explained, and this can only be done by reference to the development of class relations. To attempt to understand racial problems in terms of racial categories is to study only the ideological outgrowth of capitalism. The proper object of study should be the social structure generating that ideology. Class is, therefore, the explanatory concept, and race is no more theoretically than an epiphenomonon. This suggests a commitment to explain social facts only in terms of other social facts, which is again shared with the liberal tradition (Ben-Tovim & Gabriel, 1979; Lockwood, 1970).

Tying racism to capitalism also exposes the error of taking racial antagonism as being inherent in human nature and thus ever-present in history. This fallacy rests on the failure to distinguish between ethnocentrism, which is a cultural phenomenon evident in precapitalist societies, and racism, which infers moral qualities directly from biological attributes and is confined to the modern era. All civilizations are culturally prejudiced, regarding outsiders as barbarian to some degree. But the barbarian is a potential equal, inasmuch as the deficiency is cultural and therefore alterable; the objects of racism can never be equal because their "inferiority" stems directly from innate biological characteristics.

The conclusion to be drawn from this is that because racism is inextricably bound up with capitalism, it will only be possible to eradicate it by transforming capitalism out of existence. Because the exploitative nature of capitalist social relations gives rise to divisions in society between classes and races, these divisions can only be removed by substituting a social system based on common ownership and cooperation for one grounded in exploitation. In such a system, racial integration will follow because there are no antipathies that would preserve racism in all types of society; to suppose there are is to mistake a property of a transient social structure for a law of nature.

It is also part of the Marxist model that the transcendence of capitalism necessary for the elimination of racism will occur. Although the general contradictions of capitalism will provide the conditions for revolutionary change, the actual change will be brought about in practice by an alliance of Black and white workers who, as they become aware of their identity of interest in opposing capital, will develop sufficient power together to overthrow the system. Even if in the short term the value of racial discrimination to capitalism precludes progress for Blacks, it is the very absence of progress that will serve to build a revolutionary spirit among them, thereby hastening the demise of the prevailing social system and ushering a new era of emancipation. Marxian optimism then is of a longer-term and more apocalyptic nature than what is found in the liberal tradition. In the short run, the two models have diametrically opposed implications for the extent of possible Black progress, and in the long run they differ over the societal setting within which progress will occur. Their shared optimism, therefore, conceals more than it reveals.

The Problem of Functionalism

The first problem with the Marxist approach lies in the functionalist nature of the explanation of racism it proposes. Racism is not to be explained in its own terms; it is explained by its effects. So, as an example of this reasoning, it is argued that because racial discrimination divides the working class and this division benefits the capitalist class, discrimination exists because it has this consequence. The Marxist theory of race thus becomes a variety of the idea that every institution or behavioral pattern in capitalist society serves the interest of capital and is maintained because it serves that interest.

The point is not to dispute that racism does indeed have this effect but to question whether this of itself can explain its nature and hence the limits it places on the potential for Black progress. G. A. Cohen (1978, 1986) has argued that functional explanation is necessary to Marxism because no other treatment can preserve its central thesis, that the forces of production[1] have primacy over the relations of production[2] in the sense that relations are what they are because they have the function of furthering the development of the forces. Nor, to put it another way, can any other form of explanation reconcile the causal primacy of the productive forces with the recognition that the development of these forces causally depends on the form taken by the relations of production.

Such explanations, Cohen argues, take the form of consequence laws, which explain something in terms of a preexisting disposition of that something to have a certain consequence. The means by which a consequence law works itself out are bound to be difficult to observe before the fact, if not impenetrable, but Cohen insists that such explanations remain legitimate, even when we lack an account of the mechanism by which they work.

Jon Elster (1980, 1982), in response, has argued that functionalism can have no place in sociology. In its naive form, it is clearly untenable; phenomena simply cannot be accounted for by events that occur after they have arisen. But few would adopt such a position. The more mainstream version argues for the existence of latent functions to explain the persistence of institutions and behavior. But this still does not absolve us of the need to specify the mechanisms by which latent functions manifest themselves and so act to maintain certain institutions. And as Elster (1985, p. 28) argues, if we can identify these manifest processes, this in itself produces a conventional causal explanation. Specifying the mechanisms, therefore, amounts to substituting a causal explanation for a functional one and so makes the latter superfluous.

Functional explanation itself is often difficult to distinguish from conspiratorial interpretation of the sort that arises when direct evidence of how an outcome came about is absent. Rather than accepting that lack of direct evidence makes explanation impossible, the conspiratorial approach asks who benefits from a particular outcome and, reasoning backward, argues that the beneficiaries must have acted so as to bring about the outcome by virtue of their benefiting from it. This makes for an approach that is inherently unfalsifiable; as long as the capitalist system persists, any phenomena can, with sufficient imagination and no constraint of providing direct evidence, be interpreted in a way that demonstrates how it has helped to maintain that system. Such interpretations are particularly prevalent in the discussion of the role of the state, where an element of secrecy inevitably leaves the field open to wilder forms of speculation and conspiratorial fantasy undertaken in the name of a functionalist Marxism.

Whatever the general permissibility of the functional form of explanation, there can be little doubt that it has been widely abused in Marxism as a device for explaining everything and anything while avoiding conventional criteria concerning evidence. The identification of functions is better treated as a call for explanation rather than as an explanation itself. The Marxist framework can specify interesting problems through the identification of functions; what has to be avoided is the attempt to provide explanations of all events in terms of the continuing success of capitalism or its eventual demise. It is because Marxism claims, through the philosophy of history on which it is based, to know in advance what the end result of history is, namely the creation of a communist society, that the tendency arises to interpret everything in terms of its contribution to producing this end result. This creates an intellectual system that is self-confirming and theoretically closed, attributes that rob its analysis of intellectual conviction. The solution is to accept the discipline of specifying those mechanisms associated with the functions identified; in other words, to investigate the historical process in which these mechanisms reveal themselves, as opposed to resolving issues in terms of the ahistorical necessities of a closed intellectual system.

The corollary of treating Marxist categories in this way is to retain an open-endedness in respect of outcomes. What has to be avoided is the employment of a philosophy of history as a metanarrative by which the answers to all important questions are predetermined, if for no other reason than that of "The justification of an iniquitous act by the 'laws of history' is no more convincing than its justification by the 'laws' of racial superiority" (Todorov, 1993, p. 22). It will not do for Marxism to correctly criticize racism for its universality in the sense of its false, timeless assumption of superiority, only to replace it with its own claim to a scientific knowledge of the goal of history that is equally spurious. Considered in relation to the problem of Black progress the implication is clear; the general Marxist theory of racism cannot predetermine its possible extent. Allowing that the Marxist approach can generate interesting lines of inquiry, there can be no substitute for detailed historical investigation to determine the strength of obstacles to Black progress and the likelihood of their being overcome.

Limiting Racism to the Modern Era

A further question that must be asked of this approach concerns the definition of racism and its consequent restriction to the modern era. The hard and fast distinction between racism and culturally based ethnocentrism is only tenable if the definition of racism is confined to the biological sphere. Such a definition is, however, unable to cope with the clear evolution of racist thought from a biological to a cultural basis (Ben-Tovim & Gabriel, 1978, p. 132). Attempts to justify racial superiority in purely biological terms are rare today. Even in South Africa during the apartheid era, the justification for this most extreme form of racial separation was predominantly cultural. The point is that racism has evolved into a cultural form under capitalism. Consequently, not only has the rigid distinction between cultural ethnocentrism and biological racism fallen, but so has the attendant but equally rigid distinction between capitalism and all other societies in respect to race relations. In questioning the identification of capitalism and racism, one may ask whether, in the absence of a clear-cut distinction between ethnocentrism and racism, it is the ever-present factor of cultural prejudice that should be emphasized as the root cause of racial antagonism. If this is accepted, it would follow that, contrary to the Marxist position, structural factors, such as the mode of production, rather than being the fundamental cause of racism, would become the vehicle through which cultural antagonism was given a particular form in any society. It is not surprising that any such tendencies should have flourished in the modern era, because there has been so much more racial contact than in previous periods. To look at the matter this way need not involve a denial of the theory that racism has served to rationalize the capitalist form of exploitation. But this is not the same thing as saying capitalism causes racism. That would be to succumb to the danger inherent in the functionalist approach of confusing cause and function, of failing to distinguish between a contingent factor and a causal one.

There are other grounds, beyond a belief in the constancy of cultural antagonism as the source of racism, for skepticism as to the closeness of fit the Marxist argument proposes between capitalism and racism. The connection is much looser and more tenuous than this approach allows; there is demonstrably more room for variations in race relations within a capitalist framework than it admits.[3] Capitalism has historically taken many different forms, and these have had fundamentally different implications for the systems of race relations with which they are associated.

Is it not then the case that differences within capitalism (and by implication between capitalism and other types of society) are more important for race relations than any core properties that all capitalist societies (and only they) must have? If capitalism can accommodate widely diverging racial systems, is there any point in arguing that it has a determining effect? The variety of racial systems that historically have been compatible with capitalism suggests that the development of racism cannot be viewed as a necessary by-product, even where it is recognized as functional for the interests of certain elements within the system. If capitalism in its various forms can accommodate a wide range of race relations, is it not possible that it might be able to accommodate a system in which there was no racial exploitation at all? If this were the case, it would no longer be necessary to predicate the abolition of racism on the overthrow of capitalism. Even if we accept that capitalism is, by definition, exploitative of all workers, it is quite possible to envisage a situation in which racial minorities suffer no exploitation by virtue of their race but are exploited, if at all, only as a result of their class position. Indeed, insofar as racial equality forestalls the unrest often associated with discrimination, it might be thought conducive to social stability and so to the persistence of capitalist social relations.

This brings to the fore the contradiction that vitiates much of the classic Marxist analysis of race. Although it can show why certain types of exploitation are logically necessary for the existence of capitalism, it cannot show why this has to occur in a racially differentiated fashion. It may be necessary to appropriate surplus value from the labor of workers; it does not follow that it must appropriate more surplus from Black workers than from white. Two points arise. The first is that the only way to show the necessity for racism is therefore to introduce specified mechanisms by means of which the color-blind working of the imperatives to accumulate capital and maximize profit are transformed into a racially discriminatory social pattern. In this framework these can only be ideological. But the introduction of an ideological element in what must be an analytically primary way to explain racism contradicts the initial, economic basis of the argument (Ben Tovim & Gabriel, 1978, p. 136). Second, in the absence of any logical necessity for capitalism to produce racism, even if one accepts that they have been associated historically, it does not follow that they will continue to be so. The conclusion must again be that in this framework the outcome is open-ended. Marxist categories cannot resolve the problem theoretically; they cannot preclude a solution to the problem of Black progress because they cannot demonstrate that capitalism must prevent the achievement of equality by Blacks. Because it crucially underestimates the flexibility of capitalist society, the Marxist analysis of race can therefore provide only limited guidance in assessing the nature and extent of Black progress.

The Position of the White Working Class

A further line of criticism begins by focusing on the problematic position of the white working class in this model. The reservation here is that if the white working class is in the same objective position in terms of exploitation as Blacks, and if it is their role to challenge the system, why is there no alliance between the two groups to achieve this end? And why, far from their being such an alliance, is the white working class the repository of some of the most virulent racial prejudice in society? Is it simply "false" awareness of their position that makes them racist? If so, on what basis does the Marxist argue that they "ought" to behave differently. The task of theory is to explain the behavior that occurs, not to tell people how they should behave. Such a conflation of prescription and analysis parallels the liberal approach in its attempt to fit the Blacks' situation into a preconceived framework. The Marxist response is to argue that within the existing social structure, it is the white working class that has most to lose in the short term from Black gains in jobs, neighborhoods, and schools. So their opposition is a rational, if misguided, defense of immediate interests at the expense of their longer-term ones. We are entitled to ask, however, when the short term becomes long, especially when, as Keynes noted, "in the long run we are all dead." In the absence of a stipulated mechanism by which white workers will transcend this narrow perspective toward Blacks, it is difficult to sustain confidence in the ultimate inevitability of a Black-white workers' alliance, which the Marxist framework requires if it is to be coherent.

The problem is compounded by a further line of response suggesting that workers fail to perceive their true interests because of the effectiveness of the ideological propaganda of the ruling class. Ruling-class control of information and communication, it is argued, allows it to manufacture and disseminate myths creating the social divisions that serve its interests. This claim should be treated skeptically for three reasons. First, it imputes far too great a degree of power to a monolithic ruling class. Such a concept may be necessary to make sense of the theory, and the conspiratorial implications are quite consistent with its functionalist approach. However, the concept is imported into the analysis at great cost;

it implies such a high degree of social integration underlying ruling class hegemony that the possibility of revolutionary change proceeding from class conflict is effectively ruled out. The ultimate political objective of the Marxist analysis is thereby contradicted. Second, if we accept this argument, we are accepting that ideological factors are more powerful than material ones, that ideological manipulation can blind workers to their own material interests. This may be the case, but it cannot be reconciled with the materialist premise of Marxism. And if the reply to this is that workers will eventually see the light, we are brought back to the initial question of how and when short-term blindness will be transformed into long-term percipience. If ruling-class propaganda has been so effective in the past in instilling prejudice, what reason is there to suppose it will not continue to be so, especially given the momentum now existing to sustain it. In the absence of a transformative mechanism, this explanation of the persistence of racism suggests its indefinite continuance, a conclusion again at odds with the Marxist objective of explaining how racism will be transcended.

The central weakness underlying this form of Marxist analysis lies in its reductionism. In stressing the theoretical supremacy of class, it denies force to the category of race in explaining the position of Blacks. But by employing a narrowly economic concept of class, it also denies any independent role to ideological factors. Racism becomes an epiphenomonon located in an ideological form that itself mechanically reflects the imperatives of the base or economic level. However, because no logical necessity for discrimination at the economic level can be shown, and because no autonomy is allowed either to race itself or to ideology, all that remains is a dubious empirical proposition concerning the genesis of racism in early capitalism. If racism is not a necessary function of economic laws, it becomes at most an optional device available to capitalists to use in an attempt to weaken workers through the creation of false categories. It is an option they may or may not take, one which may or may not work. Such a set of concepts, when not internally inconsistent, develops a level of determinacy in respect to Black progress that is virtually nonexistent.

MODIFICATIONS OF MARXIST THEORY

There have been critiques of this brand of mechanistic Marxism from within the Marxist tradition itself (Genovese, 1971; Hall, 1980). One has sought to escape the functionalist trap inherent in the stress on the connection between the forces and the relations of production by giving primacy instead to the concept of class. This alternative tries to deal with the vagueness in Marxist theory about the exact relation between two of its central concepts, the forces of production and the class struggle (Cohen, 1978, pp. 207-215). Stress on the former has produced an objective, structurally oriented, determinist strand of the tradition, whereas concentration on the latter has made for a subjective, voluntarist strand focusing on class capacities and allowing scope for the working-class action to change the direction of history.

Leaving aside the difficulties of achieving a meaningful reconciliation of these two poles within a shared framework, the advantage of class analysis in this context is flexibility. It is a synthetic concept that obviates the need to choose between economic and ideological factors. Both can become reciprocal manifestations of class struggle. If this is placed at the center of history, then economic determinism can have no place because the task of a properly conceived materialism becomes to relate satisfactorily the psychological, material, and other aspects of class struggle to each other in a way that presents reality as an integrated process (Genovese, 1971, p. 46). In this process, to adopt Gramsci's metaphor, material forces are the content and ideology the form; each is thus inconceivable without the other.

The danger of this approach is that in asserting the importance of subjective elements, it goes so far beyond an admittedly untenable economism as to reject any form of structural determination (Ben-Tovim & Gabriel, 1978). By making consciousness the essence of class analysis, it can move from analyzing a complex reality involving interacting, semi-autonomous levels to taking an idealist totality as the object of analysis. This is particularly problematic when, as we have seen, the appropriate radical consciousness is lacking in the working class. To avoid these dangers, it is at least necessary to combine an awareness of structure with that of autonomy and to refuse therefore to treat racism as self-explanatory or as mere mystique. It may be seen as having its own autonomous formation, its own contradictions, causes, and so on, as well as having repercussions for, and being influenced by, the class struggle at the economic and political levels.

The real problem with even this more balanced version of Marxism is that although it is undoubtedly an advance in its recognition of complexity in the study of race, it does not take us very far beyond such recognition. If we are to discover the extent of the possibilities for Black progress in the United States, we need more specific conceptual guidance than the knowledge that levels interact, a perspective that can easily descend into saying little more than that everything depends on everything else.

If the importance of class and the relative autonomy of race, politics, and ideology are incorporated into Marxism, as they must be if an obviously inadequate economism is to be avoided, then the options available widen to the point of compatibility with almost any position for Blacks in America. The twin dangers of reductionism and eclecticism threaten to engulf the whole project: On the one hand, we have an economic Marxism that provides a simple, determinate theory but one that is internally contradictory and wrong in its prognosis; on the other, a more refined version of Marxism, which is theoretically more adequate but offers no compelling explanation of Blacks' current position or what the constraints on its development might be.

If it remains unclear as to how the Marxist approach to race can steer its passage between its own Scylla and Charybdis, one course might be to object that this model is too abstract to provide great insight into a specific, contemporary issue such as the African American predicament and that a fair assessment must include consideration of some Marxist ideas that have a direct bearing on the issue. Much Marxist analysis accepts that Blacks have made progress in the postwar era, although much of this is attributed to the unique factor of migration from the rural South during the three decades after World War II. In general, the liberal formulation that Blacks are now on the same ladder as the rest of society is accepted; the difference is that they have signally failed to move up it. As with the liberal perspective, this argument is supported with statistics on income, occupation, health, education, housing, and so on (Baran & Sweezy, 1968, pp. 251-257; Willhelm, 1980, pp. 7-60). The distinction is that in this tradition the statistics are claimed to point to the exact opposite of the liberal conclusion (Hill, 1978; Pinkney, 1984). This suggests a parallel deficiency on both sides, a one-sidedness that is the product of an expedient attempt to fit "facts" to a preconceived conclusion, in this instance that it is impossible for Blacks to progress under capitalism. In any case such data cannot in themselves explain what they purport to show. For this we must turn to concepts of a somewhat higher order of sophistication.

Changes in the Operation of Racism

The first argument worthy of note is that the modern pattern of racism has become more subtle and durable as there has been a move away from the direct oppression of Blacks toward isolation as a mechanism of subjugation. This is most graphically illustrated by the high level of residential segregation that has persistently separated whites and Blacks (Massey & Denton, 1993).[4] The image this typically conjures up is of the contrast between leafy, well-kept white suburbs and rundown, deprived inner city Black ghettos; in fact the degree of residential segregation, with all its consequences for schooling, social interaction, and mutual understanding, has persisted into the era of Black suburbanization: Blacks have made it to the suburbs in increasing numbers, but only to suburbs that rapidly become as racially separate as any inner city ghetto (Massey & Denton, pp. 67-74). The virtue of this argument is that it subsumes and reinterprets in a way consistent with Marxism those very aspects of progress upon which the neoconservative view relies so heavily.

The suggestion is that it is precisely the institutionalization of formal equality—there is after all no longer any legally enforced segregation—that has reinforced the subjugation of Blacks (Bell, 1987, pp. 13-14; Bumiller, 1988). This is because the achievement of formal equality has allowed white America to come to terms with its democratic values without having to forgo the substantive benefits it derives from racial exploitation. It therefore resolves the moral dilemma for all Americans, which Myrdal saw as the root of America's race problem, but, crucially, it does so without creating an impetus for progressive change in which he and the liberal tradition placed so much faith. Contrary to the liberal view, the principle of formal equality is pernicious because, far from generating an impetus for the implementation of Blacks' social and economic rights, it rationalizes exactly the opposite tendency. It permits white Americans to feel that all that should be done for Blacks has been done. By generating a myth of equality of opportunity, it facilitates the argument that if Blacks fail to make further progress, they must deserve their position because they now have the same chances as everyone else. Thus feelings of guilt are purged, racism and idealism reconciled. In this way overt oppression can be seen as superfluous or indeed counterproductive to the extent that it generated an impulse for change. Its elimination via the achievement of constitutional and legal equality for Blacks since World War II has therefore done less to improve their position than to rationalize their subjugation.

The theme of superfluousness arises again in the context of changes in the work process, but in this instance the Black population itself, or more strictly its labor power, is becoming superfluous (Willhelm, 1970). Blacks migrated from the rural South when their agricultural labor was made redundant by mechanization. As computer-based automation reduces the demand for unskilled labor in the manufacturing and service sectors of the economy, the same thing is happening again because Blacks are concentrated disproportionately in jobs most subject to these adverse trends. This time, however, there is nowhere for them to migrate. Whereas formerly Blacks replaced whites in low-skilled categories as those whites moved up the ladder, now, as the bottom categories shrink, Blacks are prevented from moving up by the presence of whites in all the available skilled jobs, by restrictive union practices, and by lack of the educational qualifications needed to compete. Nor do Blacks have open to them the avenue of political influence that served white immigrant groups so well. The decline of machine politics and the extension of a "civil service" ethic to local government has blocked off this patronage-based path of mobility. Consequently many Blacks have moved out of the labor market altogether into the nether world of the underclass. The problem is accentuated by the internationalization of the capitalist system, which has led American capital to farm out unskilled work to even cheaper labor in the Third World.

These trends are reducing Blacks to the status of a lumpenproletariat whose perpetual subjugation is guaranteed because they have no capacity to bring about constructive change to the system. All that remains is a capacity for destruction, which is tragic in itself and if exercised could only presage a more intense racial conflict than so far experienced, conflict from which Blacks certainly will not gain. If this were to arise, the state would reveal its true, oppressive character in defense of white privilege. Even in its absence the state still acts to perpetuate Black subjugation. This is not just because of the acts of recent conservative administrations in cutting back on welfare and unemployment programs in ways that disproportionately affect Blacks. Rather welfare itself is a form of aid that has been consistently manipulated to maintain the dependency of the beneficiaries (Piven & Cloward, 1979; Tabb, 1970, p. 96). Levels of welfare are deliberately kept to a minimum, the recipients vilified and isolated. The real purpose of welfare is not to compensate for the hardships generated by trends in the economy at large, or to help reposition people to take up a productive place in the labor market; instead it is to keep them on a string so as to ensure good behavior. Although failing to alleviate their misery, welfare neutralizes any threat they might pose to the stability of the social structure by making them dependent on handouts that can be withdrawn if they transgress the boundaries of acceptable behavior.

Even Progress Perpetuates the Problem

The Marxist view recognizes that not all Blacks are being reduced to this lumpen status, but it does suggest that even where there appears to be progress—and where the liberal tradition places most emphasis—in the rise of a new and bigger Black middle class, the reality is a mechanism for perpetuating Black subservience. Most of the income advances that have occurred in the last 25 years have been confined to the wealthiest 30% of Blacks. This means that the Black community is moving in two opposite directions simultaneously, a fact that average Black income gains, such as they are, gloss over. On the one hand, there is a poorer, less skilled element increasingly trapped in a vicious circle of poverty and alienation; on the other, a dynamic, richer group eager to exploit the opportunities being presented to them.

The effect of this is to create a section of the Black community that has a stake in the existing order and a loyalty to it. This groups exercises its influence as an intellectual and political elite to help preserve that order, to keep alive the myth of eventual incorporation, and to forestall any rise of militancy that might emanate from the mass of the Black community. It is because the new Black middle class is amenable to co-option and acts in effect to keep the Black masses in line that its expansion has been sanctioned by the white governing elite. Its very existence serves to keep alive the spark of hope for the rest of Blacks of success within the existing system. But in clinging to this, they implicitly accept the existing structure of advancement and so pose no threat to the status quo. Consequently, the rise of the Black middle class, far from being an indicator of a path more Blacks will follow, as liberals would have it, is in fact the cheapest and most effective way of ensuring that most Blacks accept their unchanging lot.[5]

Although being forced by this analysis to recognize the resourcefulness of capitalism in absorbing Blacks into the system, the Marxist argument remains that this type of incorporation is only designed to affect the minimum number of Blacks necessary to forestall disruption. Because the proportion of Blacks thought of as incorporated is up to 30%, one may question whether the terminology of masses and minorities is not being employed in a cavalier manner.

More important, this argument, both as it concerns the underclass and the middle class, leads ineluctably to conspiratorial explanations. It presupposes not only a malevolent elite but one capable of controlling the levers of society to such an extent that it can produce these outcomes. In some of the further reaches of this mentality, the drug problems of the Black ghettos are also seen, without direct evidence inevitably, as part of a master plan to perpetuate the subjugation of Blacks. It is not necessary to accept the clichés of American pluralism to treat with considerable skepticism any explanation that relies on so omnipotent a guiding hand for its intellectual coherence. The point is that even this more concrete example of Marxist analysis reverts to the same type of explanation as its more abstract form because it is driven by the same underlying functionalist principles.

Despite the control this explanation invests in a conspiratorial elite, the conclusion remains that Blacks will be emancipated. The capitalist system can only survive on the basis of two poles of wealth and poverty. The rich can only be rich if the poor remain poor. Blacks may now be represented in both poles, but the balance of power remains overwhelmingly against them under capitalism, and the condition of Blacks as a whole can only be changed as part of a revolutionary transformation of the capitalist system. But it is not enough merely to say what is necessary. It is a distinctive quality of the Marxist analysis to go beyond description and even prescription to a theory of how and why the necessary changes will occur. And indeed it is invariably argued that Blacks will not continue to be blinded by the mystifications of bourgeois ideology, to be trapped in the pathological web of ghetto life or impeded by leadership drawn from a tokenized elite. Rather they will develop the required revolutionary self-consciousness in the face of the increasingly barbarous anachronism of persistent poverty in the midst of a society with the capacity to create enormous affluence (Baran & Sweezy, 1968, pp. 272-273).

Reform Over Revolution

The problem that this framework has been unable to resolve, however, is that Blacks remain resolutely reformist in their response to oppression and show no sign of developing the consciousness ascribed to them in this model. Marxist writers have supported calls for Black power, community control, affirmative action, and so on, but they have great difficulty in specifying how these can be transformed into a revolutionary program. Such demands are, in fact, more analogous to trade union demands. They can be conceded because they challenge only the distribution of advantage within the system, not the system itself. And as with unions, the effect of a judicious level of concessions is incorporation of the dissident element and thus a strengthening of the system, as the Marxist model itself recognizes. The weakness of its position is illustrated by the policies of the American Communist Party, which once it jettisoned its view of Blacks as a submerged nation within the United States (Geschwender, 1977, chap. 4), has supported Black organizations such as the NAACP in the belief that if they achieve their goals, it will enhance the prospects for revolution. The NAACP and other such organizations show not the slightest sign of moving in this direction; moreover, the Communist Party effectively forfeits any revolutionary influence over them by taking this supporting role. And it must adopt such a role because its revolutionary analysis is so at odds with the basic fact that Black energies are almost exclusively channeled into reformist activity.[6]

In sum, the argument is pessimistic as to the prospects of Black progress, as it must be given the powerful forces in a capitalist society that foster racism. Despite this, an ultimately optimistic view continues to be plucked from the analysis. This optimism is based in large part on the belief that there will be a rising tide of Black militancy, which will provide a catalyst for a fundamental working-class challenge to the social system. Stress has been placed on Blacks as the vanguard of this process because they have given greater indications of militancy than the white proletariat, but the faith is misplaced because of their increasingly manifest reformism. This drives Marxism back into the arms of a clearly non-revolutionary and often racist white working class in what becomes a rather forlorn search for revolutionary optimism. The Marxist analysis is thus caught in a trap of its own making; it looks to Blacks because whites do not fulfill its revolutionary expectations. But without the power of the white proletariat behind them, Blacks do not have the capacity to revolutionize the system and so must settle for such reformist goals as their own energy can achieve for them. These, however, can never be sufficient to justify a claim of real progress for all Blacks. The logic of the analysis is, therefore, that Blacks are condemned to continued subjugation under capitalism, ameliorated by reformist gains for a minority. But this is a conclusion Marxists are universally unwilling to accept because it implies that their whole model of the development of capitalism in the United States is incorrect. Hence the vain search for optimism as an escape from this impasse (Cox, 1976).

The root of the problem is that this type of Marxist analysis assumes an answer to the question before analyzing it. It is assumed that Blacks cannot make progress in the United States under capitalism. Because the basic issue is taken to be resolved a priori, all that remains to be done is to provide a descriptive account of how Blacks are superexploited. This can illuminate some aspects of discrimination that liberals would prefer to ignore, but it creates in its turn an equally one-sided view of the problem. It leads to an analysis in which any aspect of Black disadvantage is seized upon as confirming the model. Because the possibility of genuine Black advance is blocked off, serious consideration of alternative explanations becomes unnecessary and the facts of discrimination are taken to speak for themselves. They do not. The indisputable facts of Black disadvantage of themselves tell us very little about the potential for progress. To come to any conclusion about that, it is essential to leave open the complete range of possible outcomes. This the Marxist analysis signally fails to do.[7]

The reason for this lies in the tension between Marxism as a mode of intellectual analysis and as a political creed. The problem is that the political commitment comes first and the analysis is used to substantiate the given political premise. The goal is the revolutionary transformation of capitalism and arguments are invoked when they support this goal, ignored or attacked when they do not. Problems are analyzed to make them fit into the framework. In the case of Black progress, this involves the assumption that it must be limited under capitalism, and the alternative is not seriously considered. We can expect no realistic appraisal of the prospects for Black progress from a framework that so prejudges the issue. It should be apparent that there is an important similarity with the liberal tradition in this. Among liberals, the undeviating commitment to the open nature of American society vitiates their analysis of Blacks. There, too, Blacks are fitted into a preconceived notion of American society and open-ended analysis is made impossible. The Marxist presupposition—of the United States as an unjust and doomed society— may be the opposite, but the process of intellectual inversion, putting the answer before the question, is the same. One tradition cannot conceive that Blacks will not be incorporated, the other cannot allow that they will. In neither case is the issue taken on its merits, and the consequence is that both lines of argument are partial, tendentious, and unsatisfactory.

The Concept of a Dual Labor Market

The question remains whether any other aspects of Marxist analysis escape these deficiencies. One possibility is a concept that has been widely employed, that of a dual labor market divided into primary and secondary sectors. The primary market is characterized by high wages, security of tenure, good working conditions, opportunities for promotion, and equity and due process in the enforcement of work rules (Piore, 1971). In the secondary market, the opposite characteristics prevail. Each market has its own institutions, recruitment mechanisms, training, and allocation procedures (Baron & Hymer, 1971). The primary market is overwhelmingly filled by whites whereas most Blacks are concentrated in the secondary market. The segregation thus imposed leads to a differential job-seeking process between the races as each tends to confine itself to its own sector. Consequently, independent supply and demand processes operate for each market. The significance of this dualism is, first, that Blacks in the secondary market act as a surplus labor force, a modern version of an industrial reserve army. The primary sector is relatively rigid and limits capitalists' flexibility in dealing with the vagaries of the business cycle. The reserve sector allows expansion of the labor force during prosperity without raising wages and so helps solve the problem created by the privileges gained by white workers. Although marginal in one sense, the role of Black labor is thus shown to be vital to the successful functioning of the economy. Its disadvantaged position is not some extraeconomic aberration or anachronism but is rather a direct consequence of the needs of contemporary U.S. capitalism.

The divided labor market has the further advantage of keeping Blacks relatively powerless in spite of their economic importance. To the extent that their labor is essential, they would normally have the leverage to extract concessions; by isolating them and making them appear a threat to white workers' privileges, the dual market keeps this leverage to a minimum. There are sufficient numbers of unemployed Blacks, on the one hand, and the opportunities for Blacks are sufficiently restricted, on the other, to keep the majority of Blacks insecure and relatively docile, with little alternative but to keep providing the flexible and relatively cheap labor capitalists require of them. Implicit in this is the underlying point of the dual market, to provide a mechanism for dividing the working class. The white working class is afforded a relatively privileged and secure position at Blacks' expense. The dual market not only gives the white working class economic protection, but also makes members aware of a clearly identifiable group that might threaten their privileges. White fears and insecurities are thereby diverted from capitalists to Blacks. Hence the development of white working-class racism as a means of preserving their privileged position. The dual market thus acts as a tool of social control and provides a cogent explanation of white working-class racism.

The division in the working class brought about by the dual labor market also helps to explain how one of the basic contradictions of modern capitalism is managed. This is the contradiction between capital's need to minimize costs while at the same time ensuring that there is a sufficient level of demand in the economy (Burawoy, 1976, p. 1083). Each employer wishes to extract the maximum surplus, and this requires them to pay the lowest possible wages. But if all employers successfully pursue this strategy, there will be chronic deficiency of effective demand in the macroeconomy because workers are consumers as well as producers, and without sufficient wages they cannot buy the goods they produce. What is rational for the individual capitalist thus becomes irrational for the capitalist class. The bifurcation of the working class helps to resolve this problem by separating out the two functions: High wages in the primary sector meet the need for adequate demand, low wages in the secondary sector help fulfill the requirement to maximize the surplus.

The fact that the dual labor market concept can be invoked to resolve so many issues is perhaps the key to its nature (Boston, 1988, pp. 115-116). Used in this fashion it becomes a tool of the functionalism that lies just below the surface of a great deal of the Marxist analysis and again only just stops short of a conspiracy interpretation. No doubt some capitalists wish they had the degree of control of society such a view implies, but although they will take advantage of any gains offered by a bifurcated labor market, it does not follow that they have the power to create one just because it serves their interests; nor does it follow that the system needs this bifurcation to survive. The tendentious use of the concept becomes apparent if we recognize that nothing in the idea of a dual labor market explains why it has to be a racial division. Although the divisions in the labor market can be described in more detail (Edwards, Reich, & Gordon, 1975; Gordon, Edwards, & Reich, 1982; Reich, Edwards, & Gordon, 1980), however sophisticated the elaboration, the concept remains an explanation of labor market organization rather than one of racial antipathy. Given this focus its view of race tends to be reductionist. But even at the economic level divisions in the labor market by no means parallel racial divisions. Not all Blacks are in the secondary market, any more than all whites enjoy secure, well-paying jobs in the primary market. Moreover, racial differences, although they may highlight the dualism, are not the only basis for labor market segmentation. Others such as ethnic, national, or gender distinctions can serve equally well. At most we can say that the dual labor market dovetails with preexisting racial divisions, reinforcing and perhaps perpetuating them. But to go further and claim it explains such divisions in society would be unwise.

Showing That Whites Lose

The theme of division within the working class is so critical to the Marxist perspective that it has been repeatedly addressed. In addition to the dual labor market thesis, econometric tests have been employed to show that white workers lose from discrimination (Legget, 1968; Prager, 1973; Reich, 1981; Szymanski, 1976, 1978). It is necessary to the Marxist position that this should be the case because if white workers, along with the white bourgeoisie, gain materially from the subjugation of Blacks, then clearly race rather than class would constitute the primary cleavage in society and Marxist hopes for a proletarian-led transformation of society would be dashed. Such tests demonstrate that where discrimination against Blacks is greatest, wage levels of whites tend to be lower and inequality among whites tends to be greater. They also show that white workers' wages do not benefit from having a large number of Blacks in their labor market. The explanation for these findings is familiar: They are the consequence of reduced working-class solidarity, which undermines the power of the unions to bargain effectively for higher wages. Exactly how far up the ladder it is necessary to go before the balance of advantage from discrimination becomes positive is difficult to specify, but the conclusion remains that there does exist a solid material basis for an alliance between Blacks and white workers to prosecute their common economic interests.

It is only fair to point out that liberal writers have used similar econometric tests and arrived at quite the opposite conclusion (Villemez, 1978). By now this should hardly surprise us. The real difficulty , however, is that although it is welcome to see the problem addressed on the basis of firm data rather than the vague psychologizing that sometimes passes for analysis in this area, even if we accept the Marxist claims at face value, we are brought up against the limitations of econometric evidence in its inability to resolve the ensuing problem of false consciousness. If the white working class loses from discrimination, why is there little evidence for the alliance for which the material basis is said to exist? The only answer is the familiar one, that white workers are manipulated into a false awareness of their own interests. But to accept this is to accept that ideological manipulation takes precedence over material interests. This is hardly a congenial proposition from a Marxist viewpoint, especially as in this context it must imply that race, the ideological factor, takes precedence over class, the material one, which is precisely the opposite of what this line of argument set out to demonstrate. If econometric analysis shows that in being anti-Black, white workers are behaving irrationally—that is, against their own economic interests—and we leave it at that, then without the assumption of rationality, the whole model is untenable. Alternatively we can argue that white workers are motivated by other considerations more important to them than economic advantage, that they have, in Becker's (1957) phrase, "a taste for discrimination," for which they are willing to make economic sacrifices in order to satisfy. Either way, the attempt to demonstrate how white workers lose from racism seems to end up further exposing the flaws in the Marxist model rather than resolving them.

The difficulty in specifying the nature of the connection between racism and capitalism has led to attempts to reverse the connection and to argue that in fact it is a departure from Marxist principles to suggest that racism is inseparable from capitalism (Szymanski, 1974). Marx himself believed that in the long run, the logic of capitalist development is to eradicate all divisions in the labor force, racial, sexual, or otherwise. This is because the largest surplus can only be realized by maximizing the pool of mutually substitutable employees. In other words, the drive to maximize profit creates a homogenous working class. Keeping Blacks segregated may make white workers more secure, but if the Blacks cannot be used for "white" jobs, then how can they act as a reserve army? It is only free competition between different sources of labor that pushes wages down, and it is therefore in capital's interest to encourage this. Racial segregation of jobs limits the ability of capitalists to replace white workers, and by weakening this basic sanction, segregation enhances working-class power and so reduces the surplus available to capital.

The argument can be taken further with the suggestion that because, as a result of discrimination, Black labor is cheaper than white, it is now in the interests of capitalists to replace white labor with Black at any given level of productivity. So it becomes capitalists who favor breaking down discriminatory barriers and white workers, especially those organized in unions, who act as the bulwark of resistance in order to defend their privilege (Bonacich, 1976). This stress on the purely economic logic of capitalism and the power of the market is reminiscent of the neoconservative analysis, although with the important difference that in this framework the homogenization generated by profit maximization is the essential precondition of interracial working-class unity and ultimately of its revolutionary potential. Nonetheless, this argument does reverse the more typical Marxist approach in suggesting that the economic benefits of homogenization, which promotes Black progress at least in the short run, outweigh the social benefits to the capitalist system of dividing the working class, which inhibits it. And by grounding the argument in the imperatives capitalism places on the individual capitalist, it can specify the mechanism by which this logic is worked out. In contrast the social argument, because the advantages it stresses accrue to the class as a whole, has great difficulty in doing the same without resorting to tautological, functionalist mechanisms. This also has the merit of reemphasizing the class nature of the problem by showing that racial conflict is rooted in differences in the price of labor and not in racial differences as such, even though historically the two have become associated (Bonacich, 1979).

The troubling aspect, however, is that this reversal can be effected in a way that is both plausible and yet entirely consistent with the logic of the Marxist analysis of capitalism. For the implication of this is that, depending on which element is stressed, the Marxist framework becomes compatible with the whole range of possibilities on Black progress, to the point even of becoming reconcilable to neoconservative analysis. Indeed it is so flexible that it can generate entirely contradictory hypotheses on this question from one set of principles. The basic tenets survive, whichever hypothesis is confirmed. The approach is therefore incorrigible, a way of rationalizing whatever happens rather than explaining it. The premise is that whatever happens in society is to the advantage of capital; its method is to observe what happens to Blacks and then find the advantage to capital in that outcome. If Blacks fail to progress, it is because this divides the working class; if they succeed it is because it helps meet the need to maximize profit. Whatever the case, it is functional for capital, and we have no means of choosing between the arguments because in either case the model is self-confirming. Once again we find that a promising line of argument cannot escape the functionalism that undermines the Marxist approach and, instead of rescuing it from its difficulties, ends up only confirming the intractability of its problems.

CONTRIBUTIONS OF THE MARXIST MODEL

If the Marxist model is so flawed the question remains, What insights, if any, can be extracted that will be of use in analyzing Black progress? Its principal contribution is to show that a problem appearing to be one of race is determined in its outcome by factors that are not solely racial. The limitation of race as an abstract concept is that it is the constant element in the equation and as a constant it cannot explain the process of change that is intrinsic in Black progress. To argue that the concept of class provides the necessary dynamic element begs as many questions as it answers, but it does at least provide a starting point that is consistent with the problem to be explained, something which, paradoxically, a focus on the racial aspect itself cannot do.

Beyond this the crucial Marxist insight is that capitalism is color-blind. Capitalists are subject to the imperative to maximize the surplus accruing to them. If they fail they will, due to market pressure, be forced out of existence. They are not subject to an imperative to discriminate racially. If racial discrimination furthers the pursuit of the surplus, for example by dividing the working class, it will be employed; if it hinders, it will be undermined. It is not an end in itself and, from the point of view of capital, it is at most a means to the end of profit maximization. Racial discrimination is not, therefore, inherent in capitalism, a conclusion that, although derived from Marxist premises, is at odds with the conventional Marxist analysis of race. What is necessary to meet the imperative of profit maximization is that capital retain control of the production process. Racial discrimination, seen as an option rather than a necessity, becomes a tactic that may be used to achieve this goal. The extent to which it is used and the degree of effectiveness capital attains in its employment cannot be determined theoretically. The logic of the Marxist approach, contrary to its practice, should be to use its insight into the nature of the system to guide empirical investigation that is open-ended in respect to outcomes, investigation that goes beyond the surface dimension of the race question but that is also the only protection against a tendency to the circularity of a self-confirming functionalism that so bedevils this approach.

It is essential to stress that concepts of class and capital accumulation can only be a starting point of the analysis of this question, or to put it another way, can provide no more than a framework for it. The fact that racism is no more than an option implies that the maintenance of capitalist prerogatives is compatible with a wide variety of racial systems. If these are to be sustained in a culture that is itself racist, that culture becomes part of the environment which acts as a given to all capitalists rather than as something which an individual capitalist can easily gain competitive advantage from overturning. If, in addition, we resist the temptation to see capital as all-powerful even in a class-based society, the tendency to follow the path of least resistance and adapt to a racial system produced by other pressures becomes intelligible (Baron, 1975; Greenberg, 1976; Johnstone, 1976). Insofar as the logic of capital accumulation is, therefore, to be seen as providing both a dynamic and a framework, as setting the limits within which racial systems evolve, it can only tell part of the story; it needs to be complemented by an account of those historical factors that have filled in the space between these limits, factors which are themselves cultural. The determination exercised by capital is therefore at the same time critical and very loose. In assessing the question of Black progress it becomes essential to complement an awareness of its influence with an appreciation of the importance of culture in shaping race relations.

The starting point of class conflict and the logic of capital accumulation provided by the Marxist perspective is superior to the idealist formulations of the liberal tradition. We must, however, reject the theoretical closure imposed by the functionalist nature of Marxism, together with both the short-term pessimism and revolutionary optimism that characterize it. But even if this means the conventional conclusions of the Marxist approach are unsatisfactory, a framework is better judged by the issues it generates for investigation than the particular answers it offers. In this sense the Marxist approach retains its promise. Equally, it is apparent that the role it assigns to culture in determining Black progress has not been articulated satisfactorily and requires greater elaboration. This remains true, even if class and culture are seen as complementary in providing a rounded response to the question of Black progress. Some, while sharing the radicalism of the Marxist approach, reject this convenient complementarity as little more than eclecticism disguised as comprehensiveness. They insist it is necessary to choose between class and cultural explanations, but in an inversion of the classic Marxist approach, they suggest that culture must be given primacy. To this alternative radical view and its relationship to Marxism we now turn.

NOTES

1. Cohen (1978) defines productive forces as follows:

> To qualify as a productive force, a facility must be capable of use by a producing agent in such a way that production occurs (partly) as a result of its use, and it is someone's purpose that the facility so contribute to production. (p. 32)

2. For Cohen (1978), "relations of production constitute the economic structure of a society" (p. 35), an argument based on a famous quotation from Marx:

> In the social production of their life, men enter into definite relations that are indispensable and independent of their will, relations of production which correspond to a definite stage of development of their material productive forces. The sum total of these relations of production constitute the economic structure. (Marx, 1859, p. 20, quoted in Cohen, 1978, p. 28)

The critical aspect is property relations, which are "but a legal expression for" the relations of production (Elster, 1985, pp. 253-254) and which are defined in terms of (a) the relations of producers to the means of production and their own labor-power, (b) the nature of the nonproducing owners, if any, and (c) the rules governing acquisition and transfer of property (Elster, 1985, p. 258).

3. To take but one illustration, in the prewar Philippines, the white ruling class kept control of all the reins of power, extending even to social aspects such as membership of the polo club. In the postwar era such distinctions between white and Asian capitalists were largely eliminated as the two groups combined. And yet throughout this transition capitalism continued. This example was recounted to me by a colleague, Professor Rupert Wilkinson, from personal experience.

4. The virtue of Massey and Denton's (1993) book is not just to demonstrate the continuing and too little recognized facts of residential segregation, which persists at a unique level for Blacks as compared to other ethnic groups; it is also to elaborate on how the fact of segregation perpetuates disadvantage, economically, politically, and culturally and so contributes to the creation and maintenance of an underclass of Black Americans. Further they show that this does not happen accidentally or through the workings of the system but is the consequence of deliberate, conscious decisions on the part of some elements in the white community. They conclude, "segmentation of Black and white housing demand is encouraged by pervasive discrimination in the allocation of mortgages and home improvement loans. . . . The end result is that Blacks remain the most spatially isolated population in U.S. history" (p. 114).

Although eloquent and convincing in its argument, their work is weaker on solutions, falling back on exhortation and legislation to outlaw such practices and the prejudice that underpins them. The contradiction underlying this is that in a democracy with a white majority, those who evidence such attitudes would have to be the ones who would pass the legislation outlawing them.

5. This too is an insight that is not confined to Marxists. The usual problem for those without a Marxist framework is the difficulty of demonstrating this gut feeling, but Derrick Bell (1987), in his *And We Are Not Saved,* employing techniques more akin to literature than legal scholarship, finds an eloquent way of expressing this truth. However, he too retains a sense of ultimate optimism in the face of a lifetime of experience to the contrary.

6. This is not to suggest that the NAACP has necessarily been naive in its faith in a gradualist, legally oriented solution. Even in the 1930s its executive secretary, James Weldon Johnson, expressed the underlying realism that justifies the gradualist approach when he said:

> We would be justified in taking up arms or anything we could lay hands on and fighting for the common rights we are entitled to and denied, if we had a chance

to win. But I know and we all know there is not a chance. (quoted in Bell, 1987, p. 70)

7. The tendentiousness this gives rise to can be illustrated in the Marxist approach to the labor process. In the context of race relations we have seen that stress is placed on the superfluity of Blacks in the labor market as the demand for unskilled labor declines. However, the general thrust of the Marxist argument on changes in the labor process, developed notably by Braverman (1974), is that it has involved a progressive deskilling of the workforce in the interest of enhancing capital's control over labor. Of course, if this thesis is correct, Blacks' ability to compete for jobs should be enhanced because the advantages of skill possessed by the white labor force have become redundant. However, this possibility never seems to be raised in the Marxist discussions of race. The two areas of analysis are kept discrete, even when they have clear mutual relevance. The suspicion must be that this occurs because the conclusions of the respective lines of argument are irreconcilable. What does unite them is the preordained need to substantiate the condemnation of capitalism, in the one case by suggesting it promotes racism, in the other by arguing it limits the autonomy of workers in the production process. This need is so encompassing that it overrides the elementary requirement of ensuring internal consistency and encourages instead the adoption of arguments that reinforce its presuppositions without any apparent need to consider their compatibility.

5

Been Down So Long:
Race, Culture, and Black Nationalism

Discussion of culture as it relates to the question of Black progress cannot proceed without further consideration of the meaning of the terms involved, not only *culture* but also of allied concepts of *nationalism, ethnicity,* and indeed of the idea of *race* itself (Banton, 1977). The meaning of these terms, and of the relations between them, has been subject to searching scrutiny in recent years, with implications that have recast the whole debate. One reason for the emphasis on culture has been dissatisfaction with economically oriented class models, the basis for which is evident from the previous chapter. The impetus has been to determine the relation of culture to class, whether it should be seen as complementary or contradictory, and in doing so to flesh out a more comprehensive radical approach to this issue. However, closer examination has not provided a single or simple answer but has opened up a whole new set of problems, which leaves the significance of culture in this context far from established.

THE MEANING OF RACE

The meaning attributed to the idea of race is prior to any discussion of the role of culture. But this meaning is now accepted as being far from constant (Banton, 1988); the evolution of its connotations has created a shifting foundation for the discussion and imbued it with an unsettling degree of indeterminacy. This is important because race had traditionally been viewed as fixed, an attribute that provided the reference point for all

101

wider debate. This fixity had its roots in physical characteristics of populations, which were for all practical purposes unchanging and unchangeable. Hence the well-known distinction: Race is determined by physical criteria, whereas ethnicity is ascribed by cultural criteria of a fluid nature (Van Den Berghe, 1967). The significance of the physiological basis of race was that it undermined choice in favor of determinacy because it suggested moral characteristics were the product of given physical traits. In doing so it transformed the idea of difference into one of superiority, and thereby justified unequal treatment of races in society. Although such a notion of difference could in principle permit tolerance and be anodyne in its social consequences, the deterministic nature of its origins meant it was used more often than not as the ultimate justification for brutality and inhuman treatment, even to the point of genocide.

If the classic Marxist perspective on race treats it as an epiphenomenon that is reducible to class, any radical perspective on Blacks in America that rejects the primacy of class has to insist on an alternative conception of race as central to what becomes a cultural explanation. This concept must link the idea of difference to inequality, because inequality provides the precondition of social transformation. But equally it must reject any biological basis for inequality, because of the implication of determinacy it entails. This in itself is not a problem because no respectable biologist would now allow any scientific taxonomy that divides the human species into discrete racial categories; the demonstrable overlap of characteristics between groups is too great to continue to accept a scientific justification of race (Todorov, 1993, pp. 91-92).[1] The problem is to determine how biology or class can be excised entirely from cultural differentiation because this must, even if implicitly, appeal to some underlying basis for differentiation; without prior distinctions of some kind, the groups to which cultural attributes are applied become meaningless at worst and tautological at best.[2] If the response is to reintroduce transcendent categories into the meaning of race, this flies in the face of the historical evidence of diversity in its meaning. Without such categories, race becomes a free-floating concept whose relation to culture, also free-floating, becomes quite indeterminate. We are again faced with a familiar dilemma: On the one hand, it is necessary to avoid grounding analysis in a fixed meaning for race because that implies a biological or class explanation that is historically and scientifically invalid; on the other hand, it is equally essential to avoid the complete indeterminacy that arises once race is cut loose from such roots, if we are to keep its relationship to the admittedly discursive concept of culture from resembling two objects floating in space.

Radical cultural approaches are hemmed in by this dilemma, needing a concept of race that is distinguishable from culture but denied the fixed points of class or biology in which to find it. Acceptance of the fundamental point that race also is a discursive concept, one that has to be constructed rather than given, is liberating to a cultural approach in that it consolidates the rejection of a spurious certainty that Marxism seeks in class or racism seeks in biology. But it is problematic, in that it collapses the distinction between race and culture and in that sense leaves the connection between them tautological rather than explanatory. Indeterminacy also opens the door to relativism by suppressing hierarchical judgments of superiority and inferiority. This is a positive development insofar as it is helpful in denying racist practices; but it can also undermine the radical intent of such an approach by privileging an idea of tolerance, an idea that within the framework of a hierarchical social structure can easily be adapted to a more subtle and therefore more effective defense of the status quo than overt or biologically grounded racism.

The Relation of Race and Culture

The path out of this dilemma for a cultural approach to race is to explore further what is meant by race as a constructed concept. The object is to encompass the dual nature of race as an idea that is at once constant and changing in its meanings, to find a common thread that can give a continuing unity to the concept while recognizing its shifting nature. As Gates (1992) puts it, "race is a text, . . . not an essence" (p. 79), but it "has become a trope of ultimate, irreducible difference between cultures, linguistic groups, or practitioners of specific belief systems, who more often than not have fundamentally opposed economic differences" (p. 49). The fact that race is a trope, however, "is not to deny its palpable force in the life of every African American who tries to function every day in a still very racist America (p. 147). To the contrary, the fact that

> literally every day, scores of people are killed in the name of the differences ascribed to "race" only makes even more imperative this gesture to "deconstruct" if you will the ideas of difference inscribed in the trope of race . . .

to reveal the latent relations of power and knowledge inherent in popular and academic usages of "race." (p. 50)

Here perhaps we glimpse the beginnings of a constructive relationship between race and culture. The key is to reject the notion that acceptance of change entails a complete lack of determination. The fact that the concept of race has to be constructed and that this is the source of its variation over time does not mean that its meanings can be plucked out of thin air or that change is therefore random. Rather it means that race has to be constructed in a given social environment, which structures and limits the meanings it is possible to attribute to race. Those meanings change because the formative considerations for race change as the social structure evolves through history. But the context provided by history is far from arbitrary and limits the fluidity of acceptable meanings that can be attached to race at any one time.

The range of formative factors will also vary in their composition and weight over time. Economic or class-based factors are undoubtedly one element in this mixture, but, as viewed from a cultural perspective, they are no more than that and not the primary element. The attributes by which racial categorization is assigned and the concept itself constructed are themselves a cultural choice, and it is in this sense that culture is the comprehensive concept. Indeed, insofar as race is not a static concept with a given meaning, its power consists precisely in its adaptive capacity to define groups at various social moments. By facilitating exclusion and inclusion, it gives specificity to social relations. Thus although it is the product of social conditions, it is not reducible to them because it helps to define them even as they define it. Its arbitrariness is also reduced by the fact that not all social conditions are external influences on the evolution of the concept; one of the social conditions at any given time is the history internal to racial thinking, a history attached to the concept itself, which provides a set of categories that further limit the acceptable meanings that can be applied to it. Although in one sense devoid of meaning then, the concept of race is both arbitrary and not arbitrary at the same time. The underlying irony is that, although fluid over time, the rhetoric of race remains that of fixity. The key to this paradox lies in the fact that the appeal of race rests in its capacity for the creation of identity, and this is a process in which the search for stability and certainty is of the essence. It is by the process of differentiation that identity is created. What we are is determined by what we are not, by the idea of otherness. The sting in the tail is that, although not logically entailed, the predominant construction of otherness is in terms of superiority and inferiority; what we are is not only different from what we are not but also better (Taylor, 1992, p. 38).

How Race Creates Identity

This has two aspects. The first, which is usually stressed, is the creation of a positive identity by means of vilification of the other. When engaged in by a socially powerful group, such a process becomes the basis for exploiting or abusing the group defined as the inferior other. The implication of this process for the abused group is the creation of a negative identity that is a mirror image of that of their oppressors.[3] Less noticed is the alternative perspective in which race can be self-constructed. Even though it might invariably arise out of the experience of discrimination, it is not necessarily a negative phenomenon. Discrimination can induce cultural connectedness and in this way be the product of, and an aid to, political struggle. It is thus not only a creature of conflict but also of solidarity, and it can generate a positive identity among the oppressed (Hall, 1990, pp. 18-20).

The creation of identity facilitated by race is therefore a double-edged process producing both exploitation and resistance. Whichever aspect is paramount in any given epoch, the continuity in the idea of race is provided by the dialectic of identity involved in the relation between these two aspects.

In taking on this character, the concept of race begins to merge with that of ethnicity; the loss of a fixed character leads to a shift to an emphasis on a common, historically shaped culture as the basis of racial identification, a property that has long been recognized as the root of ethnic affiliation.[4] This also intersects with the concept of nation, which has been the other great source of collective identity through history; in the current era the relationship is of particular moment. Although the nation state has been the principal formal unit of societal organization for centuries, it is under increasing strain as the forces of modernity create a tendency to globalization in economics, culture, and ultimately politics. These confront the individual as massive, overwhelming, and impersonal powers, creating a sense of anonymity and anomie from which respite is sought in bases of identity that are greater than the individual but smaller than the nation state. Globalization, therefore, attacks the nation state from above and below and creates a vacuum that is being filled increasingly at the ethnic/racial level.[5] The consequences are by no means benign, not only because of the instability that follows from the disintegration of traditional boundaries, disciplines, and balances of power, but also because the search for new bases of identity is conducted under pressures that emphasize the conflictual nature of this process rather than its tolerant aspect.

The construction of the self is under an even more insidious attack from the current of postmodernity, which in this context may be seen to be attacking the notion of identity from within. Here, as Stuart Hall (1990) has argued, many of the major currents of modern thought coalesce in their attack on the subject as the source of authenticity and the guarantee of stability in a world where everything is in flux. Although Marxism is associated with analysis of the external forces affecting the individual, it also undermines the notion of the self as autonomous by demonstrating its origins in social conditions; from Freud the notion of the self is destabilized by the idea of a subconscious that helps to form it but that it cannot fully know; then, deriving, from Saussure, the role of language in expressing even the most intimate notions is shown to be problematic because of the shifting meanings of words themselves; and finally from Nietzsche, the relativization of the Western idea of rationality and the awareness that Western domination has been based more on power than access to any ultimate truth that is the corollary of certainty has created a changed awareness of other cultures and belief systems.

Taken together such major currents of thought have created a confluence of relativistic concepts under which the idea of the self threatens to fragment, becoming a perpetually changing signifier without any core. Powerful as both the external and internal attacks on identity in the modern world are, they do not require us to abandon it to total collapse. Rather they compel a reconceptualization that can grasp its pluralistic and diverse character. The key is to view identity as a process, rather than an entity static across history.[6] This makes change inherent, but in an ordered and evolutionary way. History changes the concept of the self but not in isolation; change is the result of the interaction of the self and the other, not of the action of the self alone or of the self and purely impersonal forces. Identity is therefore always in the process of construction, but it is also always split because it is always the product of difference. This is where its dynamic comes from, explaining why an essentialist view of identity is no longer tenable.

Race and ethnicity are critical to this because they engender stability in individual identity through the medium of a collective identity to which the individual has the right of access. Race and ethnicity connote an historical position, an inheritance. This, too, has to be constructed; it is not given by history any more than it is given by biology or class. The historical narrative and the place of the self or group in it has to be recovered. This is a cultural act. Race and ethnicity provide a conceptual mechanism through which this act is mediated. To the extent that is possible they therefore address, if not satisfy, the need for certainty and authenticity in an era of cultural relativization.

Racial Identity and Individuality

The duality of racial identity is significant in another sense. Any stable identity based on group association defined by race or ethnicity also acts as a limit on the individual and may be seen less as a source of self-worth than as an agent that stifles freedom of expression. Membership implies restrictions on the individual, both of values and of behavior. Whether this is seen as restricting or liberating is again a function of the wider historical position. In the early stages of capitalism, society was composed of stratified groups of castelike rigidity. In this context the upheavals in traditional structures brought about by the growth of capitalism were perceived as liberating to the individual, and this energy received intellectual expression in the universal values of the Enlightenment. America is a case in point; the values of liberal universalism enshrined in its founding documents drew much of their promise and attraction from the escape they represented from the hide-bound replication of the Old World that colonial society might otherwise have become (Patterson, 1977, p. 148). Today, in contrast, the conception of liberty implicit in individualism, driven on by the power of a globalized market system, retains attractions for many. The emerging global culture can be viewed as a vigorous and exciting site for the realization of individual possibility, creating greater potential for the full expression of universalism than any previous era. Equally, it makes others feel fundamentally ill at ease because the scope of freedom is too great, the impersonal forces governing our lives too shadowy and beyond control (Jameson, 1984). These seek stability and security where they may. They may not find it in traditional status or class structures because there can be no turning back the clock. The question is whether the allure of the apparently even more intimate and comforting attachments and rituals of racial and ethnic association can be made real in this context, or whether this, too, is just a nostalgic regression.

The hope that it is not lies precisely in the discursive understanding of these forms of attachment because this gives them the adaptability to embrace change and redefine themselves in the context of the rapid evolution that characterizes the modern world. It is evident that the attempt will be made, but perhaps equally certain that it will never be fully successful. The gratification provided by group association will always have to struggle to find a balance with equally powerful needs satisfied by more individual conceptions of liberty. This struggle cannot be contained within cultural forms of expression. They must find political expression in a struggle that is informed but not determined by its cultural input, but that also feeds back into and shapes the ongoing process of cultural identification. The story of recent American politics is only one of many in contemporary history that can be written in terms of this momentous struggle.[7] The political implications of racial and ethnic identity are influenced by the negative perception of the other. Because it is impossible to excise this aspect of difference, the process of cultural identification is as likely to lead to social conflict as to harmony.[8] The very intensity of the needs addressed by the process of racial and ethnic identification makes it inimical to compromise, the shibboleths of cultural pluralism notwithstanding. Resolution of the ensuing conflict, therefore, poses a political problem of the first order and demonstrates the irreducible importance of politics in explaining the outcome of racial issues. It is in this relation to politics that we come up against the limits of the cultural approach to race. Culture informs the political struggles of the age; it cannot resolve them.

THE RADICAL CULTURAL APPROACH

How do these relatively abstract considerations connect to the radical cultural approach to the African American predicament in the contemporary United States? They demonstrate first that the very idea of race—of who African Americans are—is intimately bound up with culture. African American culture today expresses Blacks' conception of themselves, it is the realization of their identity as a group, an identity that is constructed in racial terms. Race and culture are in this sense synonymous in this context. This identity has been developed through the retrieval and interpretation of their historical experience. Although this experience has evolved through a variety of phases, its overwhelming characteristic is the fact of racial discrimination and exploitation. Blacks' self-awareness is therefore predicated on a conflictual relationship based on race. The defining experience of African Americans, that which continues to shape their culture, is one that sets them apart from, and in opposition to, whites. The idea of difference that underpins the creation of African American identity is not, therefore, neutral or benign. Rather it takes conflict and exploitation as its essence. The positive aspect of Black identity is fashioned from the reaction to, and triumph over, adversity. But there can be no escape from the fact that this adversity is the product of whites' behavior through American history. The implication for the conception of whites and of the relations between the races is unavoidable. The historical relationship between Blacks and whites which has created race as a discrete category in American society has done so in a way that makes white racism its governing feature and indeed the central fact of American history.

Faced with such an analysis of their own identity and role in American society, African Americans are led ineluctably to a nationalist response to their predicament. Nationalism deriving from this basis can only be confrontational, if not separatist, in its politics. We thus have the four defining elements of this approach; it is informed by culture, takes race as its pivotal concept, is nationalist in its implications, and is radical in its political agenda.

African America: An Internal Colony

One way to view the cultural-nationalist approach to the Black predicament, which emphasizes both its distinctiveness and comprehensiveness, is to suggest that it views the domination involved in race relations as that of one people by another as opposed to the domination of workers by capitalists suggested by more Marxist-oriented versions of a radical approach (Tabb, 1971b). As race is the characteristic that defines these populations, racism, its formation, and evolution become the key concept in explaining the central and persistent conflict that characterizes American society, a concept that is not reducible to class or any other factor (Omi & Winant, 1986, p. 13).

The idea of African Americans as an internal colony within American society provides a vivid organizing principle for this perspective (Tabb, 1971a). The analogy is drawn between Black ghettos and the former colonies of Western imperialism, or with contemporary Third World countries suffering neocolonial exploitation.[9] There are obviously limits to which this should be pressed, but the nub of the argument is that not only do internal and external colonies have common origins historically, they also serve similar functions in contemporary capitalism and are subject to similar forms of development, or the lack thereof (Bailey, 1973). Differences in location are therefore less important than the underlying similarity of condition, function, and fate (Hechter, 1975; Wolpe, 1970).

An illustration of the value of this perspective is its exposure of the inadequacy of the immigrant analogy that is a key part of the liberal approach to Black progress (Blauner, 1972; Harris, 1972). The colonial analogy highlights the distinction between immigration and colonization as the two major processes by which new population groups have been incorporated into the United States. Ethnic immigrants have always been able to operate competitively, because they have come voluntarily in search of a better life, because their movement has not been administratively controlled, and because they have transformed their ethnic culture at their own pace, using it in the process as a basis of community support. Blacks, in contrast, were brought to the country by force; their mobility was severely restricted, and their way of life and culture, far from being a source of strength, was destroyed. The fallacy of the immigrant analogy is to assume that these massive differences of historical experience can be safely ignored in analyzing current potential for progress (Lieberson, 1980). Or perhaps more accurately, it lies in the argument that in the essential fact of discrimination, Blacks were no different from other ethnic immigrant groups because the latter also faced adjustment problems arising from discrimination by the WASP (White Anglo-Saxon Protestant) mainstream (Glazer, 1971; Greeley, 1976). The only difference it allowed between Black and immigrant experience was that Blacks were subject to legal discrimination. Once that had been removed, with the laws passed in the 1960s, the playing field was immediately leveled, and opportunities for Black progress were assumed, after only a short period of adjustment, to be as great as for any other group. To ignore the differences in Black and immigrant history in this way (Cornacchia & Nelson, 1992; Tabb, 1971b) is not only an affront to the Black experience of centuries of suffering, it is also to ignore the fact that this unique experience make Blacks what they are today because, as the radical cultural perspective demonstrates, contemporary Black identity and culture are precisely the products of Blacks' reaction to that suffering.

In a cruel and contradictory inversion of the culturalist argument the liberal approach recognizes history only to condemn Blacks more thoroughly by insisting that because the playing field is now level, if Blacks fail to make the progress other groups have, then the fault must lie in their culture, whether the inappropriateness of their family structure (Moynihan, 1965) or some other legacy of the past. The truth is more nearly the opposite. Black culture and identity represent a triumph of humanity and strength in the face of centuries of racism. This racism continues today, albeit in more subtle forms, and thereby continues to impose on Blacks the necessity of creating, within the small social space of freedom available to them, a vibrant and indomitable culture that continues to confront the overarching racism of white America. If more progress has not been made, it is the consequence of a social structure that remains predicated on racism, not the supposed inadequacies of the victims of that structure.

The support for Black exceptionalism which the radical cultural approach gives may seem contradictory to its underlying presumption that conceptually the distinction between race and ethnicity has collapsed as race has come to be recognized as culturally constructed in the same way as ethnicity (Reed, in Sollors, 1989, pp. 226-229). Because the two concepts share not only their derivation in history, but also the same discursive character and a similar function in the construction of identity, the case for Black exceptionalism would appear to be restricted. The key to the difference between Blacks and other ethnic groups in American society lies, however, in history. It is because Blacks' historical experience has been different to the point of uniqueness that their present culture and potential for progress are also distinctive. So although analysis of the position of Blacks and ethnic groups shares the same conceptual framework, their current position or prospects are not necessarily similar. On the contrary, the substantive application of the common framework demonstrates why Blacks continue to be different.

Distinctiveness has implications for the most appropriate political strategy for African Americans.[10] The stress on culture as the governing element is of greatest significance here, first because it distinguishes this approach from its Marxist radical alternative (Cruse, 1967, 1968). The use of culture as an instrument of racial domination exposes how the Marxist emphasis on economics restricts understanding of the extent of control exercised by white society over Blacks. Invoking the analogy with colonial relations that are evidently national in character helps avoid the failure of class analysis. This is vital because it is the destruction of their culture in the broadest sense that is unique to Blacks in the United States; it is the factor that has incapacitated them in their struggle for progress. Integration is a myth in American society. Even when confronted with a qualitatively less severe form of discrimination (Cornacchia &

Nelson, 1992), no other group has pursued it; it does not exist. Yet it is a debilitating myth because so many Blacks, particularly intellectuals, have pursued this chimera. This has played into the hands of whites by taking away from Blacks the pride in their own culture and belief in themselves as a separate community, a pride that is the indispensable prerequisite for advancement in the ethnic competition that is the hallmark of American society.

The Black Nationalist Solution

Marxist analysis, of course, advocates integration based on class. This is no less damaging than the liberal fantasy of individualism. Neither is grounded in the reality of American life, and the pursuit of either can only prolong oppression of Blacks. Blacks will only make progress when they recognize that their unique position requires a distinctive, nationalist solution. In this light the upheavals of the 1960s were a catharsis, a rejection of Blacks' negative self-image and the aspiration to assimilation that was its corollary. These upheavals involved recognition that there are two nations in America, not one community as liberals would have it, or two classes as Marxists suggest. The inference for Blacks is obvious: They must rely on themselves for progress and will achieve it only through control of all aspects of their own communities, rather than by values of white idealism or by alliance with a white working class with which they have little in common.

The changes in the Black community since the 1960s reinforce the importance of this lesson (Burawoy, 1974). Again the transformation from colonialism to neocolonial relations in the Third World clarifies the position. As with the former colonies, Blacks have appeared to make progress when in fact all that has happened is that their oppression has become more subtle and less overt. Domestic neocolonialism is the strategy that white America has evolved to ward off the threat to social stability posed by Black disruption in the 1960s. The agents of the strategy are the new Black middle class, which has been raised up to encourage those who remain behind and to contain discontent by taking over the administration of the ghettos in which their poorer brethren remain trapped. This strategy involves elaboration of a network of welfare, which perpetuates dependency among poor Blacks and their physical isolation in inner city ghettos. But it also gives Blacks nominal political control of their own areas, the inner cities. The shift of power this appears to involve to a Black political elite is no more than a token because it is not accompanied by a transfer of the economic resources needed to redress the deterioration in the conditions of poor Blacks. Rather the consequence is to divert the focus of discontent away from whites and on to Black politicians, which has the effect of appearing to eliminate the racial element of the problem and thereby partially defuses it. The final element is policing the boundaries of the ghettos to contain crime where Blacks do damage to each other rather than to whites, again a function that has been safely devolved onto Black police chiefs because the veiled threat of severe repression, should large-scale disruption that spills beyond these boundaries be contemplated, is never far from the surface.

Domestic neocolonialism is a strategy that mixes the carrot with the stick; in this it requires concessions by whites, concessions that advocates of Black progress seize upon so avidly. But these concessions are granted as the minimum necessary to maintain existing power relations and to avoid the fundamental adjustments genuine progress for all Blacks would require. The fact that the Black middle class has cooperated in this venture should not surprise us if we bear in mind the performance of nationalist elites in former colonies. The appearance of Black progress has been as deceptive as the independence of ex-colonies. The prevailing system cannot tolerate self-determination for people of color, and neocolonialism is the strategy that has evolved both at home and abroad to strengthen the system's hold by appearing to do the opposite (Allen, 1970). It is essential that Blacks should not be deceived by this form of manipulation and the illusion of community power it involves but insist on genuine control over their own destinies. And this can only be achieved if they first build a positive self-image, developing a culture that celebrates the strength to be derived from their singularity as the basic resource to confront the racism that remains at the heart of their predicament.

CRITIQUING THE
RADICAL CULTURAL APPROACH

We have seen that, within the radical tradition, the cultural approach operates on three levels. Conceptually, it is based on a rethinking of the idea of race as discursive; substantively, it focuses on culture in its widest sense as the concept that can capture the essence of the Black experience; and strategically, it implies a nationalist politics that confronts the central issue of racism head on. Any critique must address all of these aspects.

The question conceptually is whether the efforts to reformulate race as a shifting, historically based idea in order to avoid biological or class determinism can succeed. This is of the utmost importance because the effort at reformulation is not undertaken in order to marginalize the concept, as it is with Marxism; on the contrary, it is because race and racism are perceived to be the core of the Black predicament that its correct formulation is vital. The difficulty derives from this centrality accorded to race. The very pervasiveness of racism in this approach raises the question of whether it is bound to lapse into an essentialist construction of the idea. The danger is that this approach would then come to mirror the racism it professes to criticize. On the face of it this seems unlikely. The more obvious danger is that cutting race adrift of its physical, economic, and indeed semantic roots invokes the curse of any postmodern approach, that of maintaining any rational analysis in the face of the fragmentation of meaning. The specter here is that by denying the existence of the real world, or at least the possibility of its perception other than through the use of language whose meaning is constantly shifting, it forsakes the alleviation of suffering experienced by Blacks in favor of language games that amount to nothing more than an exercise in semantics. It is led by its own premises into a futile effort to pursue the perpetually elusive meaning of race, thereby revealing the path of postmodernity to be a dead end, an attempt to capture the uncapturable, and one that denies any rational basis for action. This is a tragic conclusion and no answer to a predicament where the problem of suffering is all too obvious.

The pressing practicality of the question of Black progress tempers the excesses of postmodernity, permitting adoption of its insights without the need to give way to the temptation to succumb to its paralyzing quietist embrace.

The Permanence of White Racism

The real danger of a cultural approach lies elsewhere and becomes apparent in the construction of white racism upon which it rests. In a radical cultural approach, this becomes the primary explanation for Blacks' condition. It is the ever-present underlying factor that forestalls complete historical indeterminacy. But because it is ever present, it threatens to become unchanging; acting as a catchall, it loses the essential characteristic upon which this approach relies, its historicity. How else can such transhistorical constancy be explained than by some form of essentialism that makes the underlying character of white racism immune from the forces of change? If white racism is always and at all times the problem, this does not preclude a dialectical relationship between white domination and Black resistance, and therefore of change in this limited sense. But the intractability of white attitudes, combined with the permanent minority status of Blacks, means that change is always limited because however heroic or creative the Black response, white domination always endures. Although there will be variations on the theme, all that changes is the form of white domination, not its essence. In this sense, therefore, the essential element of change, the possibility of emancipation, is precluded.[11] The pessimistic implication of an analysis that makes an enduring racism and superior power of whites the source of the Black predicament is an equally enduring Black subjugation. This is not recognized by the radical cultural approach, even though the construction of racism on which it is based leads ineluctably to this conclusion. There is an echo here of the Marxist approach, which also refuses to recognize the pessimistic implications of a class-based analysis and attempts to sustain optimism for the prospect of radical change as a solution to the Black predicament, in contradiction to the logic of its own analysis.

The Vision of Black Identity

The more important problem with this conception of racism is that it leads to an equally essentialist and transhistorical vision of Black identity. By defining the basis of Black solidarity in some notion of Blackness, it eliminates the insight that authenticity is nothing other than a common heritage of suffering and vibrant cultural history in response; Black identity is, therefore, what the content of Black culture is at any one time. To superimpose some ethereal concept of Blackness above this is to open the pathway to the idea that cultures are incommunicable, or rather that diversity will be undermined by familiarity, "for familiarity is the first step towards the disappearance of that diversity" (Todorov, 1993, p. 71; see also Levi-Strauss, 1985). There is an evident contradiction here.

If Black culture is based on some essence of Blackness, it must mean that no one other than Blacks can have access to, or full appreciation of, its meaning; this in turn must mean that it is immune from the debasing effect of contact with whites and needs no protection or indeed special advocacy. If the threat of debasement is real, then essentialism cannot be true. Either the essence of Blackness accessible only to the chosen provides its own protection for Black identity, or it requires separatism precisely because it is not a secure basis for identity, as nationalists would propose. In this case cultural nationalism becomes a mechanism to prop up what its advocates wish were true rather than reflecting what actually is the case. It therefore reflects their fear that Black culture cannot retain its distinctiveness in the face of interaction with whites and the more general tendencies to cultural homogenization in the world today. It is not surprising, in light of this, that the practical political consequence is for cultural nationalism to lose all too easily its radical thrust and become a vehicle for a conservative Black nationalism that appropriates Black authenticity and turns it into a strategy for the advancement of a minority of the minority, a strategem for Black middle-class progress that in effect colludes with the white racism it professes to despise (Essien-Udom, 1962; Pinkney, 1976).[12]

If the conception of racism that underlies this approach is flawed, this raises the question of what weaknesses are associated with its accompanying stress on culture, because, as we have seen, the reformulation of race makes the two virtually synonymous. The idea of difference is important here because the cultural approach stresses the distinctiveness of African American culture, a sense of difference forged in response to white oppression. It can equally be argued that the oppression of slavery and Jim Crow crushed the African roots of Blacks' own culture and led them to adopt a profile of values that is much closer to the WASP culture than is the culture of many ethnic groups that arrived later and made their way in America in less harsh circumstances. The issue here is not one of authenticity but of effectiveness; African American culture is an authentic reflection of Blacks' historical experience irrespective of its degree of distinctiveness when compared to whites. But if it is not distinctive, adoption of WASP values would imply a goal of integration into white society. Blacks' values would not then be the springboard to a solution to their predicament because the problem would be one of opportunity of fulfilling their goals, not of values as such. But, of course, the radical approach denies this similarity of values on the ground that differential historical experience must be reflected in a unique culture. Even accepting these terms, the question remains, if Blacks are not like whites in their values and aspirations, how effective is their culture as a resource for achieving their own nationalist goals.

Undermining Black Culture

The danger that lurks behind the stress on culture, when judged on the criterion of effectiveness in promoting progress, is that it leaves itself open to the neoconservative argument that the distinctive cultural attributes of the Black community are precisely the reason for their lack of progress. Neoconservatives also can locate the problem in history, as with the argument concerning the destructive effects of slavery on the stability of contemporary African American family structure (Moynihan, 1965). In this way overt moral censure of Blacks is avoided. More generally a relativist line can be adopted that Black attitudes and culture may be as intrinsically worthwhile as those of whites or other more successful minorities, but they are not well-suited to success in American society as presently constituted. For neoconservatives this conveniently diverts attention from the barriers presented by the contemporary social structure it is their purpose to defend; its usefulness, therefore, is that it permits blame to be transferred to the victim, or the victim's culture, on a basis devoid of evident racism. The problem is whether any approach that stresses culture can avoid being dragged along this line of reasoning, however contrary its intentions may be.

The issue is posed most starkly in respect to comparisons with other immigrant groups that appear to have made much greater progress than Blacks. These have taken on greater force in recent years, as the changes in immigration laws made in 1965, permitting much greater immigration by peoples of Asian and Hispanic origin, have allowed contemporary comparisons, so that the case no longer has to rely on the spurious historical reconstruction of the relative disadvantage of postwar urban Black migrants and European immigrants of the turn of the century (Steinberg, 1989). The new immigrants have come from disadvantaged and even desperate backgrounds, arriving in some cases, as with the Vietnamese, as penniless refugees from persecution. And yet an increasing amount of evidence shows that significant proportions of these new immigrant communities are making substantial economic progress in little more than a generation. Having demonstrably started behind African Americans, in both chronological and socioeconomic terms, the feeling is that they are rapidly overtaking Blacks.

Furthermore they are doing so not as a result of special treatment, affirmative action or quotas, or by political means generally but by classic methods of sacrifice, entrepreneurship, family and community solidarity, and educational achievement. Anecdotal accounts abound of self-denial by Vietnamese who save to bring another family member to the United States, who is then, in turn, expected to sacrifice to continue the chain; or of Chinese and Koreans who work long hours in small retail establishments and whose children have succeeded so well in the educational system that they now occupy a disproportionate number of places in the elite universities of California and take the most difficult subjects. Even more damning are accounts of the successful entrepreneurship of Black immigrants, Carribeans from Dominica or Jamaica in New York, for example (Portes & Zhou, 1992). In short, the experience of recent migrants is taken to confirm the reality of the American dream by demonstrating that its promise can be fulfilled even today, for those who have the energy, the values, the commitment—in short, the culture—to take advantage of the opportunities American society continues to offer.

The implications for Blacks seem obvious; if these other groups can make it starting from the bottom, then there cannot be any insurmountable obstacles to progress, and so if Blacks do not make progress, the fault can only lie with them. And the advances the Black middle class has made since the elimination of legal discrimination only reinforces the idea by suggesting that the problem is neither one of race or racism but of the cultural inadequacy of certain sections of the Black community who are unwilling to pull themselves up by their own bootstraps. Instead either they demand that society solve their problems by handouts or they turn to drugs and crime in an attempt to take by antisocial means a share of the material fruits of the American dream they feel is rightfully theirs. This attempt that is at once pathological because it exacerbates rather than solves the problems of the Black underclass, and pathetic because it demonstrates a basic lack of understanding that these fruits are not given by right but won as the result of struggle in the marketplace.

Refusing to Admit Weakness

A radical approach can respond to this inversion of the role it ascribes to culture by arguing that the conditions faced by these immigrants, notably the level of discrimination, is not as intense as that met by Blacks; that many of these migrants were from relatively prosperous backgrounds and possessed of significant human capital that they could turn to advantage in the American context and that their lack of history in the United States is a positive advantage when compared to the effect on Blacks of centuries of discrimination. A radical response might add that focusing only on the present, rather than planning for the future, is a rational response for the Black underclass in its current circumstances, because the debilitating effects of white racism make superfluous any change in the attitudes of members of the Black underclass.

All of these points have some force. What weakens them is an unwillingness to admit that Black culture can be dysfunctional. The fact that it may have been conditioned by historical experience does not mean that its only role is to be positive or life-enhancing for Black identity, nor does it alter the fact that Black culture acts as a barrier to progress for certain sections of the Black community. The refusal to accept this is made in the name of a perverted sense of racial solidarity, which interprets any such criticism as itself a form of racism. This generates a vicious circle of political correctness that takes the tenets of multiculturalism to a level where rational communication and debate become impossible.

The explanation of this weakness illuminates the more important problem, however, which is that the radical cultural approach has difficulty in combating this revitalized neoconservative argument because it shares its premise of the centrality of culture. Once that premise is accepted, then the logic of the neoconservative analysis cannot be denied completely; hence the refuge in hollow abuse. The source of the weakness is the tendency to isolate culture from its relations to its material roots. Exploration of the changing economic structure of American society, which is making the labor of the Black underclass redundant, for example, and which is not a cultural problem or one of racism but of the logic of capitalist development, provides a much stronger riposte to the conservative culturalist argument, but it is an argument denied to a radical perspective as long as it insists on the primacy of culture and of racism. The solution is evidently to develop a model that allows for the complementary of economic and cultural factors in explaining the Black predicament, but this is difficult to achieve within a radical cultural framework the animus of which is insistence on the inadequacy of a class-based model.

The limitations of the radical cultural approach are further evident in its implications for a political strategy to resolve the African American predicament (Reisman, 1970; Rustin, 1966). The nationalist approach has offered Blacks an identity based on self-respect—an ethic that in opposing integration as an admission of white superiority stresses distinct Black values—and a philosophy of self-realization through self-direction and mutual support (Franklin, 1969). Its value as a movement of spiritual regeneration should not be underestimated, and to some extent the militant rhetoric associated with it has been necessary to political mobilization (Carmichael & Hamilton, 1967). But it has also served to cloud over the deeper problem of Blacks' predicament: Infatuation with its own rhetoric of emancipation and independence has obscured the fact that the segregationist strategy is as utopian as integration inasmuch as it is equally incapable of realizing its goals (Clarke, 1968; Conant, 1968; Crandall, 1972; Draper, 1969).[13]

The Political Drawback

The fundamental drawback of the nationalist approach is that the more Blacks pursue this path the more their political strategy is based on racial identification rather than on their class position. But defining the political issue in racial terms locks Blacks into a minority position. They are a group with relatively few resources relevant to the political struggle, and isolating themselves along racial lines can only accentuate this weakness. Defined by race Blacks are forever a minority; defined in opposition to whites, they ensure that the majority they face will be antagonistic. Racial identification does not create a minority position or the antagonism of whites; they would exist anyway. But it does exacerbate the weaknesses associated with them and thereby does exactly the opposite of what a political strategy should be designed to do, by undermining Black power for change rather than maximizing it.

Thus nationalism breeds racial identification, which accentuates minority status, which, combined with antagonism produced among whites, increases Black impotence, which forecloses the possibility of the radical change this approach claims is necessary to resolve the Black predicament. By polarizing the struggle along an axis unfavorable to Blacks, the nationalist approach is condemned to futility. In the circumstances prevailing in American society, nationalism itself prevents the realization of the goal of radical change. It is self-defeating. Of course, without the militancy generated by nationalism, there is unlikely to be any radical change either. That is the measure of the African American predicament. The nationalist alternative to a strategy of integration, far from resolving this predicament, therefore serves only to reveal its depths.

The Evolution of Left Liberalism

Recognition of the futility of separatism, and an effort to escape the horns of the integration/segregation dilemma, has led to the development of a strand of the cultural approach that transforms radicalism into left liberalism. Henry Louis Gates, Jr. (1992) is perhaps the most effective critic of the tendency to Black essentialism inherent in cultural nationalism, and one reason is his eloquence in arguing that Black identity has gone beyond the need to define itself in opposition to whites. Instead Black culture now

> looks beyond the overworked master plot of victims and victimizers, . . . beyond the paranoid dream of cultural autarky, and beyond the seductive ensolacements of nationalism. The new story is about elective affinities, unburdened by an ideology of descent; it speaks of Blackness without blood. (p. 151)

In making this case Gates is emphatic that "any human being sufficiently curious and motivated can fully possess another culture, no matter how 'alien' it may appear to be" (p. xv). In this vision Black culture is able to take its place in a genuinely multicultural America that is, in turn, part of a genuine emerging polycentric universal culture and not the parody of universalism that its Anglo-America regional subset claimed for itself. A positive cultural pluralism thereby replaces the negative sterility of cultural nationalism (of both Black and white varieties).

This critique of cultural nationalism is a powerful one, which redraws the cultural map and overcomes some stale and debilitating controversies; the problem with it is that while it may create an attractive vision of progress, it cannot provide a practical answer as to how it will be realized. The conservative weight of economic interest and pluralist politics as barriers to Black progress remain intact.

Cornel West (1993) is another influential critic who wishes to transcend the positive-negative dialectic that characterizes cultural nationalist strategies for Black identity formation in favor of "more multivalent and multidimensional responses that articulate the complexity and diversity of Black practices in the modern and postmodern world" (p. 20). Although radical in intent, West argues that the political basis of this must be to build upon the real-world liberalism of American society:

> I simply cannot conceive of an intellectually compelling, morally desirable and practically realizable prophetic vision, strategy and program that does not take certain achievements of liberalism as a starting point. . . . In this sense liberalism is an unfinished project arrested by relatively unaccount-

able corporate power, a passive depoliticized citizenry and a cultural conservatism of racism, patriarchy, homophobia and narrow patriotism or neo-
nationalism . . . leftist oppositional thought and practice should build on
the best of liberalism, yet transform liberalism in a more democratic and
egalitarian manner. (p. 202)

However, the subtlety and complexity of the demystification wrought
through this new cultural politics of difference mask the fact that in exposing the limits of radical cultural nationalism, it can propose only an
alternative that is ultimately captured by the theory of liberal pluralism.
The apparently radical accomplishment of its success in decentering
white male heterosexist dominance (at least in the realm of cultural
theory) only serves to broaden, and perhaps reinforce the pluralist ambit,
for pluralism can adjust to the new forms of identity and incorporate
them, so that rather than identity becoming the means to expanded
human agency, whether through grassroots coalitions or some other
method of increasing participation and effectiveness, it becomes a bulwark of the stability of a political system that has historically placed so
many limitations on Black progress.

West (1993, p. 224) sees his own left oppositional thought and practice
as building on and going beyond liberalism. He is well aware of the
accommodationist capacity of establishmentarian pluralism in relation to
literary studies, notably in the role of African American cultural critics in
the process of canonical formation and transformation (pp. 37-40). But
the experience of Blacks in this field and the elite universities in which it
is situated only confirm the resilience of the status quo, even as they
demonstrate its capacity for change.

The Rainbow Coalition

The drive toward pluralism and coalition politics continues to recognize the distinctiveness of Blacks' position and to deny a philosophy of
individualism, but it accepts that other groups also may be marginal to
the dominant culture. A coalition based on this shared condition of cultural oppression, therefore, becomes a way to broaden the power base of
those with an interest in radical change. The most prominent manifestation of this has been the Rainbow Coalition of dispossessed elements that
was the foundation of Jesse Jackson's presidential campaigns (Marable,
1985b). As the term implies, the coalition consists firstly of ethnic groups

of many colors, including Asians, Hispanics, and Native Americans. To this are added gay and lesbian groups oppressed because of sexual preference. And lurking behind this is the biggest minority, one that is in fact the majority, women who are oppressed by virtue of gender.

The numerical potential here is obvious. What is less clear is the common interest, beyond a sense of dispossession, upon which joint action may be built. A social agenda can be constructed around a common need for a greater sense of tolerance and recognition of the multicultural nature of American society. But beyond this the material circumstances of these groups are so diverse as to preclude any common strategy for furthering their interests. The same holds true within these groups generally, and for Blacks specifically. It would be naive to suggest that all women face the same material disadvantages, and their voting patterns reflect their material diversity more than any commonality derived from some essentialist notion of what it is to be female in a patriarchal society. Similarly it strains credibility to believe that the divisions within the Black community between a growing Black middle class and an increasingly wretched underclass can be conflated into a joint political agenda by a cultural appeal to racial unity.

It is evidently the strategy of the Republican Party, for example, to try to co-opt a significant proportion of the Black middle class. The means by which this would be done are illuminating (Marable, 1993). Republican leaders have sought Black support by backing claims for redistricting to create more Black majority districts. The reasoning is not that they feel they are likely to win such seats, but that redistricting will ipso facto increase the number of white majority districts that they do have the potential to win.

This reveals the flaw behind the idea of proportional representation for Blacks as a path to progress. Even if it were to prove constitutionally acceptable, it would lock Blacks into a minority position and in the process exacerbate the division between the races, not a position conducive to increased political or legislative power. As Derrick Bell (1987) puts it, "the proportional-representation remedy may increase the sense of racial difference and threat that underlie the historic resistance of white society to Black voting and political power" (p. 90).[14]

Any increases in Black representation in the Congress would then have a symbolic character, providing jobs for more middle-class Blacks while in substance increasing the power of the white conservative majority. The point is that the Black middle class willingly colludes in such a process, just as it does in acquiescing in the liberal myth that progress for a few high profile Black leaders is necessarily connected to an improvement in the lot of the ordinary Black American. The justification is a new conservative Black nationalism, which appropriates the culture of self-help in the service of self-seeking middle-class goals. In the process it uses the political resources of poorer Blacks for its own advantage while abandoning the radical content of Black culture, which is about resistance and community, in favor of their opposites.

Besides the opportunism inherent in this coalition then, it lacks the internal unity, the irreducible opposition of interest, that is the essence of the capital-labor dialectic, and the universalism of the proletariat that it is attempting to supplant as the agency of change, all of which properties are indispensable to a radical prognosis. Seen in this light a rainbow coalition can at best be a reformist movement and a relatively ineffectual one at that.

Black nationalism, if it is to avoid the utopian dead end of separatism, is driven ineluctably into the arms of the waiting politics of pluralism, which is all too ready to embrace it with a kiss of death for its radical pretensions. It is forced to sacrifice the principle of the uniqueness of the Black predicament, if not of the Black experience, in search of an effective political strategy, but the price is to confine gains to those that can be extracted from a fundamentally unchanged structure of power. Furthermore, the coalition created on these limited terms is, almost by definition within pluralism, an unstable one. Relations with other ethnic groups contain, as we have seen, as much negative charge as positive (Anthias, 1992) and the potential this creates for whites to divide and rule here is evident.

The same holds true to an even greater extent for those other components of the rainbow coalition, the fundamentally different basis of whose discrimination is obscured by the superficial similarities of a shared sense of dispossession. Exploiting such differences to create new, temporary pragmatic trade-offs with other more conservative elements around equally valid short-term goals is the stuff of pluralist politics. The fact is that Black nationalism cannot escape the fundamental truth that Blacks' position in American society is marginal by virtue both of numbers and resources, and the facts of power severely circumscribe the amount of progress they can make if they find whites in opposition to them. The incorporation of Black nationalism into the game of pluralist politics does not challenge this fact, it only confirms it.

CONCLUSION

The conclusion must be that, notwithstanding its radical veneer, the nationalist approach leads us ineluctably back to the pluralist perspective on Black incorporation. For all the insight it offers into the role of racism in the oppression of Blacks, and the basis it provides for resistance and the construction of a positive identity and vibrant culture, it nonetheless ends up reinforcing precisely the reformism it aims to reject. The reformulation of race as a discursive concept, and the centrality consequently accorded to Black culture as the means of resistance to racism, lead to a political strategy that leaves Blacks firmly impaled on the horns of the segregation/pluralism dilemma. Any strategy based on the primacy of race can, in the American context, only encroach on the system of power because its conceptual underpinnings lack the critical categories that can liberate Blacks from a position of powerlessness. The positive role of enhancing Black identity is thus counterbalanced by the trap of marginal and minority status into which this strategy locks the Black community. Demands for autonomous social and cultural institutions are not revolutionary; they are at best the means by which Blacks can obtain a share in a system whose essential structure they lack the power to change. Because the ultimate goal of separatism is unrealizable, the practical goal of the strategy becomes being separate but more nearly equal within the present system. The more confrontational tone adopted may be quite different from the gradualism implicit in the liberal model of cultural pluralism, and the underlying analysis of the role of racism in American society may be quite opposed, but the end result will be much the same as that imagined in the liberal tradition.

It would be facile to assume there is a simple way out of this impasse. The point is to face up to the measure of the predicament it entails. The criticism of the cultural approach is its failure to recognize that by taking racism as its central idea it must end up in a reformist position. For liberals, reformist conclusions are entirely consistent with their premises, and the problem is whether even this much can be achieved in practice. The class-oriented strand of the radical tradition also has the merit of a consistent premise and solution, because the racially united proletariat it sees as the agent of change is, in principle at least, capable of achieving the necessary transformation of power. The drawback is, of course, the absence of any sign of a radical, unified proletariat emerging. But for the cultural approach, the solution is inconsistent with the diagnosis of the problem, and we must conclude that it offers neither an intellectual nor a practical solution to the African American predicament.

NOTES

1. One alternative is to conceive of physical characteristics as providing the parameters that mark out a space within which culture operates as the determining variable. This loosens the chain of causation without breaking it altogether; but this does not solve the problem because "no proof has been provided for the relation of determinism or even for the interdependence of race and culture" (Todorov, 1993, p. 93). Equally, even if there is no proof, "If social differences are superimposed for a long enough time on physical differences, then racist and sexist attitudes rooted in the syncretism of the social and the physical can thrive" (p. 95). The social is so firmly superimposed on the physical in contemporary society that it would require the elimination of the latter to solve the problem. The fact that racism cannot be scientifically justified does not, therefore, give grounds for optimism as to its eventual eradication. The absence of a scientific basis for racism makes it clear that the problem is an ethical one, but the conflicts of interest that underpin racist practice make the prospect for the triumph of an ethically superior humanism a long-term one at best.

2. This is true of race to an even greater extent than it is of gender, where the facts of biology as they pertain to sexual difference, although not contradicting the socially constructed nature of the concept of gender, do set clearer parameters to the possibilities than is the case with race.

3. Todorov (1993) shows that this mirror quality betrays the nature of both ethnocentrism (pp. 1-2) and racism (pp. 93-94) as caricatures of universalism. The nature of the process by which experience is transformed into identity requires the specific values it embodies be given a universal character. The particular must become general because to be effective as a source of uniqueness, and therefore an effective basis of identity, values must have a universal quality. The alternative is relativism, which is a much less effective basis for identity formation. In the ethnocentric view, a group is unique because its values are of universal applicability. But if universality is necessary to the creation of uniqueness, it is a universality which other groups cannot share because they lack the appropriate history, culture, experience, or physical characteristics. This inherent contradiction creates the basis for antagonism in ethnic and racial identification.

4. Werner Sollors (1989), in his introduction to *The Invention of Ethnicity* (pp. ix-xx), suggests, to the contrary, that ethnicity also has been interpreted until recently as immutable and rooted in atemporal characteristics. The contradiction is, however, more apparent than real because Sollors stresses how the challenge to this view of ethnicity is part of a wider postmodern trend, in which the very notion of fixed categories is challenged by the increased recognition of language in the invention of cultural categories. This is undoubtedly the case but in its very scope this movement goes well beyond the physical/cultural distinction between race/ethnicity that is at issue here. This postmodern critique, if taken to its relativist conclusion, collapses the notion of the permissibility of such categories, a perspective which, whatever its intellectual attractions in a fin de siècle era, is unlikely to contribute much to the progress of African Americans for whom the experience of oppression remains, as does the value of the ideas of race and ethnicity, however invented, in coping with it.

5. It is, of course, quite possible that this refuge in ethnicity will come to be seen as merely a blip in the march toward homogenization of world culture. Black nationalism would then be one more attempt to turn back the tide of history, which is governed by the logic of integration inherent in a world capitalist system and against which the scope for culture to maintain significant variation is increasingly restricted. But even Auguste Comte, the first great prophet of globalization, always took the "precaution of asserting that, unification notwithstanding, distinguishing national characteristics will be respected" (Todorov, 1993, p. 29), and we may reasonably assume that, even if it will ultimately triumph, the process of globalization has a long way to go before it condemns the nationalist response to futility.

6. Patricia J. Williams (1991), in *The Alchemy of Race and Rights,* has shown how a critique that challenges certainty can penetrate even areas, such as the system of law in American society, where objectivity and rules would appear to be of the essence. She also demonstrates that the employment of critical theory does not have to lead to a relapse into relativism but can, through the process of contextualization, create a broadened awareness of the idea of justice that encompasses perspectives beyond those of the privileged and so produces better law.

7. Arthur M. Schlesinger, Jr.'s (1992) *The Disuniting of America: Reflections on a Multicultural Society* expresses a widespread fear that the cultural fragmentation resulting from the "cult of ethnicity," and Afrocentricity in particular, is threatening American national identity. In the process it may ultimately foster the fragmentation and even disintegration of society, but in the shorter term it is counterproductive because it promotes on "self-pity and self-ghettoization" (p. 102). Such fears echo those initially expressed by Glazer some 20 years ago. Their continuing resonance in conservative circles, although coming from a renowned liberal, should come as no surprise in light of the argument of Chapter 3.

8. This is particularly true in a time such as the Reagan-Bush administrations, when not only was multiculturalism attacked directly in the name of an attenuated concept of the melting pot, but economic and social policies promoted greater inequality. In view of the renewed focus on the idea of equality that was part of the legacy of the Civil Rights Movement and of the darker demographic hue of America (Takaki, 1987, p. 5), it is not surprising that the tensions caused by growing inequality would take the form of ethnic antagonism.

9. Common features include a lack of capital for investment, external ownership of resources, political dependence, a weak bourgeoisie, extreme residential segregation, and an inappropriately consumerist outlook (Savitch, 1978; Tabb, 1970, p. 17).

10. Stephen L. Carter (1991) makes the important distinction between a common history of suffering and a "single, genuine, preferred Black perspective" (p. 197). The one does not translate into the other; differences in political perspective, and even in strategies for progress, are perfectly compatible with a common history of suffering. Therefore, there can be no single, correct, "Black" view on this subject. He sees the idea that the difference between Black and white is an unbridgeable chasm as a view which, far from giving Blacks "a badge of authority" (p. 206), in fact creates "a victim-focused Black identity" (Steele, 1990, quoted in Carter p. 238) that limits and demeans Blacks and confines them to an intellectual ghetto unable to transcend their own experience. It is, as Shelby Steele (1990) has put it, "a skin which needs shedding," one which, also traps and isolates Blacks socially and politically and is therefore no avenue to progress. Taking the recognition of difference to the point of insisting on uniqueness and unanimity, and in the process denying that the Black experience can possibly be fathomed by someone who is white, is thus a comforting but ultimately

self-defeating argument. The echoes of Schlesinger supra in this are significant, inasmuch as they illustrate the growth of a more conservative strand of thinking among Blacks themselves, which takes culture seriously but, in reaction to the excesses of multiculturalism, refuses the inevitability of its radical connotations.

11. Even worse is when Black identity develops a vested interest in the perpetuation of exploitation. This arises when cultural nationalism argues that Blacks' historical legacy of white racism not only defines their identity, it also the precludes the possibility of advance in mainstream society. To the extent that Black identity comes to rely on the absence of opportunity, the existence of progress undermines that identity. Refusal to acknowledge progress thus becomes essential to the maintenance of the nationalist perspective (Steele, 1990, p. 164).

12. One ironic consequence is that this analysis uncritically accepts the categories extant in society (Bonacich, 1979; Burawoy, 1974; Wolpe, 1975). It elevates existing group ideologies to the level of analytic categories and portrays the social structure as a reflection of how the participants define it, which is to take as given what should be the object of the analysis. In the process it adopts categories created to serve the interests of particular groups. It is easy to see the political interest of middle-class Black spokespersons in portraying the Black and white communities as internally homogeneous and unalterably opposed by racism. It is also easy to see the weakness of any model whose logic is to cultivate such spurious homogeneity. In taking its lead from such ideologically loaded categories, it forfeits its analytical function and becomes itself at once ideological and merely descriptive.

13. It is because this integration/segregation dilemma is as absent from the colonial situation as it is central to the African American experience that the colonial analogy gives rise to erroneous conception of Blacks' ties to white America and arouses false hopes of emancipation. On the nature of the true colonial relationship see Memmi, 1967, and Fanon, 1965.

14. Bell (1987) himself quotes Douglas's more magisterial rebuttal:

> When racial and religious lines are drawn by the State, the multiracial, multi-religous communities that our Constitution seeks to weld together as one become separatist; antagonisms that relate to race or to religion rather than to political issues are generated; communities seek not the best representative but the best racial or religious partisan. Since that system is at war with the democratic ideal, it should find no footing here. (p. 90)

6

Power and Pluralism:
Black Progress and the Politics of Race

It is not only the cultural nationalist approach to the African American predicament that has implications for Black politics; all explanations have to address the issue. The ideas of race, class, and culture that underpin the various approaches are incomplete until their analytical and prescriptive relation to politics is understood. But more is involved than the needs of comprehensiveness. Politics is not just another discrete area of American life with which any theory must come to terms. Rather it is the arena in which the contest between competing explanations is played out and receives its most acute expression.

It is in the political cauldron that the essence of the Black predicament is distilled and revealed in its clearest outlines. The intensely practical nature of the African American predicament means that progress toward its resolution, however conceived, must involve tangible material or cultural benefits to Blacks as an underprivileged group. The political strategies inherent in the various explanations of the Black predicament can either further this goal or hinder it, and to this extent the effectiveness of these strategies stands as proxy for evaluation of the general approaches from which they derive.

It is a commonplace that since the 1960s Blacks have turned from protest to conventional politics as the most effective means of advancing their cause, and the tangible results in the election of Blacks to political office are equally familiar (Joint Center for Political and Economics Studies, annually). The significance of such progress remains open to question, however. It may be that these gains will act as a spearhead for wider improvement because Blacks have more of the resources relevant to this field—votes, political organization, and so on—than they have in other spheres (Howard, 1978). To put it another way, Blacks have more of the currency necessary to gain equality through politics than they have of the capital that would be required to compete on an equal economic footing with the rest of society. To determine whether politics as the quintessential expression of the Black predicament justifies such optimism is the object of this chapter.

BLACK POLITICS AND PLURALISM

Despite its theoretical import, there is a markedly empirical, not to say empiricist orientation to the literature on Black politics. Although the theoretical assumptions are rarely made explicit, the bulk of this literature can be squarely placed within the liberal tradition, adopting a conventional pluralist model of the American polity that engenders optimism in respect of the potential for Black progress. Although some neoconservative analysts have come to stress the market as the key to Black incorporation, and to cite as examples the success of immigrant groups who have eschewed politics, even this perspective implies a particular supportive role for politics rather than none at all (Sowell, 1981a). In general, politics has retained its central place as the basis for optimism for Black incorporation. Gaining full political rights is seen as an essential component of full citizenship (Parsons, 1965), and the importance attributed to politics in the incorporation of white ethnic immigrants is evident from the frequency with which this analogy is employed (Glazer, 1971; Kristol, 1972).

The liberal view rests on a simple extrapolation whereby Blacks, who were formerly excluded from political power, have now gained partial access and will extend this until they achieve full political inclusion (Glazer & Moynihan, 1970; Holloway, 1969). So linear a perspective can easily cause the significance of the election of Blacks to office in increasing numbers to be seen as self-evident, a tendency which at its worst assumes the facts speak for themselves and eschews argument in favor of a tedious listing of the offices Blacks have gained. Such empiricism fails to make the elementary distinction between participation in the decision-making process and influencing its outcome, between the trappings of office and the exercise of power (Jones, 1978). The point remains as valid now as when Ralph Ellison made it, "why is it often true that when critics confront the American as negro they suddenly drop their advanced critical armament and revert with an air of confident superiority to quite primitive modes of analysis" (quoted in Jones, 1978). This stricture does not, of course, apply to all writers in this tradition (Dahl, 1958), but even those who recognize the need to evaluate outcomes accept the prescriptive implications of the pluralist model. Discussion of its relevant aspects is, therefore, a necessary preliminary to judging its suitability for analyzing Black politics.[1]

The premise of the pluralist model is that politics in the United States rests on a consensus of fundamental values that determine the shape of society. Politics is therefore confined to relatively marginal issues, having more to do with the resolution of conflict over the distribution of resources than with their method of production. Within this consensus the principal virtue of the pluralist framework is that it protects democracy from the twin dangers that threaten it, tyrannical control by an elite or the rule of demagoguery characteristic of a mass society.[2] The optimum balance is achieved first by ensuring the appropriate degree of participation; a representative system with regular universal voting guarantees enough mass involvement to keep elites in check but not so much as to lead to anarchy or to the mass mobilization associated with totalitarianism. The principal guarantee of democracy, however, lies in the network of intermediary groups which is the most distinctive feature of the American polity. These groups are voluntary and interest-based in nature and have open access to the political arena. They are the vital bridge between the elite and the masses, curbing the power of each and preventing the excesses either would be prone to if unrestrained. These interest groups compete for advantage and in the process underline the key element of the American political structure, its decentralization of power. Dahl (1967) argues that the existence of multiple centers of power, none of which is or can become sovereign and which act to check and balance each other, is the most important feature of pluralism and the sine qua non of the preservation of democracy.

Given these features, politics becomes a matter of trade-offs, a bargaining process in which policy is always the result of compromise. No group ever gets all it wants but must learn to bargain over a range of issues, giving and taking, in an attempt to maximize its returns. To do this it must form alliances with other groups, alliances whose composition shifts constantly according to the issue; groups have no permanent friends or enemies, only permanent interests. By its very structure this system educates participants in the virtues of compromise and moderation; it steers them away from permanent rifts, as today's enemies may be tomorrow's friends. The absence of any fundamental cleavage differentiates pluralism from a class model of politics. It also implies that the state, rather than being the tool of one dominant class, is neutral between competing groups (Miliband, 1969), although more recent versions of the pluralist model, sometimes termed neopluralism, accept that the state itself, or rather its personnel, can prosecute interests of its own, which undermine this neutrality (Dunleavy & O'Leary, 1987). The combination of a neutral framework and a large number of relatively equal competitors is indispensable to freedom. The role of politicians in this model is to act as professional arbiters who reflect the balance of pressures rather than making policy independently. If they form an elite, it is a differentiated one, kept internally competitive by accountability to the electorate and restrained by subjection to multiple, cross-cutting group pressures. The most obvious analogy is with a perfectly competitive market; the number of competing interest groups is sufficient that if they pursue self-interest as vigorously as possible, the system, as if guided by the same hidden hand that causes consumers' self-interest to generate the most efficient pattern of production, will produce a series of outcomes that maximizes the extent of democracy and freedom and thus the greater good.

The Rewards of Participation

Where, then, do Blacks fit into this idealized pluralist model? The reason for elaborating its features is that to do so accounts for Blacks' role, because that role is not to alter the general model but simply to act as an additional group of players in the bargaining game. Blacks have legitimate and distinctive interests and will organize and participate in the political process to advance them, just like any other group. This is not to suggest that all African Americans have the same interests in every sphere, or that "Black" groups represent the whole community in all areas of public life. Ideally, there would be a multiplicity of groups representing various aspects of African American life, and individual Blacks would participate in other groups organized on the basis of interests having nothing to do with race, thereby reinforcing the complex network of overlapping groups that bind the system together. But Black participation does not alter the model except to bring an added dimension that enhances its range and democratic potential. Access to the political process is clearly crucial, but in this model there are no barriers to access stemming from within the polity itself; any discrimination that might prevent Black participation must therefore be located elsewhere in society.

The point is that if access is assumed, as has been possible since the elimination of formal discrimination in the 1960s, then the natural working of the system should in time gain Blacks rewards from politics that are equal to other groups. Although seeds of complacency can easily bear fruit in this approach (Cole, 1976), so that the office holding now enjoyed by Blacks, particularly at the mayoral level, is sometimes taken to virtually guarantee eventual equality, it is in general recognized that success in the political game is a function of those resources a group brings to the bargaining process. These take many forms: voting strength, degree of political organization, sophisticated leadership, and so on (Mathews & Prothro, 1966). It is further recognized that Blacks are deficient in most of these compared to other groups. But in the liberal tradition these deficiencies are considered remediable now that Blacks have gained access, so long as they themselves work to develop their resources. Thus even those pluralist analyses that recognize the gap between ideal and reality imply that the solution lies in hard work by Blacks because the barriers that exist are the legacy of past disadvantage and can be overcome by sufficient effort (Kilson, 1971).

The prescriptive lesson of the pluralist model is that Blacks should strive to capitalize on the access they have now gained. They should do this through the energetic but responsible prosecution of their interests within the existing political system because that system, although not giving any group all it wants, is flexible enough to accommodate many of their demands, if pressed hard enough. Blacks' best strategy is to form shifting coalitions with other interest groups rather than operating solely on the basis of race. Following the latter course would only unite other participants against them and fatally undermine their ability to take advantage of the opportunities for progress that do exist. Fortunately, it is argued, Blacks have followed the pluralist injunction; they have spurned radical strategies and have participated with increasing vigor and effectiveness in pluralist politics. The creation of a sophisticated and variegated national Black political class is taken to demonstrate that Blacks are doing exactly this. New diverse strands of Black opinion have emerged, as evidenced for example by the varied responses of Black leaders to the nomination of Clarence Thomas to the Supreme Court (Morrison, 1993). Far from being a sign of weakness or lack of solidarity, such growing diversity strengthens the Black community. The consequence, by ensuring Black input across a wider band of the ideological spectrum, is to eliminate one of Blacks' greatest weaknesses in this game. Until recently Blacks were severely disadvantaged because their most prominent leaders adopted a single, unchanging, extreme, and ideologically driven position that did not maximize their potential power in a system that thrives on compromise. Because Blacks had confined themselves to the left of the spectrum, potential allies could count on their support without having to offer much in return, whereas those on the right saw no point in proffering alliances. Increasingly, however, and in reflection of the more diverse material circumstances of the Black community, a greater ideological flexibility has emerged. This not only binds Blacks more tightly into the fabric of the community, it also ensures that, from the inside, Blacks as a whole enjoy increased leverage. By playing their part they have begun to reap the rewards predicted by the model, with increased electoral victories, bureaucratic and political appointments, and favorable policies.

Problems of the Pluralist Model

There has been no lack of criticism of the pluralist model, both in general terms and in respect of its applicability to Black politics. Much of the criticism is valid, and although it sometimes amounts to little more than demolishing a straw man, it nonetheless adds up to a powerful critique (Hamilton, 1973; Jones, 1972; Keller, 1978; Kilson, 1975; Lineberry & Masotti, 1976; Preston, 1978; Schattschneider, 1960). However, much of the criticism remains bound by the assumptions of the liberal tradition. It is primarily empirical in nature; even literature stressing the role of elites fails to pose a fundamental threat to the pluralist model because it is confined to demonstrating the model's imperfections in practice rather than emerging from an alternative theoretical perspective. It may be seen as weakening the pluralist edifice, or, paradoxically, as strengthening it by injecting greater realism; either way it fails, through lack of theoretical organization, to issue a decisive challenge to pluralism.

The first relevant criticism is that the pluralist model of the American polity takes the values that inform its operation as a given, rather than analyzing the conditions of their production. The premise of value consensus means that the pluralist analysis can amount to no more than a discussion of how well the political process is living up to its own (unquestioned) values. Through an uncritical acceptance of those values the pluralist approach comes to be part of the value system it is attempting to analyze. In other words, lacking any concept of ideology, it becomes ideological. One consequence is to rule out the idea of manipulation of opinion by elites who control access to information. This is not to propose a conspiratorial model in which the masses are duped into believing whatever elites want them to believe. But pluralism goes too far to the other extreme in its naive and simplistic conception of the relations between leaders and led. The role and importance of ideological constructions in creating a consensus are manifestly difficult to unravel (Gaventa, 1980). Nevertheless the problem must be addressed, and the failure of the pluralist model to do so raises a serious question about it. The substantive deficiency this leads to is that the pluralist model reflects the bias that the polity itself has toward the powerful. This suggests that in practice an apparently neutral framework can only serve to reinforce existing inequalities. In allowing the weak and the strong to play by the same rules, the structure systematically favors the strong. The polity is, therefore, a knife-edged system without any self-correcting mechanisms. As such it is bound to lead to increasingly clear-cut cleavages between winners and losers. Whether these are termed bourgeois and proletariat, or elites and masses, or whites and Blacks, is immaterial; what matters is the bias in favor of the powerful.

The argument is reinforced by studies demonstrating differential participation in the political system and the low level of activity of any kind, even voting, among the majority (Hamilton, 1972). The upper classes participate because it is their system, and the lower classes do not for the same reason. This suggests that the American polity is a system whose institutions and rules, although ostensibly applying equally to all, have the consequence of protecting the privilege of elites and keeping genuine democracy at bay. In such a system any group finding itself on the margin—and we may take Blacks to be such a group—will not only have to fight with opposing interests, it will also have to take on a system whose rules favor the entrenched. The appearance of free and equal political competition is, therefore, a facade that pluralism is unable to penetrate. Accordingly it is blind to the double burden borne by Blacks and underestimates the extent of the obstacles they face.

Another attribute of pluralist politics is incrementalism. This too works against the resolution of the African American predicament, because the pace of change it permits is not commensurate with the problem. The extent of Blacks' disadvantage is such that a complete remedy would require a fundamental redistribution of resources, but pluralism acts as a bulwark against change on this scale. There are too many groups whose interests would be threatened by such a shift, and in a system of checks and balances they are able to block change, or at least minimize it to the point of insignificance. Compromise is not a virtue in all circumstances; when faced with a redistributive problem of the size posed by Blacks' position, compromise means that the problem will not be solved. Whatever its virtues in maintaining stability, such a system cannot be considered effective on the criterion of fostering Black progress. The position of Blacks in American society makes them weak participants in the political bargaining process that is the essence of pluralism. They are a low resource and high demand group, and this combination makes them an ineffective player.[3] They make poor coalition partners because if their needs are to be met, the demands they must make from any alliance will be out of proportion to the power and influence they can bring to it. Thus they are not in a position to affect the incrementalist character of the system because they do not have the strength to shift it alone, and their capacity to do so in alliance with others is equally limited if each group operates according to rational self-interest. The pluralist system, whatever its other virtues, places a premium on attempts by in-groups to maintain their position and puts at their disposal a formidable array of techniques with which to pursue a strategy of social control (Gamson, 1971). Faced with this level of gatekeeping, outsiders, if they are rational, are reduced to the pursuit of individual self-interest rather than collective action as the best means of maximizing their share of the limited returns available (Olson, 1965).

This argument, which applies to any out-group, is reinforced in the case of Blacks. The pluralist model was derived, at least partially, from the experience of the succession of ethnic immigrant groups to urban America. If we adopt the ethnic framework, we find the multiplicity of groups essential to the construction of shifting alliances and thus to the working of pluralism (Glazer & Moynihan, 1963). If we adopt a racial framework, however, the groups are reduced to two, Black and white. Blacks are not one group among many, with all that implies for opportunities for successful bargaining; they are one group against all the rest. They are the weaker of the two groups, and the process is no longer one of competition between equals in which Blacks might be expected to do as well as others. Thus even though the model might work as prescribed for interethnic group conflict, it does not follow that it will work when

Blacks seek to participate. If ethnic groups, when dealing with African Americans, define their interests by race rather than ethnicity—as whites, for example, rather than as Irish or Italians—then the elaborate logic of the bargaining system becomes redundant, to the inevitable disadvantage of Blacks.

The question then becomes which basis for the definition of interests do whites employ when dealing politically with Blacks? It would be absurd to suggest they employ either exclusively, but even a cursory glance at the history of Black politics will tell us that the racial mode is adopted at least as frequently as the ethnic one. To the extent that this remains true Blacks are forced into an unequal contest in having to take on all whites, and in that event they are condemned to perpetual exclusion from the benefits of pluralism.

The capacity of the pluralist system to marginalize groups that challenge the status quo is apparent from some specific instances of Black political activity in recent years. Most change has taken place at the level of local politics, and one vehicle of Black involvement has been the community action programs that were instigated in the 1960s. These were hailed as tools Blacks could use to gain access to the political process, providing new channels through which they could affect policy and so making confrontation redundant. The improved leverage thus gained was expected to produce noteworthy consequences in redistribution of local government resources and jobs. Although some progress has been made in this area, this has happened only because these programs are relatively marginal to the real problems of redistribution upon which the question of progress turns (Fainstein & Fainstein, 1974; Greenstone & Peterson, 1973). Such programs do not threaten or even affect the major interests of business, which has abstained from direct involvement in what seems a sideshow, especially as over time they have lost their redistributive edge. So even where victories have been won against local government, they have occurred in areas where important economic interests are not threatened (Stone, 1976). The limited importance of the issues involved in community control, as it has come to be defined, means that these have had little impact on the lives of most Blacks. Their principal consequence has been to incorporate Black leaders into conventional politics, absorb their energies, and reduce the potential threat they pose, while conceding little of importance in return. Community action is then a classic instance of defeating a challenge through diversion and co-option.

The Election of Black Mayors

This theme is even more apparent in that area which has drawn most attention within the liberal tradition as evidence of the extent of Black progress in politics, the election of Black mayors in a growing number of American cities (Bryce, 1974; Levine, 1974; Nelson & Meranto, 1977; Nelson & Van Horne, 1974; Stokes, 1973; Tryman, 1974). Here the criticism of the pluralist model has been about the limited powers these mayors enjoy and the difficulties they face (Preston, 1976). In a number of cases, Blacks have gained office in what are known as weak mayor systems, where the powers of the office are virtually nonexistent and the municipalities are run by councillors or appointed executives. In such cases the only resource the mayor commands is the capacity to influence public opinion and through it those officials with executive powers. Although not to be dismissed, this is hardly sufficient to wage a successful fight against entrenched interests. Mayors are further constrained by the political complexion of the city councils with which they share power in virtually every system of local government. Although there are instances where councils are also Black-dominated, this is not always the case, and where whites form a majority, they can act and have acted to limit mayoral initiatives. Perhaps more important, because they are less susceptible to change, are the bureaucracies that mayors have to depend on to implement their policies. These are often hostile, having been appointed by earlier white administrations, and they have considerable scope for stifling initiatives of which they disapprove. The position is made more difficult by the fact that civil service rules now governing the appointment of administrators restrict the power of any new mayor to hire or fire bureaucrats on the basis of political considerations. This reform of appointment procedure came about in response to the corruption endemic in the machine-based appointments of earlier generations, but one consequence has been to reduce the power of mayors to effect rapid change just at the time when Blacks are taking over these offices.

These limitations are not racially specific. This is also true of other limitations on mayoral freedom, which include reliance on federal and state funds to initiate redistributive programs and the impact of the health of the national and international economies on the revenue base available to them. Even so, these factors impinge on Black mayors to a greater degree because they are, more than white mayors, attempting to use their office as a cutting edge in the struggle for greater social and economic equality. Their frontline position in trying to effect Black progress brings them more painfully up against the limitations of their office than is the case with white mayors, who tend to have ambitions more in keeping with the scope of their position.

The real dilemma of Black mayors and the marginality that their prominent position disguises only become apparent, however, when we consider the suburbanization and fragmentation of urban government that has occurred in recent years (Newton, 1975, 1976). This has been defended on the ground that it produces competition between government units and so allows the political consumer to maximize choice. Increasing the number of jurisdictions can also be seen to increase the access points to power centers within government and so be of particular advantage to groups such as Blacks which have been denied access hitherto. Although fragmentation may be beneficial to some groups, however, benefits tend to flow to those further up the social scale rather than to those at the bottom or on the margin. This is because political differentiation follows socioeconomic disparities. The consequence of fragmentation is increased stratification between communities and increased homogeneity within them. It therefore amounts to a device by which richer communities insulate themselves from the demands of the poor. Part of the reason for this is to avoid the public expense consequent on the presence of impoverished groups; but there is also a wider fear of association with the poor, particularly as it concerns the education of children, which is the driving force behind the development of the fortress mentality that suburban government often expresses. Weak and fragmented government is, therefore, functional for the interests of the middle class, and this includes increasingly those parts of the Black middle class that have migrated to their own largely racially separate suburban communities for the same class-based reasons as their white predecessors. But it is disastrous for poor Blacks because it reduces the tax base that might finance programs to alleviate their position. Suburbanization is the process underlying fragmentation, and its effect has been to reduce the fiscal base of the central cities without commensurately reducing the demands on their governments. This has placed an impossible burden on those left to run the central cities.

The burden is made greater for Black mayors by the high and unrealistic expectations imposed on them by their Black constituents. Black mayors have borne the brunt of expectations of a payoff from participation in conventional politics. The restrictions under which they operate have inevitably led them to disappoint those Blacks who elected them to office. The initial temptation was to try to offset this disillusionment and maintain Black support by blaming whites, both those individuals who flee to the suburbs and businesses that resist property tax increases. But such a strategy only further alienates white voters and businesspersons. Yet it is they who control the economic resources on which Black mayors must depend if they are to end up presiding over an empty shell of a city (Eisinger, 1983). Mayors cannot, therefore, afford to bait whites with racial rhetoric or make demands on their resources that would be necessary to generate the funds with which to meet the demands of their Black constituents. If they do, whites will simply take up their option of leaving the city, and the mayor will end up with yet fewer resources, even less able to meet Black expectations. If, for fear of alienating them, Black mayors make no demands on whites that they are not prepared to meet, they will have to operate within fiscal limits that severely restrict their capacity for innovation of any kind, let alone any attempt at redistribution. Thus Black mayors are faced not so much with a dilemma as with an insoluble problem; no matter what strategy they choose the economic position of the bulk of the Black community cannot be improved. The best that can be done is to walk a tightrope between the conflicting demands of the two communities, attempting to make what few gains are possible, an endeavor requiring consummate political skill. Given the impossible position they find themselves in, one cannot but conclude that the skill of those Black mayors who have walked this tightrope is incommensurate with the meager rewards it brings.

The Failure of Politics

These criticisms of the pluralist model amount to a powerful indictment. They demonstrate the limited value of the tactics recommended to Blacks, to act within the existing rules but to organize better and work harder. Such tactics can have only a minimal impact, given the structural obstacles Blacks face. Consequently, the pluralist analysis, just like the liberal tradition of which it is part, fails to come to terms with the extent of Blacks' problems or the true depth of their predicament. Viewed in this light the underlying proposition that future Black progress can simply be extrapolated from their increased occupation of political office appears facile to the point of insult.

And yet, despite the uncongenial pessimism following from this argument, many of these criticisms could be accepted by what we might term a realistic pluralist. The model could be and is defended in pragmatic terms. Even if the system limits Black progress, it evidently does not eliminate it altogether and some progress is better than none. And in any case, what is the alternative? African Americans have no alternative but to continue to participate in the system and make whatever gains they can, no matter how short of the ideal they may fall. The type of criticism we have encountered so far exposes the flaws of pluralism but does not and cannot of itself suggest a superior conceptualization. It makes pluralism more realistic and in doing so has the ironic effect of improving the model rather than refuting it. Lacking an alternative theory, this type of criticism must fall back on making pluralism work better, both as an analytic and a prescriptive device. To put it another way, although pluralist pessimism reveals that political progress does not guarantee socioeconomic advance for Blacks, it fails to analyze the relationship between these areas. It sees the limitations of Black political power as a series of unhappy circumstances, which because they are ad hoc rather than systemic in character, can only be tackled in an equally ad hoc fashion. This will remain true no matter how many or how serious the empirical obstacles uncovered. Clearly what is required is an alternative model which can incorporate this type of criticism into a more coherent framework of the relation between Black politics and Blacks' situation in American society as a whole (Walton, 1972).

AN ALTERNATIVE MODEL

The various strands of a radical approach to the question of Black progress claim to offer such a framework. The strength of the nationalist approach stems from the realization that economic interests are no longer an adequate basis for radical politics because changes in the class structure of capitalist societies have undermined the idea of a universal proletariat as the agent of radical change. These structural changes have led to an increasing differentiation among the proletariat rather than its progressive homogenization and impoverishment, as Marx predicted. Some elements have been increasingly marginalized and reduced to the status of an underclass, whereas others have been incorporated in a more complex hierarchy of stratification, permitting broader groups than pure capitalists to have at least some stake in the status quo (Wright, 1985). The differentiation of the African American community in recent decades is a case in point. The danger of a traditional approach within a radical framework is that continued reliance on the idea of the proletariat condemns any analysis to futility, as that class is reduced to impotence by the incorporation of some of its elements and the marginalization of others.

Awareness of this has been combined with an improved understanding of the role of culture as a basis for political action, both as an agent of dispossession and of empowerment. This stems, in turn, from a recognition that politics is not solely about material interests in the narrow sense of the term because exploitation cannot be successfully exercised without an accompanying ideology and therefore without the appropriate culture. It follows that the bases of discrimination can span the whole realm of ideas and vary beyond those that are economically based. This transforms the hierarchy of discrimination, dethroning economics and giving race, ethnicity, gender, and other bases equal status in the construction of the societal hierarchy. It also follows that, because culture can be a tool of resistance as well as of oppression, groups who share the experience of discrimination on theoretically equal, even if practically different, terms can and should unite in a politics of cultural resistance to further their common aims (Laclau, 1975). This insight opens up a whole new realm of political activity, or rather results in the reinterpretation of much activity formerly seen external to politics. One of the more important consequences is to redefine the concept of the state to embrace this new terrain. If the struggle for emancipation is no less political for being waged on a cultural front, the gains are no less tangible and the ground on which the battle is fought no less relevant to state power than traditional institutions. The struggle to control the state, therefore, becomes as much about the meaning of ideas—not only of racism itself but also of tolerance and respect for diversity in a multicultural society—as it is about the precise division of economic benefits. Indeed success in the battle of ideas is more likely to result in tangible material benefits for the dispossessed than a political struggle confined to an outdated conception of class unity based on an economic structure that no longer exists.

If this perspective demonstrates how struggles around popular culture are legitimate avenues for resistance, the question remains whether the broader understanding of their predicament offers Blacks enhanced political effectiveness in their efforts to escape from it. One positive legacy is an appreciation of how the forms of struggle can be expanded into areas more favorable to Blacks than conventional politics. Examples include the role of Black music, of gang culture, and of Black religion as rituals of resistance.

Equally, the struggle to influence the governing ideas of modern society in a direction that increases respect for diversity must, insofar as it undermines hierarchical notions placing white male culture at the apex, favor Blacks. This suggests the second, related positive legacy, the realization that Blacks are not alone in their marginality but share this status with other groups. Each of these may have a different basis for their own marginality, but they all share the common fate and this provides the potential for a coalition of the dispossessed, the collective power of which must enhance the position of each. However, as we have seen in the previous chapter, there is a tension inherent in an approach that insists on the uniqueness of the Black experience and yet simultaneously advocates a strategy of coalition. The major premise of the nationalist approach remains that white racism is the unique source of the Black predicament. The broader awareness of the changing nature of this racism, and the corollary of new forms of cultural resistance, do not change the fact that Blacks cannot by themselves successfully challenge white power.

The problem is that the discursive nature of racism can work against Blacks, not just for them. For every form of cultural resistance that chips away at the stereotypes that this approach makes us understand are essential to white hegemony, new forms of racism can and will be constructed to perpetuate Blacks' subjugation. The white neoethnic reaction to the campaign for affirmative action arising out of the Civil Rights Movement is plain evidence of this. Not only were whites able to turn to their own advantage the idea of ethnicity initially invoked by Blacks as a basis for their struggle, they were able in the process to eliminate their own sense of collective guilt and so lay the ground for blaming the absence of progress on the supposed deficiencies of Black culture, with all its accompanying imagery of fecklessness, criminality, and drug and welfare dependency. To the extent that Blacks define the problem as one of racism, therefore, any shift in its meaning they negotiate can be matched by whites. Making race a discursive concept may create new forms of politics, but this is a game two can play and does nothing itself to alter the underlying balance of power between Blacks and whites. Its political creativity is therefore superficial because it does not extricate Blacks from the starkness of the predicament revealed by its own analysis of the centrality of racism.

Prospects of a Rainbow Coalition

If any analysis resting on Black uniqueness remains confounded for these reasons, can the alternative strand of creating a rainbow coalition of dispossessed groups fare better? There need not be any inconsistency

here since a coalition does not preclude Blacks from organizing themselves as effectively as possible in response to their own distinctive sources
of disadvantage while joining with other groups doing the same. The
problem is rather that the combination of self-help and alliances with others
of similar but, critically, not the same source of marginality amounts in
fact to a classic pluralist recipe for change, with all the limitations we
have seen to be attendant on that. The analysis of the power of racism
gives this approach an awareness of the difficulties of making progress
within pluralism. This leads, on the one hand, to signs of progress being
greeted as evidence of Black fortitude, and, on the other, to the catalog-
ing of the still formidable array of obstacles facing Black politicians as
indications of the continuing power of racism. But this only replicates
the points made by a realistic pluralism and is rarely accompanied by the
pessimism it logically entails.[4]

The more radical rhetoric in which the approach is couched appears to
encourage Blacks and others to confront the political system rather than
to work within it, especially insofar as it enjoins extracurricular challenges to conventional politicians. But the rhetorical flourishes are misleading, for if the recommended tactics were to prove successful, the best
Blacks could hope for is to end up as conventional participants in the
pluralist system, obtaining some concessions but no radical restructuring
of a system that marginalizes them. In the event that these tactics do not
work, the explanation, the power of white racism, is easily at hand; but in
this case it will have proven an impenetrable barrier to progress. The
choice is a stark one; either the model accepts that the power of white
racism means that no progress is possible, a conclusion quite at odds with
its rainbow-oriented politics and one contradicted by the facts of progress for some Blacks, or it accepts that there has been progress based on
the efforts of Blacks and others, in which case it takes its place as a
refinement of the pluralist analysis. The difference is at most one of tone:
The nationalist approach wears its radicalism on its sleeve, its anti-
system position appearing to differentiate it from pluralism, the commitment of which is clearly the other way around. But indignation at the
status quo, understandable as it may be, offers no route out of it and
serves only to expose the contradiction at the heart of an approach that
either induces an unjustifiable degree of pessimism or duplicates in an
extreme form the pluralist model.

Some versions of the alternative, class-oriented radical approach deny
not only the importance of culture but also that of politics itself in favor
of the primacy of economics. Both are seen as epiphenomenal, that is to

say, no more than a reflection of the economic forces that determine the possibilities of Black progress. Until the development of these forces produces a revolutionary position, the contribution of politics is taken to be limited and any gains will give only the illusion of progress because true emancipation can come only with victory in the class struggle and the overthrow of capitalism. Similarly, redefining racism and the struggle against it in cultural terms can only divert attention away from the true path out of the African American predicament, the class struggle. So narrow an interpretation of a Marxist perspective cannot survive the critique of a cultural approach, and the remaining question is whether it is possible to develop a more flexible model that can incorporate the insights of the cultural approach but achieve what it so signally fails to, that is, to provide a coherent conceptual framework that can stand as an alternative to the pluralist model.

A Revised Role for the State

The key here is a revised interpretation of the role of the state under capitalism as it relates to the question of Black progress. Analysis of the state is an area of Marxism notorious for its functionalist proclivities (Miliband, 1977). To avoid this it must borrow an aspect of pluralism in seeing the state as an arena in which the struggle for progress is waged rather than as solely an instrument of capitalist domination. This does not require relinquishing the idea of the state as a class institution, as opposed to the societal role it occupies under pluralism. It remains a set of institutions whose function is to preserve the conditions under which the accumulation of capital may proceed, rather than a neutral arena for the resolution of group conflict. The point is that the execution of this role, far from making the state the servant of capital, requires a significant degree of independence from it (Evans, Rueschemeyer, & Skocpol, 1985; Jessop, 1990; Offe, 1984; Poulantzas, 1973). The class bias of the state does not imply inevitable acquiescence to the policy preferences of capitalists. Nor does it imply the subordination of political life to economic life. To the contrary, it is essential for the state to exercise its independence, if it is to serve the wider interests of capital in promoting a social system in which it can continue to prosper. In the process the state must also become responsive to pressures from a wide variety of other sources, including the dispossessed, in pursuit of the goal of fundamental stability in the mode of production. It is this independence, or relative autonomy, that injects open-endedness into the framework and so pro-

vides the conceptual underpinning that allows this approach to avoid the
pitfalls of determinism inherent in the functional analysis of politics.

This helps to demonstrate how the substance of the political struggle is
connected, as opposed to reduced, to the balance of power in society as a
whole. In this sense the state becomes the site in which the class struggle
is worked out (Poulantzas, 1978). Avoiding the liberal fiction of the separation of economics and politics permits an improved grasp of the complex ways in which a wide variety of groups within the class struggle turn
to politics to redress the disadvantages they suffer from in civil society.[5]
This is not to suggest that the state is necessarily the prime avenue of
progress. It has an inherent conservative bias inasmuch as it protects the
existing legal framework of property rights on which the power of capital
rests. This and the obvious inequalities of economic resources that are
brought to political activity are powerful arguments for seeing the state
as a barrier to the advance of disadvantaged groups. On the other hand,
the democratic basis of the American state and the constitutional guarantees that can be turned against economic power suggest a fundamental
equality of resource that makes it the most promising arena for Black
struggle. Potential for advantage exists for groups on both sides of the
class struggle. It follows that the state is intimately connected to, but not
totally dependent on, the forces emanating from the wider society. It also
follows that the outcome of the struggle cannot be predetermined and
does not necessarily confirm a radical, let alone a revolutionary, prognosis. One consequence is to suggest a key to the paradox of Black progress, the widespread impression that Blacks seem to be making it and not
making it at the same time. To resolve this it is necessary to distinguish
between material progress and the balance of power between Blacks and
whites. Improvements in income, living standards, and so on in the economic sphere do not themselves make Blacks any less subservient to
whites politically. To alter the power relationship, they need to gain a
measure of control of the state. Clearly, material advances have been
made, whereas on the question of power progress has been much less
great. Blacks' position appears paradoxical only if material progress is
equated with increased power. A more likely relationship is that the material advances some Blacks have made have forestalled demands for
increased political power, and so have acted to reinforce the stability of
the system.[6]

This suggests the essence of the role of the state in a democratic capitalist society (Castells, 1981), which is to combine the dual functions of
accumulation and legitimation. It first guarantees the conditions in which

the capital accumulation on which this type of society depends can take place, through, for example, the protection of the rights of private property or through macroeconomic policy; but it also secures in the eyes of the electorate the legitimacy of the social structure attendant on the accumulation process. Economic accumulation is an inherently inegalitarian process and thus potentially authoritarian; political legitimation is participatory and egalitarian and acts as a counterweight. It is this division of labor between economics and politics that establishes a balance that promotes stability of the social structure as a whole. Inevitably there are strains in this; it is not an equal division but a hierarchical one in which accumulation sets the framework for the process of legitimation. Because the role of legitimation is to preserve and protect accumulation, if the mechanisms employed, such as a welfare state, are taken too far, they become a threat to accumulation rather than its guarantor. Similarly, if accumulation is concerned with production, legitimation operates more in the field of consumption, or, more precisely, the distribution of the fruits of production; if accumulation is about work, legitimation is about community and culture (Katznelson, 1982); if accumulation is about class, in the American context, legitimation is about ethnicity. This duality therefore permits a conception of the state that encompasses not only ostensible political institutions but a wide range of cultural institutions, which have an equally vital role to play in determining the distribution of power in society and therefore ultimately the rate of Black progress.

Accumulation Versus Legitimation

The importance of the distinction between accumulation and legitimation to the question of Black progress is evident in the relationship between national and local politics; national politics is about accumulation, and legitimation operates primarily at the local level (Cawson & Saunders, 1983). In the United States domestic politics is ostensibly concerned with issues of consumption, distribution, community, and ethnicity. Such concerns are at the same time real and a facade for the underlying process of accumulation which shapes the discourse. Local politics provides a medium through which the class politics of accumulation is refracted. The fact that the thrust of Black political advance has occurred at the local level places racial politics firmly in the realm of legitimation (Katznelson, 1982; Tabb & Sawyers, 1978). Part of the fascination of Black politics in recent years lies in the fact that the extent of the problem posed by Blacks has tested the balance between legitimation and accumulation necessary to social stability. The fact that race itself ultimately provides too limited a basis to promote a general class crisis suggests that the challenge of potential disruption it presents can be met by some degree of incorporation of Blacks into the existing class structure, so as to leave accumulation essentially undisturbed. At the same time the fact that these concessions have to be struggled for shows how resistant to equality the accumulation process remains. It also shows that stability is not preordained. The role of the local state is to act as the first line of response to popular aspirations within a framework whose degree of flexibility is established by the national state. Although the popular struggle that is the essence of local politics in turn affects the national framework, this conceptualization demonstrates the severe limits to what can be achieved by this route.

The implications of the relative marginality of the local state deserve emphasis (Castells, 1978; Saunders, 1979). It is because the powers of the local state rarely impinge substantially on the balance between capital and labor that this area has a greater degree of autonomy and is therefore a more suitable site for the deflection and accommodation of radical forces that are central to the legitimation process. In other words, because the issues in local politics rarely pose a direct threat to the reproduction of capitalist social relations, it constitutes an insulated area in which discontent can be addressed and accommodated with the minimum threat to the social fabric. Paradoxically, the significance of this is to suggest that a capitalist society like the United States can tolerate a good deal of progress for Blacks in local politics precisely because the net effect is to strengthen the existing social structure. The point is illustrated by Edward Greer's (1979) study of Gary, Indiana. He shows how in a town dominated by one large corporation, U.S. Steel, both Blacks and local petit bourgeois capitalists were able to exert a significant influence in local politics. The power of U.S. Steel's position as the city's major employer allowed it to set the parameters within which local politics was conducted (Crenson, 1971), but within these limits there was considerable competition for control over specific policy issues by Blacks, the white working class, local capitalists, and U.S. Steel itself. As the racial composition of the city changed, Blacks became increasingly influential in determining the outcome on these issues. As Greer argues, the limits undoubtedly set by the capitalist framework of American society did not prevent monopoly capitalist interests from having, and indeed being willing, to share control in certain fields with competing interests.

Black Politics as Social Control

The burden of this argument is to see Black politics as a form of social control (Katznelson, 1976). In the era of machine politics, buffer institutions were developed to tie Blacks to the machines without conceding control over policy (Katznelson, 1973). The decline of the machines and the emergence of Black majorities in cities have led to a new pattern in which Blacks win offices that have sufficient power to make them worth striving for, but are sufficiently restricted in their scope to prevent their occupants from mounting a radical challenge to the status quo. The nub of the matter is that the increased strength of the Black challenge has led those interests that had hitherto dominated local politics to sacrifice racial exclusivity in order to protect their class power, a strategy that has meant not just accepting the election of Blacks to political office but even incorporating a few of their number into the higher echelons of the business elite. Far from threatening the economic prerogatives of the business elite, such a strategy enhances them because it transfers to Black leaders the burden of regulating malcontents in their own community. It is increasingly Black officials who suffer the vituperation of welfare recipients and public service unions when the exigencies of city budgets force reductions in services or wages. The presence of Black officials enhances the legitimacy of the political process as little else could, but the restrictions on their power resulting from a lack of control of economic resources ensures that legitimacy counterbalances rather than threatens accumulation.

The avenue permitting Black takeover of cities is also the mechanism by which their power is restricted, namely the suburbanization and fragmentation of metropolitan areas. This has created Black majorities in inner cities and so facilitated the election of Blacks; but it has also increased the problems of the poor while reducing the power of city officials to deal with them. One of the paradoxes of pluralism is the way these trends have increased the marginality of city politics even as they have increased access for Blacks to the political system. Insofar as increased access has defused a threat to domestic stability, it has been a small price for whites to pay, secure as they are in their suburban enclaves and business empires. It is because of the willingness of entrenched white interests to show the necessary flexibility and pay this price that Black political progress has taken the shape it has, one that reinforces the existing distribution of class power in the United States.

One advantage of the perspective on Black progress generated by this type of class approach is that it avoids predetermining the answer to the question of Black progress a priori. It sets limits by suggesting some progress is likely because a flexible response to Black demands enhances rather than weakens the stability of the class structure; but, by the same token, it suggests that such progress will not become generalized to the point where it threatens the prerogatives of capital. The need to rationalize every element of the Black experience in terms of its functionality for capital is thereby obviated. This, in turn, allows scope for the effects of demographic shifts, economic development, and most importantly, Blacks' own efforts to produce real concessions to be taken into account. The model suggests it is only when and if the redistributive implications of Black advance begin to threaten the class basis of the American social structure and the accumulation process at its heart that the obstacles to further progress will become insurmountable. This implies that within these limits, because capitalism remains color blind, white racism, which has developed great cumulative force over American history, is the principal barrier to further progress. But precisely because of its historical nature, racism does not remain a constant factor. Rather it can either grow or become attenuated. Many pressures will determine in which direction it moves, some relatively exogenous such as demographic trends, others directly related, as with the strength of Black resistance. But the most important factor governing its limits will be the extent of its conformity with class interests; insofar as it reinforces these racism will be enhanced, insofar as it undermines them, it will be mitigated.

The range of Black progress that can be tolerated by this combination of racism and class power is not determinate. At one extreme it could allow progress to the point where the Blacks' socioeconomic profile matches that of whites. This is unlikely, however, simply because Blacks are starting from so far behind that to achieve this form of equality would require so massive a redistribution of wealth that race and class variables would operate in conjunction to prevent it. The limit at the other extreme would be to prevent any progress at all for Blacks. This is equally unlikely because, even if it could be presumed that this would meet the needs of white racism, the repression and labor market inflexibility it would entail would cause such dislocation to the smooth operation of a capitalist society that class forces would modify such racism and cause concessions to be made. This approach, therefore, predicts an outcome of an intermediate degree of progress. If Blacks were to make no progress at all, or to achieve enough to instigate a general destabilization of American capitalism, it would be falsified. This takes the debate beyond the fruitless argument over the precise degree of optimism or pessimism warranted by African Americans' predicament. It is a familiar metaphor that their position resembles a half-filled glass, which can be seen either as half full or half empty, depending entirely on the prejudice of the observer. But progress cannot be understood in terms of a linear scale; the notion of Blacks making 50% progress is meaningless. Quantitative data must be placed in a theoretical framework if it is to have meaning, and this approach does this in a way that resolves the apparent contradiction between the fact that some Blacks are evidently making gains and the equally obvious fact that all Blacks are not, in other words that measurable material progress for some Blacks is not being translated into emancipation for all African Americans.

This shows that simple extrapolation from the gains of a minority is fallacious. In the pluralist approach, a model is derived from white ethnic experience and Blacks are fitted into it to provide an optimistic prospect of incorporation; this approach, in contrast, accepts the uniqueness of the Black experience and also the continuing weakness of their position relative both to the interests of the capitalist class and relative to a white society that identifies with this class. Furthermore, this perspective establishes the nature of the relationship between political and socioeconomic power in the American social structure. Pluralism treats the polity as a neutral reflection of the external forces on whose generation it is silent, whereas cultural nationalism remains locked into two equally unacceptable alternatives of no progress or pluralist incorporation. By placing Black political progress in the context of capitalist social relations and the distribution of power they imply, this approach explains how this progress forms part of a wider pattern of the management of society and helps to maintain its stability. In suggesting that the relationship between the political and the economic levels of power is neither completely determinate nor free-floating, it allows scope for the importance of racism in understanding the position of Blacks. The prediction of an intermediate degree of progress is the product of a situation whose essence is the interaction of class and race. If Blacks were in a position of total subjugation, a racial explanation might suffice; if they became totally integrated only class explanations would be necessary. In fact, because they are somewhere in between and likely to remain so, class analysis has to incorporate the importance of race without ceding explanatory primacy to it.

Can It Succeed?

The remaining question is whether the form of social control suggested by this approach can resolve the predicament of African Americans. Resolution in terms of equality is not on this agenda. Rather the issue is whether the elimination of the disruptive threat posed by Black disadvantage can be achieved so as to guarantee continuing social stability. Most exponents of a class approach argue this cannot be done because the contradictions within capitalism are too great and revolutionary change is the only solution. But this form of optimism is weakly based, especially in the American context. There is undoubtedly an element of the Black community willing to take on the comprador role and fill the political and administrative positions this "solution" opens up to them. To put it no higher, the opportunities for individual advancement offered would be difficult to pass up, even if the existence of a better alternative for the race as a whole were evident. Cooperation from this element will be of no avail, however, if it fails to command the support or at least the acquiescence of the bulk of the Black community. It could be argued that the process of accommodation is vulnerable because it depends for its success on the willingness of the Black working and underclasses to vote for middle-class Black administrations and accept the limits to which these are subject. On the other hand, the alternatives open to these groups are so limited that any leverage this position might give them is strictly limited. Any sizable concessions could only exacerbate the fiscal crisis in American cities, to their ultimate disadvantage (O'Connor, 1973); and a militant response would be likely only to isolate them from both the incorporated Black middle class and the white working class, their only potential allies.

Politics then reinforces what might best be termed a pessimistic class analysis. It is the area in which accommodation has been concentrated and legitimation most enhanced. It has demonstrated the flexibility that the essential color blindness of capitalism gives in respect of racial problems. The result is not to use a class perspective to deny Black progress, but to affirm that it can occur, up to a point. But insofar as there remains a trade-off between equality for Blacks and the requirements of maintaining the accumulation process and white racist privilege, political flexibility reinforces pessimism because its principal consequence is to strengthen the latter. Incorporation has been sufficiently extensive to tie enough Blacks into the existing class structure to defuse any threat they might have posed to class relations. This has not led to full equality for

Blacks, or even to a hierarchy of inequality in the Black community paralleling that among whites. Rather it has created a modus vivendi that enhances the stability of the American social structure and removes the impetus for change needed to create a more equal society. The key mechanism is the relative autonomy of the state from class and racist pressures, especially at the local level, because this autonomy has given the American political system the flexibility to strengthen the social structure through the isolation, deflection, absorption, and accommodation of Black demands for change that are generated by their continuing underprivilege.

The fact that the resulting pattern of incorporation is manifested in conventional political gains is important in its own right, and such gains are not to be dismissed. Equally, however, it would be misleading to suppose they presage the full incorporation of the Black community. The combination of class privilege and white racism which is the barrier to further progress remains too powerful to be forced to concede the fundamental redistribution of resources necessary to achieve a resolution of the Black predicament. Because Blacks by themselves, or in alliance with any combination of other dispossessed groups, are insufficiently powerful to mount a fundamental political challenge to this social structure, we are forced to the conclusion that there is no full resolution of their predicament in prospect. Neither participation nor confrontation nor any combination of strategies can provide a complete answer. The position of African Americans is, therefore, likely to remain intractable, more divided than hitherto, still both insiders and outsiders.

NOTES

1. For a fuller, standard account of the pluralist model as it applies to American politics, see Dahl (1967).

2. The specter of totalitarianism provides the animus behind the advocacy of pluralism (Kornhauser, 1960). It reflects the belief in the fragile nature of order in society. The network of pluralism and the institutionalized division of power was designed by the founding fathers precisely because the fear of disintegration was so great. The examples of Hitler's Germany and Stalin's Russia in the 20th century have only enhanced this insecurity, accounting for the vehemence of the defense of pluralism when an attack is perceived upon it in the name of Black progress. If the price of Black progress really were the descent into evil that these examples represent, then the preference for maintaining the system at Blacks' expense would be rational. The difficulty is in understanding how the threat can seriously be interpreted in such apocalyptic terms.

3. The continuing high level of residential segregation experienced by Blacks at all income levels and in suburbs as well as cities is an important factor here, for, as Massey and Denton (1993) argue, "Although segregation paradoxically makes it easier for Blacks to elect representatives, it limits their political influence and marginalizes them within the American polity" (p. 14). See pp. 153-160 for a discussion of how residential segregation translates into political weakness. It also creates a class of Black politicians with a vested interest in segregation, which in turn contributes to the nationalist chimera of community power as the path to progress.

4. There is, of course, another way out of this dilemma, which is to eschew coalitions and argue for a Black separatist party. This is the line taken by Harold Cruse (1987) in his *Plural but Equal,* in which he suggests that the civil rights politics of the 1960s and 1970s and the ethnic politics of the 1970s and '80s are dead ends for Blacks, because the former implies an individual solution and the latter a strategy of coalition. The limitations of both lie in their inability to capitalize on the essential unity and distinctiveness of Blacks' condition. Only a separatist strategy within a plural society could do this. The deficiency of this argument lies less in its exposure of the weakness of the alternatives and more in the lack of realism of its proposed solution. The fact is that Black interests are no longer sufficiently unitary to justify a separate approach, if they ever were, and even if they did they would only succeed in isolating Blacks and uniting against them a white community that would retain more than enough power to ensure that this isolation perpetuated Black subjugation.

5. The inevitability of the use of politics as the avenue for the redress of economic disadvantage exposes the fallacy of a purely entrepreneurial path to progress advocated by the market-oriented variant of neoconservatism.

6. This raises the temptation to argue that affairs have been managed (by somebody) in such a way as to produce this outcome and, further, that Blacks have been allowed to encroach upon state power through the occupation of political office only up to the point where they contribute to social stability but not to the point where they exercise real control over whites. But this would be to fall into the functionalist trap of arguing this outcome must have been consciously designed by the governors of the system because its consequences are so beneficial to that system. The issue of intention is in fact superfluous; the point is to recognize that the state provides the arena in which this outcome is produced, irrespective of whether it is produced by an all-powerful conspiratorial elite or, as is much more likely, by a complex and wide-ranging struggle between the forces in civil society.

7

The Illusion of Progress?
Race and Politics in Atlanta, Georgia

Approaches to the African American predicament tend to analyze how it governs the lives of Blacks individually or the place of Blacks in American society as a whole. But if the true value of these approaches is to be judged, they must also be considered in relation to the concrete experience of the specific communities that do so much to shape the lives of Blacks. Atlanta is a community that has enjoyed a favorable reputation for the quality of its race relations and is widely regarded as a city offering more opportunities to African Americans than any other. Its politics have been seen as demonstrating that Black progress can be combined with cooperation between the races and continuing civic dynamism. Its very success makes it a suitable community against which to complete an examination of the various approaches to the question of Black progress (Orfield & Ashkinaze, 1991, p. 4).

Atlanta's suitability is reinforced by the fact that as African Americans have made political advances there, race relations have moved away from white domination to a pattern in which class factors have taken on increasing importance. Any analysis of Blacks' position must now take as its focus the interaction of class and race, but a substantial degree of Black advancement is a prerequisite if this interaction is to be revealed in its full complexity. In the period of transition from white to Black political rule of Atlanta, following the election of Maynard Jackson as mayor in 1973, the stresses, strains, and contradictions that shape and limit Black progress were most clearly revealed. The rapid change associated with this transition brought to the surface the underlying factors that have been resubmerged by the ensuing relatively stable pattern of accommodation. This period therefore provides the best lens through which these factors can be examined.

BLACK ATLANTA'S COMING OF AGE

The historical background that shaped the coming of age of Black politics in Atlanta in 1973 begins with the effective enfranchisement of Blacks following the decision of the Supreme Court in 1946 (*Chapman v. King*), which struck down the white primary in Georgia (Holloway, 1969). Unusual for the time and place, white leaders were prepared to talk to their Black counterparts (Watters & Cleghorn, 1970).

That they did so was due to William Hartsfield, mayor of Atlanta almost continuously between 1937 and 1961 (Martin, 1978). He was the first to grasp the implications of the growth of the Black vote and to realize that it was a force with which the established white leadership would have to come to terms. It could either counter the Black vote by appealing to the city's poor whites, the group most hostile to Blacks; or it could ally itself with Blacks against poor whites. The latter was the preferred course, because an all-white alliance could only exacerbate racial tension and threaten the city's prosperity, which was the principal concern of the established leaders.

Hartsfield recognized that the Black vote would quickly come to hold the balance of electoral power because the white majority was segregationist and could outvote the white moderates who were his power base. Accordingly he solicited the support of Black leaders; he succeeded because he was preferable to the alternative of a city run by the conservative poor white element. Thus there came about the interracial coalition between Blacks and moderate whites that was to be the hallmark of Atlanta's politics for the next 2 decades, and that gave the city its reputation for having the best race relations in the South (Banfield, 1965; Wilson, 1968).[1]

One of the principal attractions of the coalition for Hartsfield was the small price that had to be paid for Black support. The Black leaders were conservative and business-oriented. Their substantive demands were not radical and could not be so, because the Blacks had little choice of partners and, consequently, little leverage. Under these circumstances, Black leader were defensive, their role confined to delivering the Black vote in return for ensuring the return of a candidate less inimical to Black interests.

Although the result may have been no more than the lesser of two evils for Blacks, it is important not to forget the context. For them to be able to maintain a moderate in power, in the South and at a time when race baiting was still common, was in itself an achievement of some note. Even so the advantages accruing from this arrangement were of mainly symbolic value. The climate was less bigoted and gestures, such as a token desegregation of the police force (Jenkins, 1970), were possible in Atlanta when they were not in other parts of the South. But the power to elect was scarcely reflected in tangible benefits for the Black community.

The Pyramid of Power

The structure of power in Atlanta at this time was a pyramid whose apex consisted of an elite group of white businesspeople (Hunter, 1953).[2] They formed a cohesive group with a strong sense of civic duty and pride (Powledge, 1965). For the South at this time (Burgess, 1962), the businessmen were politically moderate and remarkable for their vigorous and capable promotion of Atlanta's economic development. Above all, these men were pragmatic. This meant they took the attitude that because bad race relations were bad for business, they were to be avoided. Atlanta's viability as a center of finance, trade, and transportation for the Southeast depended on its ability to present a favorable image to the outside world.

So the white business elite, irrespective of personal predilection, were determined to demonstrate that Atlanta's race relations were sufficiently peaceful and harmonious to make the city a good place in which to invest. This determination made them willing to cooperate with Black leaders and to influence events so as to maintain a progressive image at a time when other cities across the South were sinking ever deeper into the obscurantism that set the stage for the turmoil of the 1960s (Hein, 1972).

Their Black counterparts were more diverse but themselves representative of an exceptional community (Bacote, 1955). Atlanta had a large Black middle class; its wealth was minute in comparison with the white community, but it was nonetheless the largest single repository of Black capital in America. The character of the middle class (Frazier, 1957) was also heavily influenced by preeminent educational institutions such as Morehouse College, which educated a high proportion of national Black leaders, and by the prominence of church leaders (English, 1967).

The Black elite contained a number of successful men who were conscious of the vulnerability of their position, achieved within a segregated society. Caution was their watchword, and they were judicious in their deployment of Black voting strength, anxious not to overtax the tolerance of white leaders. Even allowing for the restrictive standards of the era, it is true to say that most of the Black elite in the 1950s were conservative and the cordiality of Atlanta's racial coalition was as much due to the Blacks' desire not to rock the boat or openly challenge the assumptions underlying the relationship as it was to any particularly liberal spirit of accommodation on the part of the white leaders.

The Black elite were part of an upper class whose connection to the mass of Blacks was tenuous. The civil rights activity in which the elite engaged contributed little to the improvement of the living standards endured by the large number of impoverished Blacks in Atlanta. The preoccupation with symbolic gains and with conducting racial matters in a civilized style tended to result in the neglect of issues of far greater moment to the bulk of the Black community. Their approach lightened the burden of fear that had long been Blacks' lot, and to the extent that it allowed white business and political leaders to concentrate on promoting economic growth, it benefited those Blacks able to take advantage of Atlanta's expansion. Whether they did as much as could be expected in the circumstances or sought only their own advantage, events were soon to overtake them and challenge the coalition that governed Atlanta in the 1950s.

A Watershed Event

The challenge was precipitated by a series of sit-ins and demonstrations led by students from Atlanta's Black colleges in protest against the slow progress of desegregation. Although initially reluctant to negotiate, white city leaders did eventually reach a settlement permitting peaceful desegregation of school and public facilities. The crisis was weathered, but it marked a watershed in Atlanta's race relations.

It destroyed once and for all the rather coy political arrangement that had been such a comfortable power base for Black and white leaders and brought to the fore a younger, more aggressive element of Black leadership. The white business elite had found itself forced to negotiate a solution rather than permitted to impose one. The tough, often acrimonious bargaining sessions of this episode were a far cry from the informal chats between Hartsfield and a few Black leaders that had passed for consultation in earlier days.

But the white business elite was quick to capitalize on the settlement by hailing it as a classic example of the Atlanta tradition of progress through compromise. The economic benefits that this favorable image generated in the 1960s surpassed even their most optimistic expectations. To turn a potential calamity to such advantage is no small testimony to the political acumen of Atlanta's leadership group. Much of that acumen was embodied in the man who negotiated the settlement on behalf of the white business elite as president of the Chamber of Commerce, Ivan Allen Jr.

Allen used this success to launch a campaign for mayor. As a leading businessman, he was intimately connected to the white business elite (Kotter & Lawrence, 1974), but his handling of the desegregation crisis also gained him support in the Black community. His liberalism was, by his own admission (Allen, 1971), pragmatically based; nevertheless his election signaled the continuing ascendance of a combination of moderate whites and the Black vote over the majority of the white community, which continued to vote for a segregationist candidate. The coalition, although somewhat strained, remained the key to city politics in the 1960s.

Exceptional economic growth was the essential backdrop to Atlanta's racial politics in the 1960s. Allen led a dynamic, business-oriented administration, which was able to engender an extraordinary sense of optimism and civic pride. This was consistently fostered by an unending public relations campaign that gave Atlanta a reputation as a new kind of city, one that was showing the way toward solving the immense problems plaguing the rest of urban America. This image was reinforced by generally positive relations between the races.[3]

Atlanta's race relations were perhaps seen at their best in 1968, in the emotional aftermath of the assassination of Martin Luther King Jr. Many whites, Allen among them, displayed genuine concern, and Atlanta's Black student leaders, who had previously displayed no lack of militancy, took to the streets in a successful attempt to forestall the violence that was occurring in other cities across the country (Crawford, 1969).

There were also crises as well as triumphs, tension as well as amity, and a great deal of enduring poverty alongside prosperity in Atlanta in the 1960s (Powledge, 1967). Atlanta was not so exceptional as to be immune from racial riots (Paschall, 1975). The background to the disturbances was typical of American cities at the time. On the one side was to be found a large disadvantaged Black population concentrated in the inner-city ghettos and harboring particular resentment of the police as symbols of white repression. On the other side there was a white community largely oblivious to the conditions in which the Blacks were living, viewing racial inequality as the natural order of things, and responding angrily when Blacks threatened to disrupt this order with violence. A chasm of mistrust and unawareness separated Atlanta's racial communities, as it did those of the nation at large (Hutcheson, 1973).

On less explosive matters, the white business elite retained the power to bring its schemes for the economic development of the city to fruition. Generally these had little impact on Blacks, and their relative economic disadvantage did not decline during the 1960s (Jones, 1978). And even where development adversely affected Black communities, as was the case with urban renewal, their improved organization could not match the white business elite's resources and staying power (Stone, 1976).

The important point is not that the white business elite was able to overcome the opposition of Blacks but that this was done through the active agency of the city's politicians. The administration did not act as a neutral broker; instead it identified totally with the aims of the white business leaders and pursued those aims with a variety of tactics. Issues were not resolved by edict as they might have been in earlier decades and to that extent there was a greater pluralism in city politics. But it was a very lopsided pluralism in that the alliance of the white business elite and the Allen administration proved virtually unstoppable. City politics continued to reflect their priorities, despite the fact that Black votes had put Allen into office and kept him there.

During the 1960s the white business elite completed a generational transition, adding some new elements, notably from the field of property development, but retaining its cohesiveness and personal, patriarchal style. It had to some extent become a victim of its own success. The economic expansion for which it had worked had resulted in a massive influx of professionals employed by national companies. These people were typically nomadic, tended to live in the suburbs and identified little with a homegrown, downtown-oriented elite. Much of the business growth was in the suburbs and thus as Atlanta became more of a metropolitan business area the business elite's writ began to seem more confined, concentrated as it was on the central city.

The most striking aspect of this group's position in the 1960s remained the fact that one of its most prominent members was the mayor of the city. The remarkably close identification that resulted made it unnecessary for the white business elite to involve itself directly in political issues. Achieving the desired result through political mechanisms was the task delegated to Allen. This division of labor should not be taken to indicate any lessening of influence of the part of the elite (Jennings, 1964). On the contrary, it retained its dominance not by interfering in every decision but by organizing the structure and personnel of city government in such a way that it could proceed without interference but with absolute faith that their priorities would be respected.

Atlanta's Blacks in the 1960s

Where, then, did this leave the Black leaders in the coalition? Still condemned to a subordinate role, they performed the difficult dual function of representing the Black community's interests while keeping in check its discontents. The Black elite underwent its own succession; it also had become more pluralistic, with young businesspeople and a small but growing number of professional Black politicians gaining influence, mainly at the expense of some of the older church leaders.

The Black leadership as a whole was biding its time throughout the 1960s. White flight from, and Black migration to, the city made it clear that Blacks would attain a voting majority in the near future. Only then would they have the leverage that might enable them to effect some redirection of policy. Black leaders remained cautious, still preferring cooperation and negotiation with whites to confrontation.

Their caution was reflected in the 1969 election, when it was decided that the time was not yet right for an attempt to take control of city hall, and the Black leaders did not generally support the Black who ran for mayor. On the other hand, they did not support the nominee of the white business elite either. Instead they threw their weight behind a maverick white liberal, Sam Massell. It was calculated that he would be more beholden to the Blacks and less so to the white business elite than Allen, yet his victory would not give rise to the tension and conflict likely to ensue from the election of a Black mayor.

This tactical decision did not imply lack of discontent at the persistent racial inequality in the city. On the contrary, Black leaders represented an articulate and sophisticated community whose middle class felt immense frustration at not taking a place in local politics commensurate with its general level of accomplishment. Its members had no intention of waiting any longer than necessary, but their very sophistication made them aware that to push too hard too soon could only alienate whites, accelerate their exodus, and leave the city as an economic wasteland. This was not a congenial prospect to a leadership group in which the business-oriented element was becoming increasingly prominent and which wanted political power not for its own sake but as a means of socioeconomic advancement.

The changing balance of voting strength was reflected in the election of Massell in 1969, with a greater proportion of his support coming from Blacks, who had every reason to suppose their interests would be better served by the new administration (Bartley, 1970; Rooks, 1970). Despite strains in the coalition the city was a long way from being racially polarized, and a leftward shift was effected that took account of the new political realities without seriously threatening the spirit of cooperation between Blacks and moderate whites that had previously set Atlanta apart.

However, the promise that the election results held out for Blacks did not materialize as Massell began a perceptible shift to the right almost immediately after his election. His attempts in the Georgia legislature to annex surrounding suburbs to the city in order to dilute the strength of the Black vote, an effort made with the support of the white business elite, demonstrated both his shift of allegiance and the reluctance of the elite to accept the political consequences of the impending Black majority in the city.

The fact that the attempt was defeated by representatives of suburban whites was equally significant. Many white suburbanites had no intention of being brought back into a city from which many of them had moved to escape. The question of annexation brought into relief what was to prove a fundamental division in the white community between those who chose to avoid the problem of Black domination by effectively abandoning the central city and those who retained a commitment to restraining the Black challenge by working within it.

The Atlanta Compromise

The relationship between city and suburbs lay at the heart of the episode that revealed most about Atlanta's racial politics in this period, the settlement of the issue of school desegregation by means of what became known as the Atlanta Compromise (Research Atlanta, 1973). The essential provision was that Blacks accepted much less busing, especially of white children, and in return they were guaranteed greater administrative control of the school system.

The logic behind Blacks' endorsement of this plan was that busing would only hasten the transformation of the city's school system into an all-Black one. It would increase white flight and thereby defeat the aim of integration. It was better for Blacks to face this reality and at least gain control of the system in which their children were preponderant. The object, after all, was good quality education and administrative control was essential to this, more important than integration per se. Atlanta's Blacks displayed a new conviction in their own ability to develop and run first-rate community schools. They no longer saw integration as essential for equality, and they were clearly as reluctant to subject their children to long-distance busing to achieve it as whites.

This confidence was the positive side of the issue. But there was a negative side as well. These sentiments came overwhelmingly from the middle-class sections of the Black community. Poor Blacks were less confident about the equality of their own schools and far less willing to forgo the advantages of busing for their children. The settlement was typical of Atlanta in its pragmatism and hardheadedness, and it certainly succeeded in defusing a potentially explosive crisis.

Nevertheless, it was paradoxical; besides demonstrating the ability of the two communities to deal with one another, it also signaled the fact that they had given up on each other.[4] Both recognized and accepted the impossibility of genuine educational cooperation between the races. The compromise, therefore, did as much to institutionalize the gulf between them as to confirm Atlanta's moderate tradition.

Schooling provides a clear illustration of the trade-off Blacks were forced to make between autonomy and isolation. The bifurcation of the school system was almost total; city schools were 80% Black, with the proportion increasing rapidly, whereas suburban schools were more than 90% white. So although Blacks gained control of their system, which undoubtedly qualifies as progress, they did so only as whites moved out and created a newer and better-endowed system for themselves.

Black progress did not go so far as to involve Black control over whites on such a sensitive issue. When measures were proposed that might have led to this, such as extending the city's limits, they were firmly blocked by white state legislators and the courts (Weinberg, 1977). The degree of white fear is revealed by the fact that opposition to school integration was the single most important reason whites gave for moving to the suburbs. Thus the developments in Atlanta's school system represented a touchstone, revealing both Blacks' increased capacity to make progress and the structural constraints limiting that progress.

The Atlanta Compromise typifies the defensive nature of the gains Blacks made in the Massell administration. Blacks did not succeed in significantly altering the political priorities in the city, which remained as attuned to business interests as ever. The administration was not as closely tied to the white business elite as it had been and was more amenable to moderate Black interests. But the new politics had not seriously impinged on the economic prerogatives of the white business elite. The period 1969-1973 is best seen as an interregnum between the old pattern and the new. Everyone realized that the real challenges, opportunities, and strains would come about when the bifurcation of economic and political power between the two communities was made clear-cut. The Black leaders were biding their time, laying the groundwork for their political takeover; the mass of Blacks were deferring their hopes and raising their expectations in anticipation of a Black administration; the white working class was no doubt dreading the prospect; and the more moderate white voters were hoping for a continuation of the coalition with as little change as possible. The white business elite was holding its fire, coming to terms with its new role and preparing to face its biggest challenge. All in all the position was one of some excitement and not a little apprehension as the 1973 election approached (Alexander, 1974). The preliminaries were over and the real challenge of Black progress was about to be faced.

THE RISE OF MAYNARD JACKSON

The issue was made more stark by the fact that the man who was elected mayor, Maynard Jackson, was something of a maverick who was far from beholden to the established elites of either community and who was viewed by them with great suspicion as far too radical to fit comfortably into the Atlanta political scene. Jackson was the most prominent figure among a new wave of Black leaders who represented a further stage in the pluralization of Black and city politics.

This group gained its authority directly from the offices its members were elected to by Black votes, rather than from personal economic success or nomination to a brokerage with the white elite. The 1973 election marked their arrival as a new, younger political elite in the making, representing a direct, less controllable political challenge to the established elites of both the Black and white communities.

The Black elite saw in Jackson's election the key to their incorporation and that of Atlanta's Black middle class. If their rapture was not complete, it was because Jackson's rhetoric gave rise to anxiety that he might jeopardize their gains by trying to push whites too far too fast and spoil the culmination of a strategy that had taken them down a long hard road to political power and thus threaten the prospect of reaping the rewards of their patience and effort.

For its part the white business elite remained phlegmatic in the face of Black success. Despite the unease with which its members viewed Jackson, there was no panic or attempt to withdraw from the city. They were willing to wait and see whether the concrete decisions made in the new city hall reflected his rhetoric to the detriment of their interests. The scope for conflict was obvious but the Atlanta tradition of compromise, buttressed by the knowledge that their economic power gave them greater scope to influence political decisions than elections, also gave them room for hope.

The initial period of the new administration was surprisingly quiet as the mayor concentrated on implementing a new city charter that made the mayor chief executive and gave the city council a legislative role. After the early period, a gradual rise in tension in city politics became apparent.

The white business elite was feeling the effects of the first economic recession to affect Atlanta for a long time. Formerly, the intertwining of business and political priorities had been taken for granted, and naturally they looked for political facilitation of several projects on which they pinned their hopes for economic recovery. But just as their need for cooperation increased, their capacity to induce it had been reduced. Their attitude toward the new administration consequently became more negative, their criticisms more voluble and general.

Jackson too was under pressure. He had entered office with enormous expectations for change vested in him by the Black community. Most of these were quite unrealistic, being quite beyond the powers of his office to achieve. To forestall disenchantment among his Black constituents Jackson chose to compensate for practical limitations with enhanced racial rhetoric. He quickly developed a tendency to blame all his problems on white racism generally and the machinations of the white business elite in particular. This was the surest rallying point for many Blacks and helped to maintain his popularity in the Black community.

However, it had the opposite effect on whites and inspired great resentment. There was also growing disaffection among the Black business elite. Its members were uncomfortable with Jackson's confrontational style and began to fear he would abandon the spirit of compromise that had marked Black Atlanta's relations with the white business elite, and thus threaten their hard-won gains.

So within 18 months of Blacks' accession to political power the specter had been raised of a breakdown in the cooperation between economic
and political power that had sustained Atlanta for so long.

Issues of Control

The issue that more than any other provided a focus for racial tension
in this period, as indeed throughout Jackson's mayoralty, concerned the
conduct of and control over the Atlanta police department. The control of
legitimate force was a matter that aroused deep-seated fears and passions
on both sides. In the 1960s, the Atlanta police department had enjoyed a
relatively liberal reputation (Jenkins, 1970), but it had become an object
of hatred for Blacks in the Massell years as the police chief took on an
increasingly political role as spokesman for the right-wing, "redneck"
element of the white community which had been so long shut out of city
politics.

As one of his first mayoral acts, Jackson attempted to fire the chief. He
ran into legal problems, eventually resolving them by appointing a commissioner of public safety over the chief's head. This did not reduce the
tension, however; on the contrary, the new commissioner, Reginald
Eaves, was a college friend of Jackson with little experience in law enforcement. He became an object of vilification in the white community as
his appointment aroused latent fears of a takeover by racial extremists
and a subjugation to Blacks going well beyond loss of control of city
politics.

It had become impossible to please both communities on this issue,
and Jackson as the man in the middle came under intense pressure from
white business leaders to fire Eaves. He appeared to accede, but before
the deed could be done he was forced to reverse his decision under even
greater pressure from the Black community, incandescent at his apparent willingness to capitulate to whites on such a raw issue. This showed
the increased power of the Black community, but the significance was
overshadowed by an alarming degree of racial polarization the incident
produced.

Once the furor had abated, however, some of the advantages of a Black
police chief became apparent. With Eaves as commissioner, the white
business elite enjoyed a more efficient police force and a safer downtown. There was also far less resentment in the Black community because
Eaves's presence did away with one of the major sources of antipathy to
whites in general. The greater direct influence the white business elite

might have had with a white police chief might well have been counter-productive, because it would almost inevitably have caused more friction with Blacks.

The acceptability of a Black-controlled force depended on its being run conscientiously and responsibly. But there was little danger of it being otherwise. Blacks were the principal victims of crime and, contrary to some stereotypes, were extremely keen on law and order, when the term was not used as a euphemism for police brutality. This episode was part of a painful process of adjustment to a new balance of power for the white business elite, but the outcome demonstrated some of the virtues of indirect rule to them.

If the political relations between Blacks and whites barely survived the strains created by the police affair, they were soon tested again by Jackson's attempt to use political power directly to promote Black economic advance. He made it a policy that there should be substantial participation by Black-owned firms in all work contracted for by the city. This policy became particularly controversial in connection with the contracts for a new airport the city was planning to build. Friction arose over his insistence that Blacks receive at least 25% of all the contracts arising from the new airport's construction.

His demands led to charges that in wishing to employ quotas, he was introducing racism into matters that should be decided solely on the criterion of efficiency. Jackson's determination to push through his policy was met with equally determined resistance from white businessmen. The severity of the criticism to which Jackson was subjected was due to the great importance attached to the issue by the white business elite. The issue of quotas was seen as one of principle; the majority of white Atlantans felt Blacks had already been given sufficient advantages and should now compete on the basis of equality of opportunity. Such sentiment made it easy for the white business elite to mobilize support for its position.

After a period of bitter wrangling in which relations between city hall and business reached their lowest ebb, a compromise was eventually found, which endorsed minority participation through joint ventures but sought a goal of 25% rather than establishing a quota for that participation. Despite these concessions Jackson had correctly calculated that the white business elite's desire to make profits out of such a huge project would eventually get the better of their reluctance to share the spoils with Blacks. In making some concessions he enabled them to save face and so facilitated an honorable solution.

Thereafter, Jackson vigorously pursued this policy of encouraging Black business in city purchasing generally. This was clearly an area where, by showing a certain flexibility and allaying whites' fear of quotas, the Black administration was able to engineer significant economic opportunities for that section of the Black community able to take advantage of them.

The police and joint venture issues were the main vehicles through which the Jackson administration and the white business elite tested each other and came to terms with the new balance of economic and political power in the city. Once they had been resolved, the situation permitted something of a rapprochement. In retrospect, it can be seen that the turning point came with the publication of a letter to the mayor from the president of an organization, Central Atlanta Progress (CAP), sponsored by the white business elite.

The letter described the concern felt by many businessmen at the trend of Atlanta's politics and, most damningly, suggested many firms were moving, or thinking of moving, outside the city boundaries for what were termed non-economic reasons. The factors behind such decisions to relocate included perceived racist policies on the part of the administration, fear of crime downtown, and fear of higher taxes, all of which amounted to a generally hostile environment for white business. The widespread publicity the letter received reflected its importance, not just as an expression of negative feelings, but because it invoked the white business elite's ultimate deterrent to Black militancy, the threat of withdrawal from the economic life of the city.

That the threat was real there was no doubt. In fact the threats to withdraw were coming from major national companies with regional offices in Atlanta. If the trend were to become widespread, it would threaten all the investment the local business elite had made in central Atlanta. Hence their desire to stop the flight by publicizing their fears and thereby awaken Black politicians to the consequences of their actions and attitudes. The letter had its desired effect, particularly on the mayor, who became far more accessible to leading businesspeople and undertook trips around the country to convince prospective corporate investors of Atlanta's hospitable attitude to business.

The Challenge of Annexation

The new working relationship was threatened by white business sponsorship of a new attempt in the Georgia legislature to re-establish the white majority in the city by annexing some of the surrounding suburbs. This reflected continuing ambivalence in the face of growing Black political power. White business could attempt to reassert direct political control by whites through the consolidation of the metropolitan area, which would reduce Black voting strength to approximately 25%. The alternative was to limit Black advance by confining Black political power to the central city and using their economic power to ensure continued moderation by Black politicians.

The consensus at this time favored the expansion strategy. There was concern that the alternative might push whites into abandoning the city almost entirely and thus jeopardize the investment this elite had made in downtown. In contrast, the expansion option would shift the political balance against Blacks without a return to the complete subjugation of former times; any attempt to impose that would surely have led to major disruption. Most Blacks were naturally wary (Hawley, 1975). But some were also concerned that outright resistance to annexation might leave them with control of nothing more than an empty shell of a city.

Jackson and others, therefore, proposed their own variants of expansion and approached the white business elite in a spirit of compromise. Much less willing to compromise, however, were whites living in the suburbs. Both businesses and households feared that annexation would raise their taxes to Atlanta's levels. But it was the problem of schools that was the main stumbling block.

It was highly unlikely that the courts would allow any annexation plan that did not include a merger of the city and suburban school systems. A consolidated school system would revive the prospect of wide-scale busing to combat the segregation of schools brought about by residential segregation. Because the problem of busing had caused many white suburbanites to leave the city in the first place, they were determined not to have to deal with it again. The schools issue touched the core of the whites' perceptions of Blacks as enmeshed in a complex of crime, poverty, and educational deficiency, a perception that together with the fear of higher taxes made the overwhelming majority determined to resist incorporation.

The result was a stalemate and no changes were made. The white suburbanites continued to be subsidized by the city and kept themselves free of what they saw as entanglement with Blacks. The white business elite found a balance of forces it could manipulate but had to accept that its former preeminence was diminished. The Blacks maintained their political power but were given a sharp lesson in just how circumscribed were the uses to which they could put it. This episode was the swan song of annexation. Since then the outer counties of the Atlanta metropolitan area have grown so much faster than the increasingly Black central city that the option of isolating Blacks in the city has come to be the only practical one.

Jackson and the Working Class

Once this issue was settled the rapprochement between the Black political leadership and the white economic leadership continued apace, reinforced by Jackson's firm response to a strike by low-paid city workers. He was a prisoner of his office in that the city charter did not permit deficit financing and, faced with the stark choice between improving the living standards of working-class Blacks and keeping taxes down, he chose the politically safer option. Whatever his personal sympathies, he could see that it would be futile to challenge the restrictions that the balance of power in the city placed upon him.

The strike was also notable for the strong support Jackson received from the Black business elite, in a revealing example of how Black accession to political power can work to the disadvantage of the Black working class. So long as they lacked political power, Blacks had been forced to work together in order to achieve anything. Now that they had achieved a measure of responsibility in running the system, the latent class tensions in the community became apparent. Black property owners were as determined as whites to defend their interests against the workers. The fact that these particular workers were Black was of no consequence.

It was considerably easier for a Black mayor, especially one with liberal credentials, to resist a strike than it would have been for a mayor who was white. Jackson was the perfect lightning rod, deflecting the antagonism that might otherwise have been directed at the white business elite, whose interests as major taxpayers he was protecting. The incorporation of the Black business and political elites forced their members to choose in such situations between their racial and their class allegiances. Further progress depended more on cooperating with the white business elite than on solidarity with the Black working class. If the latter strategy could prove only self-defeating, then the former, although it might extract some rewards, could never alter the basic direction of who was controlling whom, and it meant that all Blacks would continue to occupy an essentially subordinate position.

The perpetuation of this subordinate role helps explain why there was little threat to continued Black occupation of city hall. Nor indeed was there any serious doubt that Jackson would be reelected mayor. By his more moderate stance at the end of his term, he had become reconciled with the Black and white business elites; his extension to Blacks of jobs, contracts, and general city patronage had won over the Black middle class; and his symbolic role and rhetoric in defense of the poor were sufficient to prevent Black working-class defection.

For Blacks the 1977 election marked the consolidation of their recently gained political power. The old Atlanta coalition of Blacks, liberal whites, and the white business elite survived, but with the critical difference that Blacks were now in the majority role. This stage of consolidation was not conducive to a high level of racial tension or even political interest. But there were few Blacks who would complain of that. The critical relationship remained that between the mayor and the white business elite.

And at the start of Jackson's second term this seemed to be in good order. It had, on both sides, a pragmatic basis, but during his first term a pattern of understanding had developed. The white business elite had learned to accept the necessity of allowing middle-class Blacks a larger share of political jobs and city contracts and had accepted, more reluctantly, the symbolic authority of Blacks in areas such as law and order. But in return Jackson had fully digested the importance of maintaining Atlanta as a city attractive to capital, with all this implied in terms of political moderation and fiscal conservatism.

Even with the achievement of this accommodation, however, there remained too many pressures for the calm in Atlanta's politics to last long. The focus of tension was again the police department and its commissioner, Reginald Eaves. Eaves had begun to stake out a position as a spokesman for the majority of Atlanta's poor Blacks, with the clear intention of trying to succeed Jackson, a prospect that filled most whites with horror. On this occasion the pressure on Jackson to remove Eaves became irresistible because of the latter's apparent complicity in a cheating scandal within his department designed to further the promotion prospects of Black officers.

The public debate was conducted mainly between different factions of the Black community. The white business elite had come to realize their open involvement was counterproductive but left no doubt as to their concern of the need to forestall Eaves's taking over the mantle of Atlanta's leading Black politician. This concern was shared by much of the

Black leadership, and this produced an unity of class interest across racial lines that was far too strong for Eaves to withstand. The opening up of new offices to Blacks accelerated the process of factionalization.[5] Jackson retained his dominant status, but there was no guarantee that the emerging factions among Black politicians would not degenerate into a multiplicity of competing and ineffective splinter groups.

Maneuvering for the succession to Jackson, who could not succeed himself, produced candidates from the left, center, and right, and the increasingly clear divisions among Black politicians gave the white business elite the opportunity to regain some leverage over the city's mayoral politics. At the least they could secure the election of a Black sympathetic to their interests, and at best they might even be able to manipulate these divisions sufficiently to effect a white victory. Black factionalism then, as well as being a sign of the increasing maturity of Atlanta's Black politics, was also a threat to their advances and a process, given the significant white minority, that was likely to favor the forces of moderation more strongly than had the earlier imperative of Black electoral unity.

A Transition Approaches

By the middle of 1980 the stage was set for an election in 1981 that would mark the end of the transitionary period in Atlanta's racial politics. The pluralization of Black politics was bringing class issues to the fore and instituting a more complex balance between these and racial factors. The balance that had been struck between Black political and white economic power remained fragile, partly as a consequence of this pluralization. It would require another election before this balance of forces could take a longer-term shape.

Before this could happen an issue arose that dominated the city, both in and beyond its politics. Between June 1979 and June 1981, 28 young Blacks, mostly children, were abducted and murdered. Atlanta became a focus of national attention as the horrific story unfolded. Eventually a young Black man, Wayne Williams, was charged with two of the murders, although he was suspected in most, if not all, of the cases. He was convicted, and after his arrest in the summer of 1981, the murders ceased (Baldwin, 1985; Dettlinger & Prugh, 1983; Headley, 1981; Jenkins, 1981).

The bare facts of the case do little to convey the tensions the episode aroused in the city. The most obvious source of tension was the suspicion among Blacks that the murders were racially inspired. Less inflammatory but more pervasive than fears of a conspiracy was the resentment caused among Blacks by the feeling that a double standard was operating. The belief was widespread that if the children had been white, there would have been much greater outrage and the culprit would have been found long before the crimes took on such monstrous proportions.

Bitterness arose, too, within the Black community. The victims were virtually all from poor working-class public housing projects, and charges of indifference and ineffectiveness of a middle-class administration, albeit a Black one, were rife (Bambara, 1983). It would be churlish to presume other than that all Atlantans, Black and white, were horrified by and concerned to some degree about these gruesome events, but the fact that working-class Blacks could have a sense of their own victimization brought home to them in such a dramatic fashion was bound to exacerbate existing racial and class tensions.

Once the arrest was made the episode faded from political consciousness remarkably quickly. No attempt was made to exploit the tragedy in the election, and the decency and community spirit shown in this respect helped the city surmount the crisis. In other respects the election was a good deal more antagonistic. Black and white leaders had their own differing concerns for the 1981 election and made their plans separately.

Members of the Black business elite were concerned at the proliferation of Black political leaders. Their principal concern was to find a candidate who could avoid splitting the Black vote along class lines and thus allow the white business elite to reassert control of city hall. They found a suitable candidate in Andrew Young, the former lieutenant to Martin Luther King Jr. Young and the first Black elected to the U.S. House of Representatives since Reconstruction. He also had served as U.S. ambassador to the United Nations in the Carter administration. Young's recruitment was establishment-sponsored rather than a grassroots phenomenon, but despite the fact that his campaign team was carefully constructed to be biracial, the white business elite played no part in his selection.

This showed how the white business elite had moved, or had been moved, from the heart of electoral politics. More importantly, it showed that despite the working arrangement that had been achieved between Black political and white economic power, at critical moments each element sought its own advantage with little regard for any pretense at unity. In earlier periods the fact that power was so heavily weighted in favor of the white business elite had kept the political alliance with the Blacks quite stable. Now that power was more equally divided between the parties and each had its own power base, the element of competition and struggle for advantage had grown and made the alliance that much more fragile.

The white business elite was not keen on the prospect of Andrew Young as mayor because they felt he would spoil their strategy of dividing the Black vote. As regards Young himself, it was thought he might find difficulty concentrating on the nuts and bolts of city administration after his experience at elevated levels of national politics and international diplomacy. His outspokenness as U.N. ambassador was also of concern; the white business elite was seeking someone with more conventional diplomatic skills for the pivotal position of mayor. The white leaders had some difficulty in finding a white of sufficient stature to run, however, and eventually settled on a candidate without enthusiasm.

The campaign was generally lackluster. Part of the reason for the lack of excitement in the campaign was the growing Black majority. They enjoyed a 57%-43% advantage of eligible voters, one that was enhanced by a slightly higher turnout among Blacks in the election. This preponderance seemed to make the likelihood of a Black victory so overwhelming that it robbed the campaign of its edge of uncertainty. In any event Young won comfortably, although after a campaign marred by some inflammatory racial rhetoric and with a lower crossover vote from whites than Jackson had achieved. His victory was well received.

The End of the Jackson Years

The same could not be said of the white community's reaction to Jackson's departure. It was painfully clear that there was no love lost in their attitude to him personally. He was variously described as vain, arrogant, overbearing, imperious, self-righteous, and verbose. There was some grudging respect for his personal honesty and integrity and the courage with which he fought some of his battles, but little or no affection. The point of substance here is that it was exactly these qualities that gave Jackson much of his appeal to Blacks. What was to whites pomposity and excessive formality was to Blacks the embodiment of the pride they took in their political advance. Just as his style symbolized Black self-respect so equally it symbolized to whites the diminution of their own control of the city. The difference in reactions was testament to the continuing gulf between the two communities.

Young moved quickly and effectively to reassure the white business elite as to his intentions. He made it clear that his priorities were public safety and attracting capital to the city. He held a series of meetings designed to assure white businesspersons that he intended to end the embittered relations that had existed between city hall and downtown. Far from opposing their interests, he recognized that policies threatening capital would only prove counterproductive to his own goals. His approach would be to work in tandem with those who controlled capital, not for its own sake but because he saw cooperation along these lines as more likely to improve the social and economic conditions of Blacks than using control of local government to try to force the owners of capital to alter their priorities. He openly embraced a new realism favoring an alliance with business on the grounds that only the latter could generate the wealth in which Blacks hoped to share.

This was balm to the white business elite; they could look forward to a more harmonious period in which they could busy themselves with creating wealth, sure in the knowledge that leading Black politicians would pursue policies that would establish a favorable environment.

So, at the end of this transition period Black leaders had made their fundamental choices. They would accept that rather than using political powers to challenge the system of wealth creation, future Black progress would come from a trickle down of the wealth created by that system. The symbol of this meeting of minds was the joint commitment by the Black political leaders and the white business elite to maintaining a vital and economically healthy downtown. It symbolized the white business elite's willingness not to abandon the city and Blacks' willingness to accept business's priorities in economic development.

The pragmatic approach adopted by Young seemed to promise an era of greater mutual understanding. Ushering in a period of harmony in the exercise of political and economic power, it marked the end of an often embattled period of transition that Blacks' accession to major political office had given rise to. And yet it would be too sanguine not to recognize that this harmony was at least as much a sign of Blacks' acceptance of the limits to progress achievable through political power as it was evidence of that progress. The transition period had witnessed great changes within Black and white communities as in the balance between them. Relative harmony had been achieved but at some cost to the aspirations Blacks had held at the start of the period. An overall balance sheet of these changes and the forces underlying the new balance remains to be drawn from this account.

ASSESSING THE BOTTOM LINE

The fulcrum of the white community, certainly as regards its influence on Black progress, was the white business elite. Its preeminence in the life of Atlanta made it the focal point of political change, and change in white Atlanta is best examined through the prism of its role. Even though the theme is one of changes, it is the continuity in the makeup of the group that is at first striking. The white business elite of the 1970s was the clearly identifiable heir to the group dominant in the 1950s and 1960s. Its approach to politics had evolved, prompted by an awareness that Black control of city hall would require more effective involvement if their interests were to be protected. Gone were the days when politics could be delegated to men like Hartsfield and Allen, and several of the group now showed an appreciation of the need to take on directly the task of dealing with the new Black political elite.

An element of growing importance in the white business elite was a group of property developers who represented the transformation of downtown Atlanta brought about by a spectacular construction boom (Keating, 1980). This enhanced its commitment to the economic health of the downtown area. Twenty years earlier virtually all business had been located downtown. That was no longer the case. It had now followed the white population into the metropolitan area at large.

Atlanta had thus come to exemplify a widespread national pattern in which a predominantly white suburban ring surrounded a majority Black city with a prosperous high-rise financial and commercial district at its center. Just as this pattern, resulting from a combination of rapid economic growth and an artificial restriction of city boundaries, gave Blacks their political opportunity, so it also transformed the position of the white business elite (Research Atlanta, 1984). Where they had formerly been completely dominant in the business community, they were now just one element, albeit a powerful one, and significantly, one with an interest in the economic health of the city proper that was not necessarily shared by their metropolitan counterparts.

The owners of businesses located outside the city had less incentive to accommodate Blacks, isolated as they were from their jurisdiction, than the white business elite that had chosen to coexist with them. But the existence of a flourishing white economy outside the city lent credibility to the white business elite's threats of withdrawal, should the Blacks create a climate too hostile to business in the downtown area. Thus although it served to diminish the position of the white business elite in the business community, the metropolitan area simultaneously enhanced its leverage in dealing with Blacks.

There were similar effects consequent upon an influx of national businesses and capital into Atlanta. The resources of the local banks were small relative to the scale of Atlanta's growth. This meant that the city had to compete with others for investment capital, and its prosperity depended on providing conditions in which this investment could flourish. Moreover, the proliferation of branch offices of major national corporations brought into the city a stratum of influential businesspeople who judged the business environment entirely on its merits and who were much more willing than the local white business elite to abandon the city if racial friction created an environment that failed to meet their specifications.

The local white business elite was the servant of those controlling capital at the national level. Its task was to maintain a favorable business climate by ensuring that Black demands were kept moderate. But this also increased its power in relation to Black leaders because, as agents of remote national overlords, its arguments carried more weight. The threat of withdrawal from the city was that much more convincing when in effect it issued from the head of a New York bank who had little interest and no sentiment as regards keeping the money he controlled in the city.

As the group in the middle the local white business elite was squeezed, but it was the Black leaders who really felt the burden of the situation, because they found themselves dealing with forces on whom Black control of city hall made only the slightest of impressions. However much Blacks' power might have grown relative to the local white business elite, their leaders recognized that in the national context, the power of capital was unchallenged by local political advance. Indeed that advance and the responsibilities it brought for the city's welfare made it incumbent upon them to compete with other cities, themselves often politically dominated by Blacks, for scarce capital resources. The consequent competitive effort to cultivate those who controlled the scarce resources of national capital was responsible for the conservative, pro-business drift among Black leaders in cities across the nation, once they had been in office long enough to become attuned to the facts of economic life.

Challenges to the White Elite

The effect of the growth of the suburbs outside Atlanta's city limits on the city's racial politics was similar. By the mid-1970s, the suburban population was more than double that of the city and although much of the growth had nothing to do with race, the racially oriented motivation of many of those leaving the city cannot be denied. Suburban attitudes to annexation, as well as the barely concealed redlining practices of realtors, demonstrated that the vast majority of whites were vehemently opposed to any form of what they perceived as Black encroachment.[6]

The white business elite's response to suburban growth was to try to keep the suburbs attached to the city, even if political realities forbade their full reintegration via annexation. To this end they put together a package of policies designed to ease the commuting problem and maximize the incentive to at least work in the city. For the suburbanites, being wooed in this way was an excellent state of affairs. They enjoyed access to the city and the economic and cultural advantages of living in a large metropolitan area; they continued to receive a subsidy from city residents for government services they used but did not pay for; and they achieved the social segregation from Blacks that was important to them.

But if the white business elite had an interest in retaining the connection with the city, for the Blacks the need to prevent complete suburban withdrawal was even greater because the economic basis of the city proper could not withstand the outflow of capital that would follow. This placed formidable constraint on Blacks' freedom of political action. Thus the suburban phenomenon, like the influence of national capital, while curbing the dominance of the white business elite, in the wider context did more to restrict Blacks.

Other forces in the white community contributed to the pluralization of Atlanta's politics. The gentrification of parts of the city produced neighborhood associations that were influential on the city council and effective opponents of white business elite schemes, such as new freeways, that put economic convenience before the quality of city life. Their influence was to put a liberal gloss on the city's politics that transcended racial lines; but this was counterbalanced by one group that remained marginal, the white working class.

Formerly the "Manhattan coalition" of Blacks and moderate whites had denied them power, and then the Black takeover ensured that even less attention would be paid to their wishes. This produced a politics of resentment voiced by those who spoke for them, but their role amounted to little more than another lever to be used by the white business elite in its dealings with Blacks. Their racial antipathy could be invoked to help counter Blacks' demands for change, although even here they were a

waning force, once Blacks had developed a sufficient numerical superiority to outvote any threatened class alliance among whites.

Of all the changes confronting the white business elite, the most important and challenging was that of Black accession to major political
office and the separation of political and economic power this entailed.
As in other cities across the nation, existing elites could respond to the
Black challenge in one of two ways. They could pursue a strategy of
outright resistance and noncooperation with the new political leaders or
they could follow the path of accommodation to the new realities. Although the former alternative was never entirely absent from the elite's
deliberations, it would at the least have meant an alliance with the white
working class that would have gone against the grain of Atlanta's traditions of moderate middle-class politics.

Despite the rise in tension it became apparent that in Atlanta the white
business elite opted for the path of accommodation. Their strategy was
premised on being able to make Blacks realize that their best prospects
for advance lay not in confrontation but in cooperation with those who
possessed economic power. It rested on a class analysis arguing that
the large Black middle class would recognize they could make progress
within the existing system. While avoiding conflict on inessentials it
necessarily implied a willingness to impose economic sanctions if Black
cooperation was not forthcoming, to use the stick if the carrot proved
insufficient. That these sanctions were available was evident to all, and
the consequent prospect meant that although continually threatened, they
did not need to be applied.

The extraordinary preeminence, both political and economic, of the
white business elite made it difficult for them to adjust to any sharing of
power, and to make matters more difficult, the balance it involved was a
delicate one. Economic recession, for example, undermined their capacity to make the necessary concessions to Blacks and was partly responsible for the precipitate decline in relations with city hall in the first part
of Jackson's term. And the growing imbalance between an increasingly
Black city and overwhelmingly white suburbs shifted the center of grav-
ity outside central cities to an extent that threatened their capacity to
manipulate the factions in city politics.

But more important than such exogenous factors was the fact that the
accommodation strategy itself involved confrontation as a necessary
component. If overt racism was to be avoided, personal criticism of the
new mayor was an acceptable way of exercising discipline on Blacks

while leaving room for future cooperation, as was criticism of Black failings on ostensibly neutral criteria such as honesty and administrative efficiency. Both tactics were employed, but perhaps the principal issue on which this element of the strategy was brought to bear was the struggles over the conduct of the police department.

A matter of great moment to both communities, the police issue enjoyed a symbolic importance that made it a suitable ground for showing Blacks how far they could go. But because it touched such a raw nerve, any confrontation staged here was liable to go off the rails and bring about an almost irretrievable breakdown in relations, incommensurate with its role in the overall strategy. Despite these dangers the trend was toward stability. As both sides learned where relations might get out of hand, they also learned to deal with potentially volatile confrontations. This was gradually apparent in Jackson's term, and in Andrew Young's term of office this stability reached new heights.

The Role of Class Unity

The promotion of class unity at the elite level across the racial divide was a vital factor in ensuring this stability. To this end a few selected Blacks were co-opted into the inner councils of the business elite, which benefited from their inclusion because the support they enjoyed in the Black community helped to deflect some of the opposition to Atlanta's political and economic system. There was no doubt that Black leaders would capitalize on this support in order to realize business elite goals, which as successful businesspeople they shared; had it been otherwise they would not have been admitted.

But the recognition that, far from being just a painful necessity, having Blacks in political office was a positive advantage did most to reconcile the business elite to the accommodation strategy. This advantage arose from a division of labor in which Black politicians were left to cope with the problems of crime, strikes, welfare, unemployment, and so on. They were thus placed in the front line as the visible face of authority. It was they who became the object of discontent and thereby relieved the white business elite or its direct representatives of having to cope with many of the conflicts produced by the prevailing economic system. And because Black politicians had a claim of loyalty on the poorer Blacks among whom discontent was concentrated, they had a great deal more room for maneuver than pro-business white politicians would have had in their place.

Given that the economic realities prevented Black politicians from going beyond this role and challenging the class power of the elite, a hierarchy of roles congenial to the business elite was established. White leaders could continue to occupy the commanding heights and pursue their economic interests, while Black politicians pursued the no less vital but essentially subsidiary task of reconciling the population to the consequences of that pursuit. By employing Black political leaders as a *comprador* group in this manner, the "culture of accommodation" (Eisinger, 1980) preserved the structure of power in Atlanta even as it brought about shifts within that structure.

Although this division of roles was extremely useful in drawing the legitimacy of a democratic political system into the service of their class interests, the element of genuine independent power it gave to Black politicians meant there was a price to be paid by the white business elite. It was, in essence, to permit some Black progress; not just occupancy of a handful of political offices but more substantively, an improved economic position for a significant proportion of the Black population. In fact, the price is a small one (Hunter, 1980).

The elite is better served by the indirect influence implicit in the accommodation strategy than by more direct control because the indirect system allows Blacks to fulfill some of their aspirations without seriously challenging the business elite's prerogatives. Clearly, indirect control is a complex and difficult strategy. Nevertheless, by curbing Black aspirations without suppressing them, by not exposing the economic order to direct conflict, and by incorporating Black elite and middle-class elements so that these too develop an interest in maintaining the system, it increases the stability of that system and so proves its worth.

To sum up, the virtue of the strategy of accommodation was that it maximized the position of the white business elite by keeping Blacks more dependent on the balance it involved than they were. The higher level of resources and mobility enjoyed by the white community as a whole rendered the power struggle one-sided. Its power to make investment decisions enabled the white business elite to create an economic framework that constrained Black advances. By comparison Blacks control only a minute amount of capital and could not possibly create a prosperous environment on their own. Their well-being depends on the white business elite's sympathetic deployment of its resources, and this can only be achieved if the Blacks employ moderation in the use of their newfound political power.

The current of dependency ran both ways. The prospect of abandoning the city was hardly attractive to the white business elite, given the extent of its existing investment. For this group then the state of racial politics in Atlanta did not constitute the best of all possible worlds. Even so, the constraints on it were minor relative to the advantages it continued to enjoy. Moreover, these advantages were not threatened by Black progress. In the event of a fundamental clash its trump card lay not simply in its economic power per se but in the mobility of capital as compared to the static basis of Black power, votes. So long as this card was recognized by both sides it would not have to be played and Atlanta could continue to engage in the delicate balancing act that was its foremost political achievement.

Divisions in the Black Community

The evolution of this balance between the races was reflected in the pluralization of Atlanta's Black community. Fragmentation was consequent on the achievement of majority status, which brought with it more resources and so more to fight over. The conservative oligarchy of the 1950s was succeeded by a new elite consisting of businessmen and civil rights activists brought to prominence by the sit-in movement of the early 1960s. This group was joined in turn by a third wave of electorally based leaders who won both city and state offices in the 1970s.

But these waves capture only one dimension of pluralization. By the late 1970s the Black community had reached a sufficient level of political maturity for its leadership to manifest clear, class-based as well as generational dimensions. Indeed the class dimension became dominant as leaders struggled with each other to establish themselves as representatives of various points on the class spectrum. The pivotal group in this respect was the Black business elite that rose to prominence in the 1960s.

Its members' attitudes, like those of their white counterparts, reflected a hardheaded pragmatism. Their explicit aim was to extend the benefits of the American system to themselves rather than to offer a fundamental challenge to that system. They possessed a keen awareness of the realities of power in Atlanta and knew it came from control of economic resources. They were convinced that gaining access to these was the only rational strategy for the Black community because Blacks did not have the power, even potentially, to overthrow the system. Thus they viewed their strategy as one of practical necessity, not of choice.

It followed that Blacks would continue to need white cooperation because the economic power in the city was in the hands of whites. So, although Black leaders recognized the need to exert pressure on the white community, they knew it would be self-defeating to go so far as to alienate whites. Accordingly, the Black business elite attempted to exercise the power it had gained in a prudent fashion, using its leverage judiciously and for limited ends. This confirms that class took precedence over race in the calculations of both white and Black business elites. Both were willing to forsake racial antipathy when it became apparent that unity would better serve their common class interests.

However, the Black business elite's role was based on the political power it represented, not the economic power. Although its economic base was insubstantial relative to whites, its political role remained essential in the transition period. That role was to act as an intermediary or broker between the white business elite and the Black community, its function being to ensure that Blacks' demands remained moderate. In return it acted as a conduit for increased resources to the Black community. This became an increasingly precarious position.

To the white business elite, the Black elite presented itself as the group best able to control the Black community and supervise its demands. This, however, made it dependent on the Black community's willingness to follow its leadership. To Blacks, the Black elite presented itself as the group with the ear of the white leaders—as the group, therefore, that could gain most for Blacks. This in turn required that the white business elite be prepared to acknowledge its influence. Without recognition from one side it would be useless to the other.

As Blacks became the majority, their reliance on the business elite to represent them in the bargaining process decreased. If dissatisfaction arose, there was an alternative leadership, which had emerged as a consequence of Blacks' increased role in city politics. Because such dissatisfaction did arise, the new wave of Black political leaders staked out independent, class-oriented positions that distinguished them from the elite and challenged its authority (Salamon, 1973). This dissatisfaction stemmed from the feeling that the business elite had used its influence for too narrow a sectional advantage. Its strategy of incorporation for a minority of Blacks, however realistic, was questioned by many Blacks, whose trust the elite forfeited as a result.

As pressure on the Black business elite grew and its position as intermediary became increasingly difficult, the middle ground came to be occupied by moderate elements of the new political elite. The Black business elite thus fell victim to the very progress its realism helped to bring about. As a result its role tilted away from its racial aspect and toward its class function. Gradually it came less to represent Blacks' demands and more to act as agents of the power of capital, exercising a moderating influence on Black politicians. Although parasitic on Blacks' principal source of strength, the Black business elite's position—being both co-opted into a class-based economic elite and retaining ties to the Black community denied to the white elements of that class—meant it would retain at least some part of its role as a fulcrum of Atlanta's racial politics.

New Black Leadership

The political leaders who were taking over the central role in the Black community were not a homogeneous group, due to the fact that the Black majority permitted more of the class complexities of the Black community to be represented. Their political philosophies varied; although preponderantly liberal they ranged from the far, although democratic left to what in white politicians would be seen as a conventional new right stance. Common to them all, however, was the fact that their power was based on political office.

Not surprisingly, this gave rise to a tendency to place their faith in politics as the most effective means of improving the condition of the Black community, an attitude that appeared naive when contrasted with the more realistic assessment of the relationship between political and economic power held by the Black business elite. This created the appearance of a significant philosophical difference in the Black leadership and generated a certain antagonism between its component groups in the early stages of the Black majority. The differences proved more rhetorical than actual and were largely the product of a period of inexperience in which many of the new political leaders not only engaged in militant populist rhetoric but also made the mistake of believing their own rhetoric. As the transition progressed, more moderate voices prevailed and it became clear that, with the exception of some Black working-class leaders, the antagonisms were a short-term phenomenon resulting from difficulties inherent in any shift of power.

After some initial unease the Black business elite's response to these new politicians was to try to co-opt them. Accommodation was not difficult to achieve because the political elite lacked a distinctive philosophy of progress beyond the clichés of its militant rhetoric. Once the limitations of this had become apparent, the Black business elite needed only to provide a brief lesson in economic realities to convince most of the new leaders of the desirability of cooperation with the white community. The common objective was to reorder the distribution of resources within the existing system of generating them, to increase the number of Blacks able to participate in and benefit from the system, rather than to overturn its priorities in any radical fashion. Whether this limited goal was adopted out of inclination or necessity is of little consequence; once the new political leaders had become reconciled to it they began to pursue a course alternating between pressure and compromise, as had been the Black business elite's tactic toward the white community for some time.

The outcome of these moves was in part a division of labor between the two groups with each operating in a way most appropriate to its position, the politicians publicly, the business elite behind the scenes. To some extent this paralleled the divisions in the white community. In the Black community, however, the political element was gradually gaining the upper hand, because they were better able to deliver support on various issues than rather shadowy business figures.

It would be misleading to think of all Black politicians as fitting comfortably into this co-optive mold. Some seemed never to completely shake off a disruptive tendency; an element persisted that sought a Black working-class constituency through an approach marrying substance to radical rhetoric. Its effectiveness was limited, however. Occasionally an issue such as police brutality gave it a stronger, more distinctive presence, but it did not succeed in transforming it into anything more than a ginger group. Moreover, to the extent that a radical politics implied a class perspective, it had little resonance among a community that continued to define its problems in racial terms; to the extent that radical politics implies an alliance with Atlanta's white working class, they meet with virtually no response at all on either side.

The more significant impact of the radical element was to act as a bargaining weapon for moderate Black leaders in their dealings with the white business elite, in much the same way as the suburbanites were employed by the latter. Although this hardly eliminated the frustration felt by leaders of the Black working class, it did place them in a symbiotic relationship with mainstream Black leaders that helped ensure them a continuing significance in city politics. Put another way, the Black working-class leaders had the potential to upset the delicate overall balance between the races. Even though such threat as they did represent arose out of their capacity for disruption rather than any constructive capability, the elites of both communities were forced to take heed of it.

Such cognizance did not involve any fundamental redistribution of wealth to poor Blacks—hence their continuing frustration. Rather it took the form of economic palliatives such as federally funded jobs and welfare programs, combined with a reliance on the trickle-down effects of economic growth, and the occasional political concession. If their voting strength and capacity for disruption ensured that working-class Blacks were not ignored in city politics, their overall position remained weak. They faced harsh competition for resources, not only from whites but now also from their former allies in the Black middle class.

As a significant number of middle-class Blacks achieved some measure of incorporation, the Black working class found itself in an even more difficult position. The domination of the political process by the Black middle class and the white business elite left it facing a continuing dilemma of whether to accept such residual gains as are available from a system that works to the advantage of whites and, to a lesser extent, middle-class Blacks, or whether to attempt to challenge this distribution of rewards and risk being crushed by the combined weight of the opposition from the whole of the white community and a good part of its own. The balance of forces in Atlanta—a hostile white working class on one side and a dominant Black middle class in alliance with the white business elite on the other—left them with very little choice.

Maynard Jackson: Progress Through Balance

The focal point for all these currents was the first Black mayor of Atlanta, Maynard Jackson. His task was to try to balance the many conflicting pressures generated by racial and class competition, but to do so in such a way as to achieve maximum feasible progress for Blacks. The strategy he employed to carry out this task is clear. He began by seeking to secure his own political base. This involved taking on the Black and white business elites, leaving them in no doubt as to the new balance of forces, and in so doing establishing his credentials as leader of the Black community. When all parties had been forced to recognize the new situation, he began gradually to shift toward the business community, but from a position that allowed him to make the necessary compromises on a more equitable basis than if he had been accommodating from the start. His tactics no doubt owed as much to the pressure of the moment as to conscious strategy. Nevertheless he succeeded in attracting the support of most of the significant elements in city politics, at least to the extent of preventing them from uniting around another candidate.

He was perhaps less successful in consolidating his position in his second term than might have been anticipated from the commanding nature of his reelection. This was partly because the criteria for success were less clear-cut. Certainly the extent to which the disaffection of the white business elite was made obvious, once the end of his term approached and the pragmatic imperative to cooperate with him as mayor was eased, was surprising.

Relations had seemed more than cordial in the middle of his term, but the combination of his combative bearing and the fact that it was he who had forced them to face up to the new political realities meant that their personal resentment had only been suppressed. He seemed to symbolize, both by his own personality and by his role, their own diminution. Young's considerably more low key manner and his avowedly accommodationist approach were enough to restore at least the appearance of cordiality. Nonetheless, the rather sour atmosphere in which Jackson left office must have been a disappointment to him, even if it was as much a testament to the unresolved tension in the racial politics of Atlanta as to any problems arising from his own role.

Despite this mixed record these tensions were never such as to seriously jeopardize Blacks' continuing occupancy of the mayor's office. Given how limited his powers were, the unrealistic nature of Blacks' expectations, and the intransigence of many whites, Jackson showed considerable political skill in maintaining his position on the mayoral tightrope. But it was always clear that Blacks would rally round an incumbent at election time, whatever the dissatisfactions. Because these dissatisfactions were of a conflicting kind—middle-class Blacks thinking him too militant, working-class Blacks regarding him as not militant enough—the possibility of an active coalition to oppose him was remote.

And much the same logic applied to Young, once he had established himself as a clear front-runner. Blacks were not prepared to risk the loss of office by allowing themselves to be openly divided at election time. Their majority in the city was still too slender to permit such luxuries and the electoral balance between the races remained a powerful force for discipline, healing wounds and concentrating minds.

How Much Progress?

The question, therefore, is not whether a Black can stay in office in Atlanta, but to what extent he or she can use office to promote Black progress. In Jackson's case the answer is that he had to settle for limited socioeconomic gains, primarily accruing to elements of the Black middle class. The appointment of Blacks to senior administrative posts in city government and public agencies, the rapid rise in the proportion of city contracts awarded to Black-owned firms, and the concessions he extracted over the airport issue all testify to the efficacy of political office in winning economic gains for this group. More generally, his rapprochement with the white business elite demonstrated that he was prepared to offer moderate behavior in return for modest gains. It would be unfair to suggest that Jackson or any of his peers were behaving in any way dishonorably, that they were betraying Blacks' interests. Jackson recognized that political power, when it is as restricted as it is in Atlanta, simply does not provide a platform for radical change.

Andrew Young, relieved of the personality and transitional problems attending Jackson, far from overturning this strategy only pursued it the more vigorously. From the beginning of his tenure he embarked enthusiastically on a path involving judicious use of his power, with fewer qualms and more single-mindedness than Jackson. Indeed it was his assumption of office rather than Jackson's that saw the culmination of the patient, prudent strategy that Atlanta's Black middle class had, via its elite representatives, been engaged in ever since winning an effective voice in the city's politics.

This strategy exposed some of the myths of Black solidarity, showing that, given the opportunity, groups of Blacks would pursue sectional rather than racial interests. One must, however, ask what the alternative was. In the Atlanta situation those gains that could be achieved through political pressure were of the sort that accrued to middle-class Blacks with appropriate skills and resources. If these were rejected, then the alternative would not be greater progress for working-class Blacks, but an absence of progress for all Blacks. Racial solidarity could not bring about changes of the kind necessary for the incorporation of all Blacks. As most Atlantans came to realize, no matter how unfair, the fact was that those likely to gain most were those who already had the most.

Jackson realized that there was nothing he could do to alter this fact. He was determined, therefore, to steer a course that would enable Blacks to extract the maximum number of concessions but, at the same time, would not press the political advantage so far as to jeopardize their chances of obtaining such gains as were possible. To achieve even this much under the circumstances was a mark of his and the Black community's sophistication and not one of betrayal. On the other hand, that their freedom of action remained so restricted reflects less favorably on the ability of the political system to satisfy Black aspirations.

In sum, the transition period in Atlanta required the establishment of new norms of political behavior to reflect the changed balance of power between the races. Difficulties resulted from groups testing each other out to determine the limits of what could be achieved. By the end of the period the principal protagonists had come to understand the new rules of the game well enough to avoid this kind of superfluous conflict, and by the time of Young's election the trend to stability was well established, to such an extent that an earlier tension was replaced by an air of torpor in city politics.

The Atlanta transition thus fits into a pattern that may be broken down into four stages: In the first, Blacks are a minority, constitute no threat to white control of a city, and make the best coalition they can with the more liberal elements of the white community. In the second stage, Blacks approach a majority but fail to achieve office; even so, racial tension and bloc voting rise. The polarization continues in the third stage, when Blacks win significant office and conflicts arise as each party seeks to maximize its position within the new political framework. Thereafter, in the fourth stage, Blacks reach such a plurality that their incumbency becomes unchallengeable by whites; the sense of political competition and fear is replaced by a relatively comfortable division of roles, which permits the establishment of a new stable form of interracial coalition. The pattern, therefore, has a circular as well as a transitory character. By its completion whites' peace of mind is reestablished after an upheaval that is marked equally by Black advance and a reversion to the status quo ante.

This pattern is accompanied by a process of pluralization. The monolithic control formerly enjoyed by the white and Black business elites in their respective communities was replaced by a much more complex pattern of competing groups. Underlying this proliferation on both sides of the racial divide was the increasing importance of the politics of class. The waning preeminence of the white business elite, for reasons to do with Black advance and independent of it, led it to search for class partners irrespective of race to help protect its fundamental interests. But the bifurcation of the Black community provided the main opportunity for interracial, class-based alliances. The Black middle class settled for gains that accrue principally to itself; its progress brought it to a position where it has a class interest in maintaining the status quo.

To the extent that the interests and demands of poorer Blacks threaten this, they become a threat to their own middle class, which finds itself in a precarious position because it continues to need the support of poorer Blacks to maintain the political power on which advance is based. The fact that the Black middle class also continues to need the cooperation of the white business elite creates the range of possibilities lying at the heart of the balance between race and class that Black political progress brought about in Atlanta.

CONCLUSION

How then are we to assess the consequences of the new balance established in Atlanta? We must conclude that although the Jackson administration did succeed in achieving some redistribution of resources in favor of Blacks, these gains did "not represent a re-ordering of the city's priorities, but only a more equitable share for the Black community within existing priorities" (Jones, 1978, p. 116). These gains were not insignificant; but in the process of winning them, Blacks retreated from their original position, which did challenge the existing priorities, if only at the level of rhetoric. In the end Blacks were forced to accept the limitations those priorities entailed. The outcome can best be summed up as a working compromise. The Black business and political elites showed a willingness to renounce some short-term gains, and the white business elite reciprocated with a sacrifice of a few of its privileges. The biracial commitment to economic growth was perceived by both sides as vital, and the pursuit of conflicting interests was conducted in such a way as not to jeopardize it.

There can be little doubt that this moderation was the result of a deliberate policy. Both sides had the power, in their different ways, to pursue more hard-line goals. The fact that they chose not to do so prevented the city's economic disintegration and a decline into racial animosity and political trench warfare. At least in Atlanta, this alliance around economic growth was the only viable solution to the city's racial problems, even if it did favor only a minority of Blacks.

A united racial stance by Blacks insisting on a wider distribution of benefits for the whole of their community is unrealistic in the face of continuing white economic power. The idea of the Black working class obtaining a greater share of benefits through an alliance with the white working class is equally implausible. And contemporary notions of a rainbow coalition of the dispossessed amount to little more than fantasy in the Atlanta situation. Viewed in this light, the moderate "solution" achieved in Atlanta takes on a force of inevitability as the only path to Black progress.

The assumption of office revealed more starkly the limited options available to Blacks and created new dilemmas in the form of questions about what they should be prepared to settle for. The trend in Atlanta was clearly to settle for what gains the existing system allows. There is no evidence, however, that these have extended or will extend to the Black workingclass and underclass. Their relative income is no higher and their unemployment rates are no lower than in cities where Blacks are not politically prominent. And perhaps most significantly, inequality increased among Blacks in Atlanta during the 1970s (Smith, 1985; Stone, 1991).

For the bulk of the Black community the virtue of the new order is the same as the old: It precludes something worse. In previous decades that something worse was a reactionary, redneck city government; now it is whites abandoning the city proper. The nature of the threat has changed, but for poor Blacks the end result is the same. Atlanta thus demonstrates that if it is to remain stable, the political system can tolerate some gains for a minority of African Americans as a means of securing Black cooperation, but nothing more. This calls into question the conclusions of those in the liberal tradition who, attaching immense significance to the election of Blacks to local office, have seen it as the key to Black incorporation and as the solution to America's racial problem.

For the white business elite the modus vivendi proved acceptable because the political concessions it involved did not threaten the economic prerogatives that are the essence of its class interest. Its position was secure enough that it could afford to be relatively flexible over political arrangements. Although the white business elite might have preferred an enlarged city with a white majority more amenable to its control, it was able to accept the alternative toward which Atlanta had moved: an isolated Black community wedged between a business-dominated city center and a ring of predominantly white suburbs.[7]

The advantages of this arrangement were substantial because Black leaders took responsibility for managing the conflicts produced by an unequal distribution of resources, without themselves challenging that distribution. The ring of white suburbs also served the white business elite's interest inasmuch as it maintained social peace by keeping the races as far apart as was practical while confining Black power within an area where it would remain unthreatening. Thus the system of indirect control practiced in Atlanta sacrificed some of the lesser interests of the white business elite in the service of the greater.

The further implication of this is that to describe the situation as one embodying a "culture of accommodation" (Eisinger, 1980) is misleading in that accommodation did as much to preserve existing power relations as to change them. Changes in specific measurable indices, such as the occupancy of high-level political administrative offices, is too often taken as an unambiguous indicator of Black progress. So narrow a focus overstates its extent and is excessively sanguine about the culture that permits it. It cannot capture the sense in which these forms of progress, far from being extendable in linear fashion to all Blacks, are rather palliatives that reconcile conflicting interests, but only within a given framework that itself offers no possibility of full incorporation for Blacks. To describe this resolution as benign is to miss its essentially dialectical nature as one that simultaneously promotes and restricts Black progress.

The advantages of this situation for the white business elite do not imply a conspiracy interpretation of how it came about. It did not arise out of a deliberate design on the part of an all-powerful clique. The fascination of Atlanta's transition was precisely that both racial and class conflicts were genuinely present. The Black elite was pivotal in that it was attached to the white business elite on a class basis and to the Black working class on a race basis. The constant danger was that in attaching itself too strongly to either it would forfeit the cooperation of the other and so upset the balance between a variety of competing interests. The overall structure of Atlanta's political economy may have continued to favor the white business elite, but within this, the dual role of the Black elite required it constantly to press for further concessions from its white counterpart even as it cooperated with it as the obverse of its double relationship of representation and exploitation with the Black working class. Politics, as the area in which Blacks' resources were greatest, became the principal arena where these conflicts were worked out. It is in this sense that politics is central to the issue of Black progress rather than by virtue of Blacks' occupation of political office.

At the same time, politics was marginal in that the white business elite retained sufficient power for it to protect its interests adequately no matter what political system eventually emerged from the struggle. This enabled it to be flexible in the political sphere in response to the increasingly difficult problem of race. White leaders deflected and absorbed the Black challenge to their authority by co-opting the Black economic and political elites. Moreover, their political concessions served to increase the economic freedom they enjoyed: If their policy had been to resist Black political advance at all costs, the ensuing disruption would certainly have spilled over into the economic sphere and made the conduct of business more difficult. As it was, political accommodation brought them not only stability but also new partners in pursuing their economic goals, thereby enhancing the value of the political system as a safety valve for the tensions created in the economic sphere.

In the final analysis, the prevailing political arrangements in Atlanta are safe from the white business elite's point of view because its resources are potentially mobile whereas those of the Black elite are tied to its constituency. Although political office provides incumbents with considerable legal authority to influence the course of events, this authority is severely circumscribed when its writ runs only to an island in a hostile sea. The threat of withdrawal from the city by the white business elite has been the most effective mechanism for inducing Black moderation and demonstrates how the white business elite's control of economic resources gives it more independent power than Blacks have obtained through their political control of the city.

This is the fundamental reason for the conclusion that the obvious manifestations of political progress did not alter Blacks' essentially dependent and subordinate position in Atlanta. Blacks will only achieve control over their own lives if they control their own economic resources. To increase their share of these, however, requires that they support the existing economic system. Yet that system will only tolerate a minority of Blacks gaining access to these resources. The rest of the Black community has little prospect of securing the kind of gains that would enable it to become independent or would bring it equality with the white community. In the face of this harsh reality, Blacks in Atlanta have pursued an increasingly conservative strategy of accommodation with the interests of white-controlled capital as the best path to maximum feasible progress. Their choice is a realistic one: The experience of Atlanta may represent only a form of semiprogress, it may be inadequate to the scale of the problem, but it is all that can be achieved.

NOTES

1. For alternative forms of coalition in American cities, see Davidson (1972), Hayes (1972), Wirt (1974), and Greer (1979).

2. The reputational methods used by Hunter to estimate the power of this group were heavily criticized and initiated a widespread and long-running debate about the study of power in American communities. For contributions see Mills (1956), Wolfinger (1980), Dahl (1958), and Polsby (1963). Although the pluralist approach adopted by Hunter's critics did enjoy greater methodological soundness, it too came to be heavily criticized. Hunter's approach, for all its methodological weakness, did at least have the virtue of accurately representing the reality it attempted to analyze, a distinction some of his more methodologically rigorous successors in the study of community power found it harder to lay claim to (Mintz, Freitag, Hendricks, & Schwartz, 1976).

3. Allen's commitment was symbolically demonstrated by his decision to testify in favor of the 1964 Civil Rights Act, at the time an act of courage for a white Southern politician (Allen, 1971).

4. It could equally be argued that Blacks' acceptance of a plural system of education represented a coming to their senses because the previously dominant objective of integration was based on a fallacious assumption about the nature of American society. This is the view of Harold Cruse (1987, especially pp. 245-255), who sees America as a plural society in which the goal of integration is a chimera for Blacks; unfortunately it is a chimera that deceived and attracted both white liberals and most Black leaders (Cruse, 1967). The consequence was the diversion of Blacks' struggle and energies into a dead end because whites would never accept or permit integration. This approach was represented most forcibly by the NAACP, became ascendant with the Brown decision in 1954, and thereafter, while always retaining particular influence in education, underpinned the whole of the Civil Rights Movement throughout the 1950s and '60s. It was only when its limitations became apparent that a renewed awareness of the implications of American pluralism for Blacks' struggle shifted the emphasis of that struggle toward more nationalist forms (Cruse, 1968). The problem with this diagnosis, as the long-term consequences of the Atlanta Compromise demonstrate (Orfield & Ashkinaze, 1991, chap. 5), is that the plural approach is subject to equally severe limitations as a tool of progress and can as easily lead to continued subjugation through isolation as to liberation through self-help.

5. One indication of this was Eaves's subsequent election from a Black working-class constituency to a seat on the increasingly powerful county commission.

6. The Atlanta Standard Metropolitan Statistical Area as a whole and not just the central city has experienced a higher than average index of segregation (Massey & Denton, 1993). This was evident in the 1970 U.S. Census but persisted in the 1980 census (see tables on pp. 64, 68, and 71); evidence from the 1990 census suggests it has yet to be substantially ameliorated (p. 222).

7. The rapid growth of predominantly Black suburbs in the succeeding period does not alter the dynamics of segregation, fragmentation, and mobility that were apparent in the debates about annexation during the transition period.

8

Conclusion:
Progress or Impasse? The Continuing Tragedy
of African Americans

The question posed at the outset of this book was how long the Black experience in America must continue to be one of suffering and discrimination not experienced by other Americans. The answer is a pessimistic one, and the prospects for the resolution of the African American predicament are not good. However, the intervening chapters have demonstrated that there can be no simple response to this question; any answer depends on the rate of progress Blacks are making toward incorporation into American society, and there is no prospect of an agreed-upon definition of what would constitute progress. It is a term whose meaning is variable and fluctuating and whose construction is dependent on the intellectual framework within which it is employed. In addition to the inherent contestability this gives rise to, the idea of progress tends to be used in one-dimensional terms, and this makes it unsuitable for capturing the enduring dualism that characterizes the position of African Americans, who remain *in* but not *of* American society. It is this fundamental ambivalence that accounts of the African American predicament find so difficult to grasp.

THE INADEQUACY OF THEORIES

For the founding fathers of the liberal tradition, Park and Myrdal, the idea of what constituted progress was relatively unproblematic. It implied integration of Blacks into the existing structure of a society that would remain unchanged except for the elimination of differentiation by race. The social structure did not need to change because it was assumed that there were no structural obstacles to racial integration. The problem was perceived to lie in prejudicial attitudes by whites, but it was assumed that prejudice would become attenuated through enlightened education in the tenets of the American creed.

Later liberal perspectives, although maintaining an emphasis on decline in the level of prejudice as the key indicator of progress, invoked the social structure as a benign influence that fostered the decline of racism. The forces of modernization were seen as promoting pluralism and, although this implied a degree of conflict between interest groups, it also promoted the process of inclusion so that no group would be left out of the bargaining, compromise, and equitable distribution of rewards that characterized America's increasingly pluralist social structure.

As it became apparent during the 1960s that the process of inclusion was not working smoothly for Blacks, that the impact of the social structure was not so benign, and as Black protest rose, the liberal response became more prescriptive. In part this took the form of blaming Black militancy for alienating the rest of society and so further retarding Blacks' prospects for incorporation. More significantly, it involved a shift of emphasis in the criteria for progress away from equality of result between Blacks and whites and toward equality of opportunity. It was claimed that the latter had been achieved by the passage of the Civil Rights Acts of the 1960s. This permitted the argument that a significant period would inevitably be required before Blacks could capitalize on their new opportunities and translate them into substantive equality. It followed that a slow rate of current progress was primarily a legacy of historical oppression rather than any fault in the contemporary social structure.

This neoconservative response put both Blacks and radical critics on the defensive, because if structural barriers had been eliminated, to suggest Blacks would fail to achieve equality over time could only be explained in terms of the inadequacies of their own attitudes and culture. It also absolved whites of guilt for continuing Black poverty and so provided a respectable basis for opposition to special measures, such as job quotas, busing, or affirmative action, designed to help Blacks to overcome their disadvantages. This defense of the liberal structure of American society was constructed by altering the definition of progress so as to make it consistent with continuing Black disadvantage. It then became a relatively simple matter to highlight those aspects of the multifaceted experience of African Americans that indicate improvement—and there are bound to be some—and generalize from them to argue that progress is occurring. Thus the central tenet of the liberal tradition—that Blacks are making a gradual movement toward the ultimate goal of incorporation without the need to change the existing social structure—was renewed.

The full import of this only becomes apparent if we consider the radical tradition, in which progress is given an alternative set of meanings. In the Marxist analysis, true progress for African Americans can only come with the overthrow of the capitalist system, because capitalism is the root cause of their oppression. Black progress is therefore tied inextricably to the political activity of the white working class and is dependent on a biracial class alliance. This gives it an apocalyptic character in which the alternatives appear to be reduced to all or nothing. Apparent improvements within the existing capitalist framework of American society are dismissed as illusory or the product of a tokenism, inevitably confined to a minority of Blacks and designed only to buy off discontent and forestall the working-class alliance that would create a real threat to the power structure. What passes for progress under capitalism is the product of ruling class manipulation, and the only criterion remains equality of result and the overthrow of the social structure necessary to bring it about.

The inflexibility of this perspective in refusing to acknowledge that genuine progress is possible for Blacks under capitalism appears to be mirrored by the alternative radical approach, which stresses the causal role of white racism rather than of class exploitation. This is because the enduring nature of white racism, combined with the superior power of the white community, would seem to preclude progress for African Americans. However, despite its deep historical roots, racism is increasingly seen as a cultural artifact and therefore as malleable in character. This insight, in turn, gives a whole new connotation to progress by reconstructing it as an essentially subjective idea. Progress can now be measured in terms of the degree of positive self-worth experienced by African Americans. The very racism that has constituted the prime fact of their history, although it has shaped their identity, is no longer seen as having inevitably negative implications; rather it becomes a resource out of which the oppressed can generate a distinctive culture and affirm their identity. In this sense, progress ceases to be directly correlated with the objective facts of their condition.

Although racism retains its structural dimension within this radical cultural approach, there is also a sense in which this brings us full circle back to the idealist perspective of the early liberal tradition, which also focused on the subjective aspect of race relations. Apart from differing emphases on the subjective/objective axis, the measure by which progress can be assessed is an association with equality variously interpreted in terms of opportunity, result, and identity; in respect to its rate, the variations are just as great, ranging from the gradual and inexorable, through the personal and irrelevant, all the way to the absent and impossible. We are evidently dealing here with discrete intellectual frameworks, each of which proceeds in a relatively self-contained fashion from its own definition of progress to its own explanation to its own conclusions. There is no necessary overlap between perspectives with such differing fundamental assumptions and hence none in the concepts of progress they employ.

This suggests that the debate around the question of Black progress is best seen as an exploration of the meanings that can be associated with the concept and not as an attempt to reduce it to one universally accepted set of attributes because its intellectual provenance will not lend itself to such uniformity. This is not necessarily a bad thing; tolerance for a diversity of approaches to the question of progress, if it eliminates the manipulation of the Black experience in the attempt to bring it into conformity with any one framework, can maintain the legitimacy of a range of insights and so deepen our understanding. Nonetheless it remains instructive to ask why it is that no approach captures more than a partial perspective on the African American predicament.

The answer lies in the wider agenda that each approach is committed to: The liberal agenda is clearly to defend and justify the prevailing social structure in the United States. As the shibboleths of traditional liberalism became increasingly unable to bear the weight of this task, a neoconservative response developed in which the manipulation of the Black experience to make it support the virtue of American pluralism reaches its most sophisticated and yet most contorted level. Similarly, the Marxist approach places the analysis of Black oppression in the service of a general indictment of American capitalism. The revolutionary strategic implications of this are thoroughly unrealistic, and the attempt to reconcile them with Blacks' position distorts the undoubted insights this approach can provide into the nature of their oppression. Its neglect of racism in favor of a class explanation is not only unsatisfactory in its political implications, but it is also intellectually unconvincing. These weaknesses prompted an alternative radical critique that takes racism as its focus and thereby comes much closer to capturing Black culture.

Partly because of this, it is prey to the danger of romanticizing that experience. This again distorts the analysis and leads to a stress on only those aspects that contribute to the creation of a positive Black identity, a process that makes subjective self-worth a substitute for any objective path to emancipation and so belies its own optimism.

The problem with the one-sidedness of all these approaches is that they give rise to a form of theoretical closure whereby the conceptual underpinnings of each perspective are employed to predetermine the outcome, and empirical evidence is relegated to a supporting role designed only to demonstrate movement toward the preordained solution. All fail to come to terms with the depth of the African American predicament because their wider agendas prevent them from facing squarely the fact that there is no solution in sight. Blacks are caught in an impasse out of which the promise of escape offered by every approach to the question turns out to be a cul-de-sac. We need a new way of looking at Black progress, or its limits, if we are to appreciate the strength of the iron cage that entraps African Americans. The best way is to reduce this impasse to its constituent dimensions, beginning with the individual and graduating through its community, national, and global levels. This will allow us to incorporate the best insights of the various explanations while demonstrating the cumulative weight of the burden under which most African Americans still live.

INDIVIDUALS AND PROGRESS

The experience and interpretation of race for African Americans as individuals has become the focus of increased attention in recent years, with the growth of a radical analysis that takes the racism of American society as its central idea (Omi & Winant, 1986). This in itself is a form of progress because it has brought with it a revised attitude toward Black culture and given more positive connotations to racial identification. This contrasts with the historical associations of race as an internalized instrument of oppression which deformed African American culture and demoralized individual Blacks because of the conceptualization of racial inferiority as immutable. Now the same experience of oppression is more likely to be seen as having generated an independent culture of resistance that has strengthened Black life in the United States.

Both elements are stressed: resistance, not because of episodes of confrontation but because of its more enduring subversive character

(Genovese, 1974), and culture, because of its importance in creating a breathing space for Blacks in the interstices of oppressive conditions. Both aspects are the product of Blacks having been ignored by whites for so much of American history. The relative invisibility that resulted permitted the creativity of Black culture as an affirmation of an independent life with American society. This has given shape to an African American sensibility that is the linchpin of their contemporary identity. Because it is rooted in a common experience, feelings, and emotions, this is not easily controlled. It therefore becomes an instrument of resistance in what remains a racist society.

The wider significance of reconstructing race as a historical idea is to remove the shadow that its immutability cast over the lives of African Americans. By bringing together race and culture it subsumes Blacks' experience under the rubric of ethnicity, simultaneously affirming their uniqueness and allowing them entry into the network of ethnic groups that make up American pluralism. The validation of Black identity which this combination permits does not require denial of their continuing oppression; on the contrary, awareness of it is an essential building block of that identity. But it does undermine the crippling equation of difference and inferiority, and this is why it is such a liberating perspective.

The new emphasis on the centrality of race in radical analyses of the Black question can be partially accounted for by the life-enhancing effect of its reinterpretation as a discursive idea. It is, as well, a reflection of the wider currents of a postmodern era whose intellectual climate rejects finality, absolutism, and closure of categories in favor of a reemphasis on both the irreducible diversity of meaning and the importance of being in its construction. In this context the rediscovery of race is a positive consequence of the postmodern: What elsewhere produces a sense of crisis, of angst appropriate to the fin de siècle, of the specter of irrationality and the impossibility of action, creates among African Americans renewed vitality, confidence, and self-belief (Simone, 1989).

This perspective is also a reaction to the failure of other approaches to come to terms with Black life in America. From within a radical framework, Marxism, with its focus on structure at the expense of experience, with the primacy it accords economics over culture, and with its attempt to subsume the uniqueness of Blacks' position under the alien categories and imperatives of class, is perceived as irrelevant at best and opportunist at worst. Rejection is reinforced by the absence of any Marxist strategy for the emancipation of Blacks beyond advocacy of an alliance with a radicalized white working class, an alliance so lacking in credibility in the American context as to become insulting.

Differences with the liberal approach are not so clear-cut: Although there may appear to be a shared emphasis on white prejudice or racism, this is deceptive to the extent that in the liberal view prejudice is in secular decline whereas for the radical cultural approach, racism continues to be the primary factor governing the life chances of Blacks. Similarly, the shared emphasis on the importance of history conceals more than it reveals; liberals employ it to absolve the present social structure of responsibility for Black disadvantage, whereas radicals deny any historical break and see the history of racism as a seamless phenomenon in which the past and present merge to enhance the cumulative weight of contemporary oppression. There is also a common emphasis on the victims of oppression, but the ascendancy of neoconservatism has widened the difference here, too, making the culture of the victims responsible for their deprivation, whereas for radicals, culture is their greatest source of strength. One area of some common ground, and where the liberal argument is stronger, is in the focus on modernity as a benign force fostering a freer, more articulated social structure, suggesting it is thus emancipatory for African Americans.

The critique of other approaches which prompted the renewed focus on the individual's experience of racism is well founded but, as this last point reminds us, any benefits accruing at the level of the individual remain limited by their relation to the social structure because a cultural critique cannot deny the determining effect of structure but must rather explore how the two interact. The growth of the Civil Rights Movement provides a good illustration here. The cultural impact of its struggles was both a cause and a consequence of the movement's success and had a significant and positive effect on the lives of individual African Americans. But it could not have achieved that success without structural changes in the South's system of agriculture, which reduced the need for Black labor and so curbed the intransigence of the white oligarchy in defending the old system. This did not obviate the need for struggle, but it did provide the essential precondition for its success; heroism, let alone morality, would not have been enough in a different structural environment.

The question therefore remains as to what in general we can say about the effect on the social structure of the positive impact a radical cultural approach has had at the level of the individual. This takes us back to the problem of modernity. The liberal perspective on modernity is essentially that of a reinforced pluralism, and the radical cultural approach builds on the tolerance and equality this facilitates. But it must also accept the limitations of such a vision. Having rejected the fantasies of cataclysmic change associated with Marxism, it insists on a reconceptualization that breaks the equation of radical change and major structural transformation. By importing subjectivity into the equation, it creates new dimensions along which dispossession may be measured; it follows that this also creates new possibilities for coalitions among the dispossessed to promote change that is meaningful to them. But such coalitions, although innovative, still operate within the pluralist paradigm; indeed their very innovation may be seen to strengthen it by extending its inclusive properties. In this context the emphasis on Black culture is as likely to provide the opportunity for a middle-class, conservative Black politics to play the pluralist game more effectively as it is to generate a radical coalition that could challenge the status quo.

This brings us squarely to the aspect of the impasse Blacks find themselves in that this approach manifests: however liberating for individuals, however cogent its critique of other approaches, and however much it redefines the criteria for progress in terms favorable to Blacks, the political implications it carries can do no more than reinforce the pluralist framework, with all the limitations that implies. It is a curious terminus for an avowedly radical perspective to reconfirm the liberal solution. But it is explained by the intellectual weakness underlying this approach, which is that of essentialism. The centrality accorded to race as an explanatory concept makes it impossible to deny it a transcendental quality which carries it across time and space and gives it an air of permanence. This cannot be denied by an insistence on the historically variable meaning of the term, a competing emphasis that only reveals the confusion at the heart of the radical cultural approach, which is thus driven by its own premises into a form of idealism that makes it fundamentally indistinguishable from liberalism. Once this is grasped the similarity of their respective solutions become less surprising, as do their limitations.

THE COMMUNITY AND PROGRESS

If these problems are insoluble in an approach that takes the individual as its focus, then we must look to the next level, that of community, for an avenue of escape from this predicament, because it is of equal importance but potentially broader scope. Here the issues are encapsulated by the case study of Atlanta, which takes up the problem of politics, because that is where the limits of an individual approach become apparent. The initial question to be posed here is how are the intangibles whose importance a cultural approach highlights to be translated into concrete improvements in the lives of Blacks? An answer requires more precise specification of the limits the pluralist political system puts on this path to progress. This, in turn, requires the reintroduction of the concept of class as a complementary explanatory tool to race in explaining the position of African Americans.

Atlanta provides a favorable environment in this context, because its Black population has a particularly strong sense of community identity. In recent years it has a distinguished history of activism in the Civil Rights Movement and a continuing strong and sophisticated leadership class, which was partly forged in the crucible of that era. It has become something of a mecca for middle-class Blacks, attracted not just to a dynamic city but by the sense that opportunities it offers have been extended to the city's Black community. The combination of a relatively enlightened white power structure, which adopted a pragmatic approach to race relations, a sophisticated Black community with a strong sense of its own traditions, and the correct political arithmetic created the conditions for Blacks to achieve the leading role in the city's politics, and this, too, enhanced its attractions.

Nevertheless the simple answer is that this promising backdrop did not produce significant material gains for the mass of Atlanta's Blacks. This was true in the transition to Black rule, and it has remained true in the period since then (Stone, 1991). Extensive poverty has persisted; there has been very little natural trickle down from the growth of the metropolitan area's economy (Orfield & Ashkinaze, 1991), and it has been beyond the powers of Black politicians to reorient its dynamics in a more equitable direction. On the contrary, the reduction in federal government support for welfare programs in the 1980s has contributed to an increase in inequality that the powers of local government were unable to counteract. And the city has remained not only economically unequal but also socially divided, with one of the highest levels of residential segregation in the country (Massey & Denton, 1993). In schooling, too, the gains achieved in the Atlanta Compromise have not prevented the city's public school student body from becoming overwhelmingly Black in the space of a generation, with white children educated separately in private or suburban schools.

Takeover of the city's political offices is progress in itself and one with positive consequences for the Black community's pride, maturity, independence, and confidence. But these advantages accrue primarily to a middle class that enjoys most of the basic economic necessities; they have not translated into more tangible benefits for the large number of Atlanta's Blacks who lack them. The result has been disillusion, apathy, and a slide into the demoralized condition that typifies underclass existence in America. Gaining political office is evidently not the answer then; and yet it is an essential component of the pluralist prescription for Black progress.

Whether this amounts to an indictment of pluralism depends on whether it should be expected to achieve a solution to the question of Black progress. If it is, then the failure is clear; if, on the other hand, its role is to foster the maximum feasible progress that is consistent with the maintenance of the prevailing social structure, then it may have achieved its purpose. In fact pluralism has both positive and negative implications for Blacks. Black progress in Atlanta was clearly part of a process of political pluralization, both in the sense that there were more groups competing on an inter- and intra-racial basis and that they were doing so on a more equal footing than before. Political behavior in Atlanta also displayed some of the positive features associated with a pluralist framework. The consensus reached by the politically active members of both races on the desirability of economic growth, and the restraint shown in the bargaining process so as not to jeopardize it, is perhaps the most significant. Equally, the limitations of pluralism were also in evidence. The separation of executive and legislative power curtailed the freedom of action of a Black mayor, and the formal limits on his areas of responsibility and the material resources at his command made his ability to effect change incommensurate with the problems of the community he represented. His role was therefore primarily a symbolic one in relation to the question of progress.

The fragmentation of governmental units is further evidence of pluralization of the politics of the Atlanta metropolitan area. Although it facilitated increased access for Blacks, it also confined their writ to a central city that whites were rapidly deserting. By providing units of government safe from Black encroachment, it lent credence to the threat of complete economic withdrawal from the city by the white business elite. The creation of a ring of predominantly white suburban communities helped ensure Blacks' moderation by providing white taxpayers with an obvious alternative if the administration of the city became too onerous.

Fragmentation, then, maintains Blacks' second-class status by replacing direct subjugation with a milder but more flexible and sustainable pattern of isolation.

The vise of restraint gripping Black politicians was completed by whites' continuing control of economic resources. The white suburban ring and the increasingly Black central city accentuated the advantage of the white business elite's principal asset, mobility of the capital it controlled. The contrast with Blacks' principal asset, votes, which are effectively tied to the central city, is critical in giving the white business elite the upper hand. The permanent threat of capital withdrawal, to the suburbs or to other cities eager to compete for capital investment, is the lever with which capital protects its interests.

The balance of power was not established through overt economic conflict, however. Racial quotas, the conduct of the police department, and other ostensibly noneconomic issues were at the forefront of politics in the transition period, but one of the weaknesses of the pluralist approach is that it cannot establish the connection between the mechanics of the political process and the wider struggle for Black progress. Viewed for their implication for the latter, with its necessary intertwining of politics and economics, these issues were a displaced struggle for the defense of economic prerogatives that would materially affect the distribution of wealth in Atlanta. This displacement permitted their defense within the bounds of conventional democratic politics and so disguised the exercise of class power involved.

Black Leaders as a Comprador Class

The pattern of isolation is given an extra layer of insulation by the division of labor between white economic and Black political leaders which devolved on to the Black political class the task of dealing with Black demands for services and the redistribution of wealth. In other words it creates a comprador class that has taken on the work of defending the existing system of social relations, a group that, moreover, would probably have spearheaded the challenge to that system if the white business elite pursued a more uncompromising line. As a buffer between the owners of capital and poor Blacks, the legitimacy it enjoys has been used to contain the threat from below while the comprador class itself has been constrained by the logic of its dependence on white economic power. The bargain struck by this element, willingness to administer its own community in return for the maximum obtainable progress under the prevailing social system, has driven a wedge into the Black community that gives the white business elite continued scope for manipulation of city politics even as their ostensible power is reduced by the assumption of Blacks to political office.

The development of a comprador class of Black leaders is the most positive aspect of an accommodation strategy that accomplished the remarkable feat of turning the Black challenge around so that ultimately the stability of the class system has been reinforced rather than undermined. Faced with a situation in which the balance of power against them was reinforced by a political system that offered many opportunities for resistance to change and so restricted it to an incremental rate, Black politicians were forced to recognize their inability to effect a change commensurate in scale with the needs of the Black community. The disparity between the resources Atlanta's Blacks brought to the bargaining process and the rewards they needed to obtain from it meant that their position remained fundamentally weak and the benefits they derived were correspondingly small. Accordingly, the strategy of the Black leaders was to seek a culture of accommodation in order to maximize their gains within a context in which the limits on progress remain structural and long-term.

The implications of this are first to confirm the importance of race in community politics. Racial origin is by far the best indicator of voter preferences, crossover allegiance remains small, and the issues of everyday politics are dominated by those that divide the races. But the element of class is also vital. When subject to pressure for change by Blacks, American society has responded by neutralizing that pressure through bifurcation of the Black community. This has entailed advances by sections of the Black community, but there is nothing in the logic of this response to suggest that it will be carried further. It is the foregoing of the lesser privilege to maintain the greater, and once that pressure is neutralized the concessions will stop.

In such circumstances the idea that Blacks have now achieved sufficient progress to be able to rely on the natural working of market forces to achieve full incorporation is a convenient neoconservative illusion. The market is a competitive phenomenon, and outside the cozy world of perfect competition, its workings favor the strong. Most Blacks are not able to compete and will suffer accordingly. They have exhausted their capacity to extract concessions from white America, the appeal to conscience is forlorn, and white America no longer feels guilty. The power of the Black vote has achieved much but has now run its course and is hemmed within the safe confines of the central cities. Blacks do not control sufficient capital to be able to dictate terms in the struggle that has always been their only mode of advance. We should not be deceived by the concessions the new accommodation has brought. Their effect, and perhaps their point, has not been to raise Blacks as a whole from the bottom of American society but to eliminate the possibility of their doing so at the lowest practical cost to the rest of society.

So even when politics is conducted largely in terms of racial categories, these are best understood in their relation to the prevailing class structure. Its essence is the resolution of tension between Blacks' aspirations and the preservation of a class-based economic system rather than racism as such. When faced with a choice between preserving racial privilege by attempting to prevent all Black incorporation and strengthening class privilege by incorporating some Blacks into the higher levels of the class structure, those whites in a position to make such a decision have opted for the latter strategy. Were racial privilege their primary commitment they would not have done so. To suggest that racial categories provide the form of the struggle is not to imply that they are superficial or likely to disappear. They will persist even as class divisions within the Black community become more apparent. But it is to argue that to treat race as analytically primary because it is politically visible is to mistake appearance for essence.

Racial conflict is important in and of itself but its implications for Black progress can only be understood within a conceptual framework able to accommodate the complexity of the interaction between race and class. Class analysis confirms that Blacks can make genuine progress within a capitalist framework. The flexibility shown by the white business elite in Atlanta demonstrated that defense of privilege need not require a closed social system. Indeed the defense of class privilege prompted the flexibility under pressure on the race issue that gave Blacks scope to advance. The example of Atlanta amply confirms the concept of racial privilege as an option rather than a necessity under capitalism by showing the willingness of those who control capital to make the compromises with Blacks that are necessary to maintain social stability. The workings of the local state in response to the Black challenge have reinforced the class structure of American society at the expense of the racial status quo. They thus support the case for the essential race blindness of capitalism.

The local state has distinctive features that make it the most suitable arena for meeting the Black challenge. As the level most directly accessible to popular intervention, it might be thought to be more subject to instability. But the fact that the issues arising in local politics rarely threaten the accumulation process means that the local arena can maximize the outlet for expression of discontent while minimizing the danger of this causing instability. The politics of the local community tend to emphasize consumption rather than production, specifically competition over the balance between consumption of and payment for government services. Such issues need not fail to generate heat, and the role of the local state in providing services has important implications for the accumulation process that go beyond its significance for race relations, via infrastructural and social wage expenditure and general demand maintenance. But this service orientation also keeps local politics within an ostensibly apolitical, managerial frame that puts a premium on fiscal responsibility. The consequence is to place Blacks in the position of competing as supplicants for resources from the local state while confining the amount they can receive within a fiscal framework established overwhelmingly by whites and primarily by white owners of capital who directly or indirectly provide the bulk of the revenues available for dispersal.[1] More generally it is the advantage of local politics as a means of deflecting, absorbing, and containing discontent, of neutralizing the disruptive consequences of a productive system based on inequality, that has made the white business elite willing to make the relatively small concessions political accommodation required of them.

But if race is in this sense of declining significance, the implications for Black progress are not sanguine, because the strengthening of class inequality that is its corollary condemns a large part of the Black community to continuing poverty at the bottom of America's class structure. Although full incorporation for Blacks is theoretically possible under capitalism, there is no sign that it will be achieved. In the United States, class and race privilege are closely intertwined, and what we are witnessing is a change in the relation between the two types of privilege. Race privilege has been modified but simultaneously, and partly as a consequence, class privilege has been reinforced. Maintenance of the prerogatives of capital and general social stability have been shown not to require the full incorporation of Blacks.

The price of stability has been a form of semi-incorporation. It may well be that the pluralist system is sufficiently strong that redistribution of wealth to the extent required by Blacks would not be achievable even by a group without any racial signifier attached to it. However, this does not alter the fact that the level of the community or local state fails to offer Blacks a way out of their impasse. Some Black progress—or more precisely, progress for some Blacks—is possible, and the maximum available has been wrung from the system by a sophisticated Black community in Atlanta. But so many Blacks are left out of this form of progress that the result is a bifurcation of the Black community that, far from resolving the African American predicament, only confirms it.

THE UNITED STATES AND PROGRESS

At the national level the picture is hardly brighter. The impact of national government policies on local Black communities was negative during the 1980s and reinforced the constraints on Black advance at that level (Young, 1991). Cutbacks in federal funding of welfare and training programs for the inner cities and a general reorientation of policy toward the suburbs were not surprising developments in view of the fact that the heartland of support for Republican administrations lay in the predominantly white suburban rings of major cities. Again the policy was less one of overt antipathy than of isolation and neglect. The significance of this lies in the fact that in the classic liberal perspective as expounded by Parsons (1965), the federal government is the principal agency of universalism, which will promote the decline of the forces of particularism that perpetuate Black disadvantage. The ascendancy of power sharing and the general philosophy of cutting back the role of the state demonstrated the dangers of relying on this idea as a source of Black progress almost as soon as it was expounded in the 1960s.

The possibility of national Black politicians having the power to remedy this situation is remote. Although the Black congressional caucus has grown in size and importance, it remains victim to the same divergence between Blacks' resources and the demands they need to make of the political system that is apparent in local politics (Swain, 1993). However well organized, it is therefore obliged to play the game of pluralist politics, with all the compromises and limitations this implies for any outgroup. The more charismatic campaigns of Jesse Jackson threatened to challenge this pragmatic approach but ultimately fell victim to the same contradictions. His specific problem was the inability to build a majority either from his Rainbow Coalition of the dispossessed or a more conventional alliance of the Black and white working classes, and perhaps from a confusion between which of the two was his strategic aim. In the face of this, his bravura performance only accentuated the gap between symbolism and substance that is so characteristic of Black politics, a gap that reflects the divergence between the benefits it results in for middle-class Blacks when compared with the rest of the Black community.

The impasse at this level is also manifest in both the liberal and Marxist traditions of thought, which approach the question of Black progress at this level. Each generates insights but uses Blacks as a case study to confirm their wider views of the trajectory of American society and thereby produces an unwarranted optimism that is too one-sided to capture the predicament of African Americans.[2] The liberal tradition is strong on delineating such progress as Blacks have made and on explaining the stability of the American pluralist system. The account of pluralism it offers can provide a clear understanding of both the possibilities for and the limitations of the gains open to Blacks. However, the former element is unduly stressed and the claims made for pluralism in facilitating Black progress are more than it can be expected to deliver, or indeed than a system whose prime virtue is to guarantee social stability should be expected to deliver.

As the arguments employed to fortify the positive case for Black progress became increasingly threadbare, the dominant form of the liberal perspective has been transmogrified into a neoconservative mutation. But the underlying argument remains the same. Warnings of the dangers of affirmative action in undermining the essential balance within American society between formal individualism and informal group competition are well taken. But the reasons why Blacks have been forced onto this unique path are not addressed. Instead the need for special measures is decried and a defiant optimism reasserted on the grounds that pluralist politics and a free market will eventually eliminate Black inequality. Whites' unwillingness, as expressed in the neoconservative argument, to alter a system that has worked well for them places severe limits on Black progress. The problem, therefore, is not so much the absence of liberal principles among whites as it is the adoption of a malleable form of liberalism that reconciles adherence to ideals with the maintenance of material advantage.

The weakness of the liberal approach lies in its idealism, both in the sense of a belief in the virtue of American society and in that it has no theory of power, either as it applies to class or to race. It neglects the facts and implication of the unequal distribution of power in America because its purpose is not to expose them and their pessimistic implications for Black progress but to provide a rationale for the structure that generates them. Its success as an intellectual edifice stems from the fact that it has the weight of the American social structure, which has worked well for so many other groups, on its side.

Full Black inclusion is a threat because it would jeopardize this structure, with no guarantee of putting anything better in its place. The value placed on it by whites leads them to exercise the power they hold to force Blacks to pay the price of semi-incorporation in defense of the greater good. This is a perfectly defensible position; the problem is that rather than stating it clearly, liberal writers cling to the camouflage that the system that has worked to incorporate others will do so for Blacks as well. The fact remains that the social structure is too powerful and precious to those who benefit from it for Blacks to force the changes that would be necessary to gain them full entry into it. This is the impassse that the rationalizations of the liberal tradition attempt to conceal.

The Marxist tradition has different strengths. It goes beyond the surface level of racial conflict and employs the inherently dynamic concept of class to create a framework that will explain the constraints a capitalist society places on changes in race relations. This injects greater realism because it focuses on the structure of power that liberalism neglects and so generates a clearer understanding of the forces of conservatism in American society. The starting point of a properly construed class analysis is the recognition that the imperative to accumulate capital is fundamental because only if it is met can the capitalist system of social relations survive. This requires not only direct control of the process of production, but also the stable reproduction of a system of social relations within which accumulation through profit maximization may be pursued. The problem comes from the fact that the former threatens the latter. Profit maximization in its nature produces growth but also inequality and exploitation, and this threatens social stability, especially when the exploited feel identified by group characteristics such as race that give "natural" basis for struggle.

There are a number of mechanisms that operate to prevent this contradiction from becoming acute, but the arena of tension management with the greatest relevance to Black progress is politics, the state. Blacks in America historically have had an interest in challenging the social system. Even if their capacity is limited to disruption, the threat they pose is sufficiently great to require a political response. The first alternative is the repression of discontent, ultimately through physical force. Although hardly absent from the Black experience, this has become much less prominent. It is potentially counterproductive and at best can secure only short-term stability. Its role therefore is that of last resort. Much more important is the alternative response of accommodation to Blacks' demands, a strategy that is more commensurate with the limited threat they pose. It is also a response that concedes no more than is necessary to preserve stability. In addition it is consistent with a relationship between racism and capitalism that both permits flexibility on the part of capital and explains the incentive to adopt this strategy.

Although this offers a fuller explanation of the process of accommodation, isolation, and bifurcation that has shaped Black progress in recent years, the Marxist approach also has its weaknesses. The importation of class can lead to an economistic and objectivist bias that discounts the subjective aspect of race relations too heavily in favor of a supposed essence that is not always amenable to investigation. This approach can become internally contradictory because it imports race only as an idealist accretion to a materialist framework and is forced into minimizing the importance of race in order to avoid contradicting the materialist premise. Of more direct relevance to Black progress is the close connection between capitalism and racism, which can be posited in such a way as to make the latter a necessary component of the former and the elimination or even serious diminution of racism impossible in a capitalist society. The problem with this is that the Marxist approach cannot demonstrate anything in the logic of capital accumulation that requires discrimination on a specifically racial basis.

To resolve this tension recourse is often made to a functionalist mode of explanation which attempts to explain any level of progress in terms of the needs of capital. This gives rise to post hoc rationalizations and conspiratorial interpretations that take flexibility to the point of incorrigibility. Functionalism does provide a defense of the approach but only at the cost of making it vacuous, able to explain anything and therefore nothing. By permitting the Marxist perspective to generate a plausible interpretation compatible with any degree of Black progress, it improves its internal consistency only by robbing it of its explanatory power and confirming its status as a worldview rather than a falsifiable model.

The disposition toward functionalism, economism, and opportunism undermine a conventional Marxist perspective and preclude it from resolving the question of Black progress. The pressure for these contortions stems from the political character of the Marxist approach; its revolutionary commitment and the apocalyptic form of optimism is quite at odds with the pessimistic logic of the analysis. The practical counterpart of this is advocacy of a political strategy of a transracial working class alliance whose lack of realism only confirms the underlying flaws of the approach. Even when these tendencies are avoided and a more flexible version of class analysis is developed, the result is to demonstrate the strength of the forces ranged against Black progress. It leads therefore ineluctably to the pessimistic conclusion we have already encountered, that the forces governing Blacks' position are too powerful to make anything more than a form of semi-progress within capitalism possible in the foreseeable future. The irony is that even the model with the greatest potential for revealing the nature of the condition of African Americans only ends up confirming the impasse that is its hallmark.

GLOBALIZATION AND PROGRESS

If neither tradition provides either an intellectual or a practical solution, a final and new dimension of difficulty for African Americans completes the grim picture. Ascending from the national level to the international, the globalization of the capitalist system in recent years has negative implications for Black progress. The economic aspect of this process has its roots again in the mobility of capital whose significance is so apparent at the community level. Now, however, the scope of that mobility has made a quantum leap. Facilitated by improvements in technology and transport and by the political openings brought about by the collapse of communism, and driven by the unrelenting imperative for capital accumulation, corporations are increasingly having to maximize their efficiency by viewing their operations in terms of a single, integrated global economy. This applies not only to the markets in which they seek to sell their products, but also to their sourcing of raw materials and of the labor used in the production process.

This has important consequences for nation states, including the United States. Its role has had to evolve in light of the momentous developments in international affairs in recent years. Perhaps the most important effect has been to place a premium on the competitiveness of the U.S. economy. America's role as a world leader will depend much more on this in the future than it did in the Cold War era, when military and political power underlay its leadership. This creates intense pressure for the United States to improve the productivity of its economy. One of the ways it will have to do this is to find new and cheaper sources of labor (Wood, 1994); the development of the North American Free Trade Agreement is plainly intended to meet this need.

In addition to the more rapid circulation of capital, global integration will also give rise to a vast increase in the migration of labor, in the Americas as elsewhere. This will bring culturally and ethnically distinct groups into greater contact and so raise afresh the problems of social stability and absorption, of opportunity and competition in an expanded multicultural context. American society has experienced these pressures because of its history as an immigrant society. Its response has been the development of a form of pluralism that reconciles diversity with opportunity for most immigrant groups and so combines relative social harmony with evolutionary change.

It thus provides a model for other societies that will face the challenge of establishing these virtues in circumstances in which economic pressures are likely to produce a new level of intensity in ethnic competition. America will not be exempt from these pressures and its past success is no guarantee that it will remain an exemplar of how to deal with the challenge of multiculturalism.

This is all the more true when it is recognized that the historical flaw in American pluralism has been the relative exclusion of Blacks from its benefits.

What then are the implications of these momentous international shifts for Blacks in American society? It seems unlikely that they will promote inclusion, as previous eras have not. On the contrary, the relocation of capital that will result from global integration is likely to make the labor of many Blacks superfluous to the needs of capital in the American economy. Trapped as they are in high-cost areas of the inner cities but with low levels of skill, many Blacks cannot compete with new sources of labor in Mexico and farther afield. The consequences of their combination of high cost and low skill will become increasingly severe as jobs and capital move elsewhere with ever more speed as part of an intensified search for profits. Those with economic power have no responsibility for the welfare of those, like inner city Blacks, who cannot contribute; they are subject to the laws of the market, which compel profit maximization for survival, and if the pursuit of this leaves some groups redundant, then so be it.

Furthermore, the American state, which does have some responsibility for dispossessed groups, cannot interfere with this way of increasing productivity if the economy is to retain the competitiveness on which America's world role depends. It can either provide better training to improve the skills of the dispossessed, or provide a compensatory safety net of welfare to ameliorate the harshest consequences. But each remedy is expensive, and in the current climate it is hard to gain acceptance for even these palliatives from a white majority that itself feels hard-pressed by the cold winds of international competition and declining living standards. The result is the rapid transformation of large segments of the Black working class into an underclass that lives outside the mainstream economic system, condemned to survive as best it can on its wits, which all too often means struggling to escape against the odds from a web of drugs, crime, and welfare dependency.

The cultural changes that parallel economic restructuring do not offer any relief for Blacks. The plight of the Black underclass is easy prey to the revival of the blame the victim syndrome. Personal inadequacies are so much easier to grasp and vilify than the impossible circumstances that impersonal, objective, and shadowy forces of globalization create. The replacement of race by ethnicity attendant on the growth of multiculturalism is potentially liberating for Blacks because it accords them equal respect with other groups and frees them from the inherent weakness of any definition of their position that is couched in Black-white terms. And yet the uncomfortable evidence that even recent immigrant groups of Asian and Hispanic origin are climbing the ladder of success in a way Blacks have never done reinforces the pluralist mythology and in the eyes of many whites confines Blacks to an historical backwater separated from the march of pluralism by their own inadequacies. If the new trends arising from globalization do revive the U.S. economy and reinvigorate its cultural pluralism, the great swath of the Black community firmly excluded from this rosy future will become ever more marginalized. Not all the Black community is caught in this trap, of course. A new and expanded Black middle class is sufficiently well established to be able to find an economic and cultural niche in the new order. But this only confirms the extent of the division within the Black community and reinforces the bifurcation that is the contemporary curse of its struggle for progress.

Globalization, then, forms the final circle in the inferno to which African Americans are condemned. Their purgatory consists of a set of immovable constraints that operate at all levels of the Black experience, from the intimacy of individual identity, across the politics of their local communities, into their place in the ideological scheme of the American nation, and now beyond even that to the reconstitution of the world order. The dualism of the Black condition—that of a divided community in which progress is possible for some but incorporation for all lies beyond the iron cage that entraps them—is the measure of the African American predicament. Contrary to both the liberal and radical traditions, no solution to the question of Black progress is in prospect. The advances Blacks have made are deeply ambiguous, serving as much to lock them into continued subjugation as to emancipate them. The latest solutions offered by each tradition, faith in the power of the market or of a rainbow coalition, belong to the fairy-tale land where rhetoric takes the place of analysis and simple solutions are promised to intractable problems. They contribute to yet another false dawn to the experience of African Americans, whose struggle will be confined for the foreseeable future to maintaining the form of semiprogress they have so far achieved. Unpalatable as such a conclusion may be, unless it is recognized, there can be little possibility of developing an analysis commensurate with the continuing tragedy of African Americans.

NOTES

1. The restrictions placed on Maynard Jackson's handling of the sanitation workers' strike in a city where it is illegal to run a budgetary deficit illustrate perfectly how Blacks' demands can be channeled in a safe direction by local political mechanisms that obviate the need for direct suppression.

2. Among recent writers, Roy L. Brooks (1990) perhaps comes closest to recognizing the unpalatable fact that there may be no solution to the African American predicament. Certainly he makes a strong case for not relying on government to provide the answer. But even he suggests that a program of self-help by African Americans can fill the gap left by the failure of will at government level. This begs the question of why, if such a program is evidently in the interests of African Americans but has not worked in the past, it should prove effective in the future.

References

Alexander, S. (1974). *The Atlanta elections of 1973*. Atlanta: Voter Education Project.

Allen, I. (1971). *Mayor: Notes on the '60s*. New York: Simon & Schuster.

Allen, R. (1970). *Black awakening in capitalist America*. New York: Doubleday.

Anthias, F. (1992). Connecting "Race" and ethnic phenomena. *Sociology, 26*, 421-438.

Aptheker, H. (1946). *The Negro people in America: A critique of Gunnar Myrdal's "An American Dilemma."* New York: International Publishers.

Arendt, H. (1958). *The human condition*. Chicago: University of Chicago Press.

Arrow, K. (1973). The theory of discrimination. In O. Ashenfelter & A. Rees (Eds.), *Discrimination in labor markets* (pp. 49-63). Princeton, NJ: Princeton University Press.

Bacote, C. A. (1955). The Negro in Atlanta politics. *Phylon, 16*, 333-350.

Bailey, R. W. (1973). Economic aspects of the Black internal colony. *Review of Black Political Economy, 3*, 43-72.

Baldwin, J. (1985). *Evidence of things not seen*. New York: Holt, Rinehart.

Bambara, T. (1983). What's happening in Atlanta? *Southern Exposure, 11*, 25-35.

Banfield, E. C. (1965). Atlanta: Strange bedfellows. In *Big city politics* (pp. 18-36). New York: Random House.

Banfield, E. C. (1974). *The unheavenly city re-visited*. Boston: Little, Brown.

Banton, M. (1977). *The idea of race*. London: Tavistock.

Banton, M. (1988). *Racial consciousness*. London: Longman.

Baran, P., & Sweezy, P. M. (1968). *Monopoly capital*. Harmondsworth, England: Penguin.

Baron, H. (1975). Racial discrimination in advanced capitalism. In R. Edwards, M. Reich, & D. M. Gordon (Eds.), *Labor Market Segmentation* (pp. 173-216). London: Heath.

Baron, H., & Hymer, B. (1971). The dynamics of the dual labor market. In D. M. Gordon (Ed.), *Problems in political economy* (pp. 94-101). Lexington, MA: Heath.

Bartley, N. V. (1970, Winter). Atlanta elections and Georgia political trends. *New South*, pp. 22-30.

Baudrillard, J. (1988). *Selected writings* (M. Poster, Ed.). Cambridge: Polity Press.

Becker, G. (1971). *The economics of discrimination* (2nd ed.). Chicago: University of Chicago Press. (Original work published 1957)

Bell, D. (1975). Ethnicity and social change. In N. Glazer & D. P. Moynihan (Eds.), *Ethnicity: Theory and experience* (pp. 141-174). Cambridge, MA: Harvard University Press.

217

Bell, D. A., Jr. (1987). *And we are not saved: The elusive quest for racial justice*. New York: Basic Books.

Ben-Tovim, G., & Gabriel, J. (1978). Marxism and the concept of racism. *Economy and Society, 7*, 118-154.

Ben-Tovim, G., & Gabriel, J. (1979). The conceptualisation of race relations in sociological theory. *Ethnic and Racial Studies, 2*, 190-212.

Berman, M. (1983). *All that is solid melts into air: The experience of modernity*. London: Verso.

Boggs, J. E. (1970). *Racism and the class struggle*. New York: Monthly Review Press.

Bonacich, E. (1976). Advanced capitalism and Black/white race relations in the USA: A split labor market interpretation. *American Sociological Review, 41*, 35-41.

Bonacich, E. (1979). The past, present and future of split labor market theory. In C. B. Marett & C. B. Leggon (Eds.), *Research in race and ethnic relations* (Vol. 1, pp. 17-64). Greenwich, CT: JAI Press.

Boston, T. G. (1988). *Race, class and conservatism*. Boston: Unwin Hyman.

Braverman, H. (1974). *Labor and monopoly capital: The degradation of work in the twentieth century*. New York: Monthly Review Press.

Breitman, G. (1965). *Marxism and the Negro struggle*. New York: Pathfinder Press.

Brooks, R. L. (1990). *Rethinking the American race problem*. Berkeley: University of California Press.

Bryce, H. J., Jr. (1973). *On the progress of Blacks: A comment on Wattenberg & Scammon*. Washington, DC: Joint Center for Political and Economic Studies.

Bryce, H. J., Jr. (1974). *Black mayors of medium and large cities*. Washington, DC: Joint Center for Political and Economic Studies.

Bumiller, K. (1988). *The civil rights society: The social construction of victims*. Baltimore, MD: Johns Hopkins University Press.

Burawoy, M. (1974). Race, class and colonialism. *Social and Economic Studies, 23*, 521-550.

Burawoy, M. (1976). The functions and reproduction of migrant labor: Comparative material from Southern Africa and the United States. *American Journal of Sociology, 81*, 1050-1087.

Burgess, E. M. (1962). *Negro leadership in a southern city*. Chapel Hill: University of North Carolina Press.

Burman, S. (1991). *America in the modern world: The transcendence of U.S. hegemony*. London: Harvester/Wheatsheaf.

Burman, S. (1994). America in transition: Domestic weakness and international competitiveness. In G. Thompson (Ed.), *The United States in the twentieth century: Markets* (pp. 269-288). London: Hodder & Stoughton.

Busby, M. (Ed.). (1992). *Daughters of Africa*. London: Jonathan Cape.

Carmichael, S., & Hamilton, C. V. (1967). *Black power: The politics of liberation in America*. London: Jonathan Cape.

Carter, S. L. (1991). *Reflections of an affirmative action baby*. New York: Basic Books.

Castells, M. (1978). *City, class and power*. London: Macmillan.

Castells, M. (1981). Local government, urban crisis and political change. In M. Zeitlin (Ed.), *Political power and social theory* (Vol. 2, pp. 1-19). Greenwich, CT: JAI Press.

Cawson, A., & Saunders, P. (1983). Corporatism, competitive politics and class struggle. In R. King (Ed.), *Capital and politics* (pp. 8-27). London: Routledge.

Clarke, K. B. (1968). Thoughts on Black power. *Dissent, 15*, 92.

Cohen, G. A. (1978). *Karl Marx's theory of history: A defence.* London: Oxford University Press.

Cohen, G. A. (1986). Marxism and functional explanation. In J. Roemer (Ed.), *Analytical Marxism* (pp. 221-234). London: Cambridge University Press.

Cole, L. (1976). *Blacks in power: A comparative study of Black and white officials.* Princeton, NJ: Princeton University Press.

Conant, R. W. (1968). Black power: Rhetoric and reality. *Urban Affairs Quarterly, 4,* 15-25.

Cornacchia, E., & Nelson, D. C. (1992). Historical differences in the political experiences of American Blacks and white ethnics: Revisiting an unresolved controversy. *Ethnic and Racial Studies, 15,* 102-124.

Cox, O. C. (1959). *Caste, class and race: Study in social dynamics.* New York: Monthly Review Press.

Cox, O. C. (1976). *Race relations: Elements in social dynamics.* Detroit: Wayne State University Press.

Crandall, G. (1972). *Black power in the deep South.* D. Phil. thesis, University of Oxford.

Crawford, F. R. (1969). *A report of certain reactions by the Atlanta public to the death of the Reverend Doctor Martin Luther King, Jr.* Atlanta: Emory University, Center for Research in Social Change.

Crenson, M. (1971). *The Un-politics of air pollution: A study of non-decisionmaking in the cities.* Baltimore, MD: Johns Hopkins University Press.

Cruse, H. (1967). *The crisis of the Negro intellectual.* New York: Morrow.

Cruse, H. (1968). *Rebellion or revolution.* New York: Morrow.

Cruse, H. (1987). *Plural but equal: A critical study of Blacks and minorities and America's plural society.* New York: Morrow.

Dahl, R. (1958). A critique of the ruling elite model. *American Political Science Review, 52,* 463-469.

Dahl, R. (1967). *Pluralist democracy in the United States: Conflict and consensus.* Chicago: Rand McNally.

Davidson, C. (1972). *Bi-racial politics: Conflict and coalition in the metropolitan South.* Baton Rouge: Louisiana State University Press.

Dettlinger, C., & Prugh, J. (1983). *The list.* Atlanta: Philmay Enterprises.

Draper, T. (1969). The fantasy of Black nationalism. *Commentary, 48,* 27-55.

Dunleavy, P., & O'Leary, B. (1987). *Theories of the state.* London: Macmillan.

Edwards, R., Reich, M., & Gordon, D. (Eds.). (1975). *Labor market segmentation.* London: Heath.

Eisinger, P. K. (1980). *The politics of displacement: Racial and ethnic transition in three American cities.* New York: Academic Press.

Eisinger, P. K. (1983). Black mayors and the politics of racial economic advancement. In *Black power in American cities, Draft Conference Proceedings* (No. 1, pp. 1-22). Chicago: Peoples College Press.

Ellison, R. (1967). *The shadow and the act.* London: Secker & Warburg.

Elster, J. (1980). Cohen on Marx's theory of history. *Political Studies, 1,* 121-128.

Elster, J. (1982). Marxism, functionalism and game theory. *Theory and Society, 2,* 453-482.

Elster, J. (1985). *Making sense of Marx.* London: Cambridge University Press.

English, J. W. (1967). *The prophet of Wheat St.* Elgin, IL: Cook.

Essien-Udom, E. U. (1962). *Black nationalism.* Chicago: University of Chicago Press.

Etzioni, A. (1959). The Ghetto: A re-evaluation. *Social Forces, 37,* 255-262.

Evans, P. B., Rueschemeyer, D., & Skocpol, T. (Eds.). (1985). *Bringing the state back in.* Cambridge: Cambridge University Press.

Fainstein, N., & Fainstein, S. (1974). *Urban political movements: The search for power by minority groups in American cities.* Englewood Cliffs, NJ: Prentice-Hall.

Fanon, F. (1965). *The wretched of the earth.* London: Macgibbon & Kee.

Farley, R. (1977). Trends in racial inequalities: Have the gains of the 1960s disappeared in the 1970s? *American Sociological Review, 42,* 189-218.

Farley, R. (1984). *Blacks and whites: Narrowing the gap?* Cambridge, MA: Harvard University Press.

Farley, R. (1985). Three steps forward and two back? Recent changes in the social and economic status of Blacks. *Ethnic and Racial Studies, 8,* 4-28.

Farley, R., & Allen, W. R. (1987). *The color line and the quality of life in America.* New York: Russell Sage Foundation.

Forsythe, D. (1977). Race relations from liberal, Black and Marxist perspectives. *Cornell Journal of Social Relations, 12,* 157-181.

Franklin, R. S. (1969). The political economy of Black power. *Social Problems, 16,* 286-300.

Frazier, E. F. (1957). *Black bourgeoisie: The rise of a new middle class in the United States.* New York: Collier.

Frazier, E. F. (1972). Sociological theory and race relations. In P. L. Van Den Berghe (Ed.), *Intergroup relations: Sociological perspectives* (pp. 15-25). New York: Basic Books.

Freeman, R. (1974). *Black elite: The new market for highly qualified Black Americans.* New York: McGraw-Hill.

Freeman, R. (1978). Black economic progress since 1964. *Public Interest, 52,* 52-68.

Friedman, M. (1962). *Capitalism and freedom.* Chicago: University of Chicago Press.

Gamson, W. (1971). Stable unrepresentation in American society. In E. S. Greenberg, N. Milner, & D. J. Olson (Eds.), *Black politics: The inevitability of conflict* (pp. 55-70). New York: Holt, Rinehart & Wilson.

Gates, H. L., Jr. (1992). *Loose canons: Notes on the culture wars.* New York: Oxford University Press.

Gaventa, J. (1980). *Power and powerlessness: Quiescence and rebellion in an Appalachian valley.* Oxford: Clarendon Press.

Genovese, E. (1971). *In red and black.* London: Allen Lane.

Genovese, E. (1974), *Roll, Jordan, roll: The world the slaves made.* New York: Pantheon.

Geschwender, J. (1977). *Racial stratification in America.* Dubuque, IA: Brown.

Giddens, A. (1968). Power in the recent writings of Talcott Parsons. *Sociology, 2,* 257-272.

Glazer, N. (1969, April). Blacks, Jews and the intellectuals. *Commentary, 48,* 33-39.

Glazer, N. (1971). Blacks and ethnic groups: The difference and the difference it makes. *Social Problems, 18,* 444-461.

Glazer, N. (1975). *Affirmative discrimination.* New York: Basic Books.

Glazer, N. (1979). American Jews: Three conflicts of loyalties. In S. M. Lipset (Ed.), *The third century* (pp. 223-241). Stanford, CA: Hoover Institute Press.

Glazer, N. (1988). *The limits of social policy.* Cambridge, MA: Harvard University Press.

Glazer, N., & Moynihan, D. P. (Eds.). (1963). *Beyond the melting pot: The Negroes, Puerto Ricans, Italians and Irish of New York.* Cambridge, MA: MIT Press.

Glazer, N., & Moynihan, D. P. (Eds.). (1970). *Beyond the melting pot: The Negroes, Puerto Ricans, Italians and Irish of New York* (2nd ed.). Cambridge, MA: MIT Press.

Glazer, N., & Moynihan, D. P. (Eds.). (1975). *Ethnicity: Theory and experience.* Cambridge, MA: Harvard University Press.

Gordon, D. M., Edwards, R., & Reich, M. (1982). *Segmented work: Divided workers: The historical transformation of labor in the United States.* New York: Cambridge University Press.

Gordon, M. (1964). *Assimilation in American life: The role of race, religion and national origins.* New York: Oxford University Press.

Gordon, M. (1978). *Human nature, class and ethnicity.* New York: Oxford University Press.

Gray, J. (1984). *Hayek on liberty.* Oxford: Blackwell.

Greeley, A. (1974). *Ethnicity in the United States: A preliminary reconnaissance.* New York: John Wiley.

Greeley, A. (1976). The ethnic miracle. *Public Interest, 45,* 20-36.

Greenberg, S. (1976). Business enterprise in a racial order. *Politics and Society, 6,* 213-240.

Greenstone, J. D., & Peterson, P. E. (1973). *Race and authority in urban politics.* New York: Sage.

Greer, E. H. (1979). *Big steel: Black politics and corporate power in Gary, Indiana.* New York: Monthly Review Press.

Grunberg, I. (1990). Exploring the "myth" of hegemonic stability. *International Organisation, 44,* 431-477.

Gutman, H. (1976). *The Black family under slavery and freedom 1750-1925.* Oxford: Blackwell.

Hall, S. (1980). Race, articulation and societies in structured dominance. In *Sociological theories: Race and colonialism* (pp. 305-345). Paris: UNESCO.

Hall, S. (1990). Ethnicity: Identity and difference. *Radical America, 23,* 9-20.

Hamilton, C. V. (Ed.). (1973). *The Black experience in American politics.* New York: Capricorn.

Hamilton, R. (1972). *Class and politics in the United States.* New York: John Wiley.

Harris, D. J. (1972). The Black ghetto as colony: A theoretical critique and alternative formulation. *Review of Black Political Economy, 11,* 3-33.

Harris, M. (1964). *Patterns of race in the Americas.* New York: Walker.

Hartz, L. (1991). *The liberal tradition in America: An interpretation of American political thought since the Revolution* (2nd ed.). San Diego: Harcourt, Brace, Jovanovich. (Original work published 1955)

Hawley, W. D. (1975). *Blacks and metropolitan governance.* Berkeley: University of California Institute of Governmental Studies.

Hayek, F. (1960). *The constitution of liberty.* London: Routledge & Kegan Paul.

Hayes, E. C. (1972). *Power structure and urban policy: Who rules in Oakland?* New York: McGraw-Hill.

Headley, B. D. (1981). Class and race in Atlanta: A note on the murdered and missing children. *Race and Class, 23,* 81-86.

Hechter, M. (1975). *Internal colonialism: The Celtic fringe in British national development 1536-1966.* London: Routledge.

Hein, V. (1972). The image of a "city too busy to hate." *Phylon, 33,* 205-221.

Higham, J. (1975). *Send these to me: Jews and other immigrants in urban America.* New York: Atheneum.

Hill, R. B. (1978). *The illusion of Black progress.* Washington, DC: National Urban League.

Hills, S. L. (1970). Negroes and immigrants in America. *Sociological Focus, 3,* 85-96.

Holloway, H. (1969). *The politics of the southern Negro.* New York: Random House.

Horton, J. (1966). Order and conflict theories of social problems as competing ideologies. *American Journal of Sociology, 71,* 701-713.

Howard, J. R. (1978). A framework for the analysis of urban Black politics. *Annals, American Academy of Political and Social Science, 439,* 1-15.

Hughes, E. C. (1963). Race relations and the sociological imagination. *American Sociological Review, 28,* 879-890.

Hunter, F. (1953). *Community power structure: A study of decision-makers.* Chapel Hill: University of North Carolina Press.

Hunter, F. (1980). *Community power succession: Atlanta's policy makers revisited.* Chapel Hill: University of North Carolina Press.

Hutcheson, J. R. (1973). *Racial attitudes in Atlanta.* Atlanta: Emory University, Center for Research in Social Change.

Jackson, W. A. (1990). *Gunnar Myrdal and America's conscience: Social engineering and racial liberalism 1938-1987.* Chapel Hill: University of North Carolina Press.

Jameson, F. (1984). Postmodernism, or the cultural logic of late capitalism. *New Left Review, 146,* 53-93.

Jameson, F. (1991). *Postmodernism, or, the cultural logic of late capitalism.* London: Verso.

Jaynes, G. D., & Williams, R. M. (1989). *A common destiny: Blacks and American society.* Washington, DC: National Academy Press.

Jencks, C. (1983, March 3). Discrimination and Thomas Sowell. *New York Review of Books,* pp. 33-38.

Jenkins, H. (1970). *Keeping the peace.* New York: Harper & Row.

Jenkins, J. S. (1981). *Murder in Atlanta.* Atlanta: Cherokee.

Jennings, M. K. (1964). *Community influentials: The elites of Atlanta.* New York: Free Press.

Jessop, B. (1990). *State theory: Putting the capitalist state in its place.* Cambridge: Polity Press.

Johnstone, F. (1976). *Class, race and gold: A study of class relations and racial discrimination in South Africa.* London: Routledge.

Joint Center for Political and Economic Studies. (annual). *National register of Black elected officials.* Washington, DC: Author.

Jones, M. H. (1972). A frame of reference for Black politics. In L. Henderson (Ed.), *Black political life in the U.S.* (pp. 7-20). San Francisco: Chandler.

Jones, M. H. (1978). Black political empowerment in Atlanta: Myth and reality. *Annals, American Academy of Political and Social Science, 439,* 90-117.

Katznelson, I. (1971). Power in the reformulation of race research. In P. Orelans & W. R. Ellis, Jr. (Eds.), *Race, change and urban society* (pp. 51-82). Beverly Hills, CA: Sage.

Katznelson, I. (1973). *Black men, white cities: Race, politics and migration in the United States 1900-30 and Britain 1948-68.* London: Oxford University Press.

Katznelson, I. (1976). The crisis of the capitalist city: Urban politics and social control. In W. D. Hawley & M. Lipsky (Eds.), *Theoretical perspectives on urban politics* (pp. 214-229). Englewood Cliffs, NJ: Prentice-Hall.

Katznelson, I. (1982). *City trenches: Urban politics and the patterning of class in the United States.* Chicago: University of Chicago Press.

Keating, L. (1980). Camelot to containment: John Portman in Atlanta. *Southern Exposure, 8,* 76-85.

Keller, E. J. (1978). The impact of Black mayors on urban policy. *Annals, American Academy of Political and Social Science, 439,* 40-52.

Kennedy, P. (1988). *The rise and fall of the great powers: Economic change and military conflict 1500-2000.* London: Unwin Hyman.

Kilson, M. (1971). Black politicians: A new power. *Dissent, 18,* 333-345.

Kilson, M. (1975). Blacks and neo-ethnicity in American political life. In N. Glazer & D. P. Moynihan (Eds.), *Ethnicity: Theory and reality* (pp. 236-266). Cambridge, MA: Harvard University Press.

Kornhauser, W. (1960). *The politics of mass society.* London: Routledge.

Kotter, J. P., & Lawrence, P. R. (1974). *Mayors in action: Five approaches to urban governance.* New York: John Wiley.

Kristol, I. (1972). The Negro today is like the immigrant of yesterday. In P. I. Rose (Ed.), *Nation of nations: The ethnic experience and the racial crisis* (pp. 197-210). New York: Random House.

Kristol, I. (1978). *Two cheers for capitalism.* New York: Basic Books.

Lacan, J. (1968). *The language of the self: The function of language in psychoanalysis.* Baltimore, MD: Johns Hopkins University Press.

Laclau, E. (1975). The specificity of the political. *Economy and Society, 5,* 87-111.

Lasch, C. (1991). *The true and only heaven: Progress and its critics.* New York: Norton.

Legget, J. C. (1968). *Class, race and labor: Working-class consciousness in Detroit.* Oxford: Oxford University Press.

Levine, C. (1974). *Racial conflict and the American mayor.* London: Lexington Books.

Levi-Strauss, C. (1985). *The view from afar.* New York: Basic Books.

Levitan, S., Johnston, W. B., & Taggart, R. (Eds.). (1975). *Still a dream: The changing status of Blacks since 1960.* Cambridge, MA: Harvard University Press.

Lieberson, S. (1980). *A piece of the pie: Black and white immigrants since 1980.* Berkeley: University of California Press.

Lineberry, R. L., & Masotti, L. H. (Eds.). (1976). *The new urban politics.* Cambridge, MA: Ballinger.

Livingston, J. C. (1979). *Fair game?: Inequality and affirmative action.* San Francisco: W. H. Freeman.

Lockwood, D. (1970). Race, conflict and plural society. In S. Zubaida (Ed.), *Race and racialism* (pp. 57-72). London: Tavistock.

Lyman, S. M. (1972). *The Black American in sociological thought: A failure of perspective.* New York: Capricorn.

Lyotard, J. (1984). *The post-modern condition: A report on knowledge.* Manchester, England: Manchester University Press.

Marable, M. (1985a). *Black American politics: From the Washington marches to Jesse Jackson.* London: Verso.

Marable, M. (1985b). Jackson and the rise of the rainbow coalition. *New Left Review, 149,* 3-44.

Marable, M. (1993). Clarence Thomas and the crisis of Black political culture. In T. Morrison (Ed.), *Race-ing justice, en-gendering power* (pp. 61-85). London: Chatto.

Marshall, T. H. (1950). *Citizenship and social class.* Cambridge: Cambridge University Press.

Martin, H. H. (1978). *William Berry Hartsfield: Mayor of Atlanta.* Atlanta: University of Georgia Press.

Massey, D. S., & Denton, N. A. (1993). *American apartheid: Segregation and the making of the underclass.* Cambridge, MA: Harvard University Press.

Mathews, D., & Prothro, J. (1966). *Negroes and the new southern politics.* New York: Harcourt.

Medalia, N. Z. (1962). Myrdal's assumptions on race relations: A conceptual commentary. *Social Forces, 40,* 223-227.

Memmi, A. (1967). *The colonizer and the colonized.* Boston: Beacon Press.

Metzger, L. P. (1971). American sociology and Black assimilation: Conflicting perspectives. *American Journal of Sociology, 76,* 627-647.

Miles, R. C. (1980). Class, race and ethnicity: A critique of Cox's theory. *Ethnic and Racial Studies, 3,* 169-187.

Miliband, R. (1969). *The state in capitalist society.* London: Weidenfeld & Nicholson.

Miliband, R. (1977). *Marxism and politics.* Oxford: Oxford University Press.

Mills, C. W. (1956). *The power elite.* New York: Oxford University Press.

Mintz, B., Freitag, P., Hendricks, C., & Schwartz, M. (1976). Problems of proof in elite research. *Social Problems, 23,* 314-324.

Morrison, T. (Ed.). (1993). *Race-ing justice, en-gendering power.* Princeton, NJ: Princeton University Press.

Moynihan, D. P. (1965). *The Negro family: The case for national action.* Washington, DC: U.S. Department of Labor.

Moynihan, D. P. (1972). The schism in Black America. *Public Interest, 27,* 3-24.

Moynihan, D. P. (1993). *Pandaemonium: Ethnicity in international politics.* Oxford: Oxford University Press.

Murray, C. A. (1984). *Losing ground, American social policy, 1950-80.* New York: Basic Books.

Murray, C. A. (1988). *In pursuit of happiness and good government.* New York: Simon & Schuster.

Myrdal, G. (1968). *Asian drama: An inquiry into the poverty of nations.* New York: Twentieth Century Fund.

Myrdal, G. (1974). The case against romantic ethnicity. *Center Magazine, 7,* 26-30.

Myrdal, G., *An American dilemma: The Negro problem and modern democracy.* (1944/ 1962). New York: Harper & Row.

Nelson, W. E., & Meranto, P. J. (1977). *Electing Black mayors.* Columbus: Ohio State University Press.

Nelson, W. E., & Van Horne, W. (1974). Black elected officials and the trials of office. *Public Administration Review, 34,* 526-533.

Newton, K. (1975). Social class, political structure and public goods in American urban politics. *Urban Affairs Quarterly, 11,* 241-266.

Newton, K. (1976). Feeble governments and private power: Urban politics and policies in the US. In R. Lineberry & L. H. Masotti (Eds.), *The new urban politics* (pp. 37-58). Cambridge, MA: Ballinger.

Novak, M. (1973). *The rise of the unmeltable ethnics: Politics and culture in the '70s.* New York: Macmillan.

Nozick, R. (1974). *Anarchy, state and utopia.* London: Blackwell.

Nye, J. (1990). *Bound to lead: The changing nature of American power.* New York: Basic Books.

O'Connor, J. (1973). *The fiscal crisis of the state.* New York: St. Martin's Press.

Ofari, E. (1970). *The myth of Black capitalism.* New York: Monthly Review Press.

Offe, C. (1984). *Contradictions of the welfare state.* London: Hutchinson.

Olson, M. (1965). *The logic of collective action public goods and the theory of groups.* Cambridge, MA: Harvard University Press.

Omi, M., & Winant, H. (1986). *Racial formation in the United States: From the 1960s to the 1980s.* New York: Routledge/Methuen.

Orfield, G., & Ashkinaze, C. (1991). *Closing the door: Conservative policy and Black opportunity.* Chicago: University of Chicago Press.

Park, R. E. (1950). *Race and culture.* New York: Free Press.

Parsons, T. M. (1965). Full citizenship for the Negro American?: A sociological problem. *Daedelus, 94,* 1009-1054.

Parsons, T. M. (1966). On the concept of political power. In R. Bendix & S. M. Lipset (Eds.), *Class, status and power* (pp. 240-265). New York: Free Press.

Parsons, T. M. (1968). The problem of polarization on the axis of color. In J. H. Franklin (Ed.), *Color and race* (pp. 349-369). Boston: Houghton Miflin.

Parsons, T. M. (1975). Some theoretical considerations on the nature and trends of change in ethnicity. In N. Glazer & D. P. Moynihan (Eds.), *Ethnicity: Theory and experience* (pp. 53-83). Cambridge, MA: Harvard University Press.

Parsons, T. M., & Clarke, K. B. (1966). *The Negro American.* New York: Houghton Mifflin.

Paschall, E. (1975). *It must have rained.* Atlanta: Emory University, Center for Research in Social Change.

Patterson, H. O. (1972). Toward a future that has no past—Reflections on the fate of Blacks in the Americas. *Public Interest, 27,* 25-62.

Patterson, H. O. (1973). The moral crisis of the Black American. *Public Interest, 32,* 43-69.

Patterson, H. O. (1976). The Black community: Is there a future? In S. M. Lipset (Ed.), *The third century: America as a post-industrial society* (pp. 244-284). Stanford, CA: Hoover Institute Press.

Patterson, H. O. (1977). *Ethnic chauvinism: The reactionary impulse.* New York: Stein & Day.

Perlo, V. (1975). *The economics of racism, USA.* New York: International Publishers.

Pinkney, A. (1976). *Red, black and green: Black nationalism in the United States.* Cambridge: Cambridge University Press.

Pinkney, A. (1984). *The myth of Black progress.* Cambridge: Cambridge University Press.

Piore, M. (1971). The dual labor market: Theory and implications. In D. M. Gordon (Ed.), *Problems in political economy* (pp. 90-94). Lexington: Heath.

Piven, F. F., & Cloward, R. A. (1979). *Regulating the poor: The function of public relief.* New York: Pantheon.

Polsby, N. W. (1963). *Community power and political theory.* New Haven, CT: Yale University Press.

Popper, K. (1959). *The logic of scientific discovery.* London: Hutchinson.

Portes, A., & Zhou, M. (1992). Gaining the upper hand: Economic mobility among immigrant and domestic minorities. *Ethnic and Racial Studies, 15,* 491-522.

Powledge, F. (1965, April). Black man, go South. *Esquire,* pp. 42-46.

Powledge, F. (1967). *Black power-white resistance: Notes on the new civil war.* New York: World.

Poulantzas, N. (1973). *Political power and social classes.* London: New Left Books.

Poulantzas, N. (1978). *State, power, socialism.* London: New Left Books.

Prager, J. (1973). White racial privilege and social change: An examination of theories of racism. *Berkeley Journal of Sociology, 27,* 87-102.

Preston, M. (1976). Limitations of Black urban power: The case of Black mayors. In
    R. Lineberry & L. H. Masotti (Eds.), *The new urban politics* (pp. 111-132). Cam-
    bridge, MA: Ballinger.
Preston, M. B. (1978). Black elected officials and public policy: Symbolic or substantive
    representation? *Public Administration, 9,* 23-39.
Rainwater, L., & Yancey, W. (1967). *The Moynihan report and the politics of controversy.*
    Cambridge, MA: MIT Press.
Reich, M. (1981). *Racial inequality: A political-economic analysis.* Princeton, NJ: Prince-
    ton University Press.
Reich, M., Edwards, R., & Gordon, D. M. (1980). *Labor market segmentation in U.S. capi-
    talism.* New York: Cambridge University Press.
Reich, R. (1993). *The work of nations: Blueprint for the future.* London: Simon & Schuster.
Reisman, D. (1970). Some reservations about Black power. In A. Meier (Ed.), *Transforma-
    tion of activism* (pp. 155-161). Chicago: Aldine.
Research Atlanta. (1973). *Analysis of the Atlanta compromise school desegregation plan.*
    Atlanta: Atlanta Research Inc.
Research Atlanta. (1984). *Economic development in metropolitan Atlanta: Part 1: Suburban
    office growth and the future of downtown.* Atlanta: Atlanta Research Inc.
Rooks, C. S. (1970). *The Atlanta elections of 1969.* Atlanta: Voter Education Project.
Rose, A. (1964). *The Negro in America.* New York: Harper & Row.
Rustin, B. (1966). From protest to politics. *Commentary, 42,* 35-40.
Ryan, J. (Ed.). (1973). *White ethnics: Life in working class America.* Englewood Cliffs, NJ:
    Prentice-Hall.
Ryan, W. (1971). *Blaming the victim.* London: Orbach & Chambers.
Salamon, L. M. (1973). Leadership and modernisation: The emerging Black political elite in
    the South. *Journal of Politics, 35,* 615-646.
Saunders, P. (1979). *Urban politics: A sociological approach.* London: Hutchinson.
Savitch, H. V. (1978). Black cities—white suburbs: Domestic colonialism as an interpretive
    idea. *Annals, American Academy of Political and Social Science, 439,* 118-134.
Schattschneider, E. E. (1960). *The semi-sovereign people: A realist's view of democracy in
    America.* Hinsdale, IL: Dryden.
Schlesinger, A. M., Jr. (1992). *The disuniting of America: Reflections on a multicultural
    society.* New York: Norton.
Simone, T. M. (1989). *About face: Race in postmodern America.* New York: Automedia.
Smith, D. (1985). *Inequality in Atlanta, Georgia, 1960–80.* Occasional Paper No. 25, Depart-
    ment of Geography and Earth Science, Queen Mary College, University of London.
Snidal, D. (1985). The limits of hegemonic stability theory. *International Organisation, 39,*
    579-614.
Sollors, W. (Ed.). (1989). *The invention of ethnicity.* New York: Oxford University Press.
Southern, D. W. (1987). *Gunnar Myrdal and Black-white relations: The use and abuse
    of "An American Dilemma," 1944-1969.* Baton Rouge: Louisiana State University
    Press.
Sowell, T. (1975). *Race and economics.* London: Longman.
Sowell, T. (1976). Affirmative action reconsidered. *Public Interest, 42,* 47-65.
Sowell, T. (1978). Are quotas good for Blacks? *Commentary, 65,* 39-44.
Sowell, T. (1979). *American ethnic groups.* Washington, DC: The Urban Institute.
Sowell, T. (1981a). *Ethnic America: A history.* New York: Basic Books.
Sowell, T. (1981b). *Markets and minorities.* London: Blackwell.

Sowell, T. (1983). *The economics and politics of race.* New York: Morrow.

Sowell, T. (1984). *Civil rights: Rhetoric or reality?* New York: Morrow.

Spero, S. D., & Harris, A. L. (1931). *The Black worker.* New York: Columbia University Press.

Steele, S. (1990). *The content of our character: A new vision of race in America.* New York: St. Martin's Press.

Steinberg, S. (1989). *The ethnic myth: Race, ethnicity and class in America.* Boston: Beacon Press.

Steinfels, P. (1979). *The neo-conservatives: The men who are changing America's politics.* New York: Simon & Schuster.

Stokes, C. (1973). *Promises of power.* New York: Simon & Schuster.

Stone, C. N. (1976). *Economic growth and neighborhood discontent: System bias in the urban renewal program of Atlanta.* Chapel Hill: University of North Carolina Press.

Stone, C. N. (1991). *Regime politics: Governing Atlanta 1946-88.* Lawrence: University of Kansas Press.

Swain, C. M. (1993). *Black faces, Black interests: The representation of African Americans in Congress.* Cambridge, MA: Harvard University Press.

Sweezy, P. M. (1953). Capitalism and race relations. In *The present as history.* New York: Monthly Review Press.

Szymanski, A. (1974). Race, sex and the U.S. working class. *Social Problems, 21,* 706-725.

Szymanski, A. (1976). Racial discrimination and white gain. *American Sociological Review, 41,* 403-414.

Szymanski, A. (1978). White workers' loss from racial gain. *American Sociological Review, 43,* 776-782.

Tabb, W. K. (1970). *The political economy of the Black ghetto.* New York: Norton.

Tabb, W. K. (1971a). Capitalism, colonialism and racism. *Review of Radical Political Economics, 3,* 50-59.

Tabb, W. K. (1971b). Race relations models and social change. *Social Problems, 18,* 431-444.

Tabb, W. K., & Sawyers, L. (Eds.). (1978). *Marxism and the metropolis: New perspectives in urban political economy.* Oxford: Oxford University Press.

Takaki, R. (Ed.). (1987). *From different shores: Perspectives on race and ethnicity in America.* New York: Oxford University Press.

Taylor, C. (1992). *Multiculturalism and "The Politics of Recognition."* Princeton, NJ: Princeton University Press.

Thurow, L. C. (1985). *The zero-sum solution: Building a world class American economy.* New York: Simon & Schuster.

Todorov, T. (1993). *On human diversity: Nationalism, racism and exoticism in French thought.* Cambridge, MA: Harvard University Press.

Tryman, M. D. (1974). Black mayoralty campaigns: Running the race. *Phylon, 35,* 346-358.

Tyson, L. (1992). *Who's bashing whom?: Trade conflict in high technology industry.* Washington, DC: Institute of International Economics.

Valentine, C. A. (1968). *Culture and poverty: Critique and counter-proposals.* Chicago: University of Chicago Press.

Van Den Berghe, P. L. (1967). *Race and racism: A comparative perspective.* London: Wiley.

Van Den Berghe, P. L. (1981). *The ethnic phenomenon.* New York: Elsevier.

Vander Zanden, J. W. (1973). Sociological studies of American Blacks. *The Sociological Quarterly, 14,* 32-52.

Villemez, W. (1978). Black subordination and white economic well-being. *American Socio-logical Review, 43,* 772-776.

Walton, H., Jr. (1972). *Black politics: A theoretical and structural analysis.* Philadelphia: Lippincott.

Warner, W. L. (1936). American caste and class. *American Journal of Sociology, 42,* 234-237.

Washington, J. R. (Ed.). (1979). *The declining significance of race?* Philadelphia: University of Philadelphia Press.

Wattenberg, R., & Scammon, R. (1973, April). Black progress and liberal rhetoric. *Commentary,* 35-44.

Watters, P., & Cleghorn, R. (1970). *Climbing Jacob's ladder: The arrival of Negroes in southern politics.* New York: Harcourt.

Webb, M. C., & Krasner, S. D. (1989). Hegemonic stability theory: An empirical assessment. *Review of International Studies, 15,* 183-198.

Weinberg, M. (1977). *A chance to learn: The history of race and education in the United States.* Cambridge: Cambridge University Press.

West, C. (1993). *Keeping faith: Philosophy and race in America.* New York: Routledge.

Willhelm, S. (1970). *Who needs the Negro?* Cambridge, MA: Schenkman.

Willhelm, S. (1980). *Black in a white America.* Cambridge, MA: Schenkman.

Williams, E. (1944). *Capitalism and slavery.* Chapel Hill: University of North Carolina Press.

Williams, P. J. (1991). *The alchemy of race and rights.* Cambridge, MA: Harvard University Press.

Williams, W. (1983). *The state against Blacks.* New York: McGraw-Hill.

Wilson, J. Q. (1968). The Negro in politics. In L. H. Fuchs (Ed.), *The Negro in politics* (pp. 217-246).

Wilson, W. J. (1978). *The declining significance of race: Blacks and changing American institutions.* Chicago: University of Chicago Press.

Wilson, W. J. (1987). *The truly disadvantaged: The inner city, the underclass, and public policy.* Chicago: University of Chicago Press.

Wirt, F. M. (1974). *Power in the city: Decision making in San Francisco.* Berkeley: University of California Press.

Wolfinger, R. (1980). Reputation and reality in the study of community power. *American Sociological Review, 25,* 636-644.

Wolpe, H. (1970). Industrialism and race in South Africa. In S. Zubaida (Ed.), *Race and racialism* (pp. 151-179). London: Tavistock.

Wolpe, H. (1975). The theory of internal colonialism: The South African case. In I. Oxaal (Ed.), *Beyond the sociology of development* (pp. 229-252). London: Routledge.

Wood, A. (1994). *North-south trade, employment and inequality: Changing fortunes in a skill-driven world.* Oxford: Clarendon Press.

Wright, E. O. (1985). *Classes.* London: Verso.

Young, A. (1991). Foreword. In G. Orfield & C. Ashkinaze (Eds.), *Closing the door: Conservative policy and Black opportunity* (pp. vii-xi). Chicago: University of Chicago Press.

Zashin, E. (1978). The progress of Black Americans in civil rights: The past two decades assessed. *Daedelus, 107,* 239-262.

Index

About the Author

Stephen Burman is currently a Research Fellow at the United Kingdom Foreign and Commonwealth Office in London, England. He is on leave from the University of Sussex, where he has lectured in American Studies since 1979. He was born in Wales, and after taking a B.A. in Economics at Fitzwilliam College, Cambridge, in 1970, he completed his graduate studies at Balliol and Nuffield Colleges, Oxford. He has visited the United States regularly and frequently and has lived in Georgia and California. In 1982 he was a visiting Professor at Hampshire College in Massachusetts. In recent years he has been involved in the development of international educational exchanges programs between the United States and Britain. He has published in the fields of international relations and American foreign policy, and his current research is on the international political economy of race and ethnicity.